T0305293

Public Policy Instruments

NEW HORIZONS IN PUBLIC POLICY

General Editor: Wayne Parsons
Professor of Public Policy, Queen Mary and Westfield College,
University of London, UK

This series aims to explore the major issues facing academics and
practitioners working in the field of public policy at the dawn of a new
millennium. It seeks to reflect on where public policy has been, in both
theoretical and practical terms, and to prompt debate on where it is going.
The series emphasises the need to understand public policy in the context of
international developments and global change. New Horizons in Public
Policy publishes the latest research on the study of the policy making process
and public management, and presents original and critical thinking on the
policy issues and problems facing modern and post-modern societies.

Titles in the series include: .

Innovations in Public Management
Perspectives from East and West Europe
Edited by Tony Verheijen and David Coombes

Public Policy Instruments
Evaluating the Tools of Public Administration
Edited by B. Guy Peters and Frans K.M. van Nispen

Beyond the New Public Management
Changing Ideas and Practices in Governance
Edited by Martin Minogue, Charles Polidano and David Hulme

Public Policy Instruments

Evaluating the Tools of Public Administration

edited by
B. Guy Peters

Maurice Falk Professor of American Government,
University of Pittsburgh, USA

Frans K.M. van Nispen

Associate Professor of Public Administration,
Erasmus University, Rotterdam, The Netherlands

NEW HORIZONS IN PUBLIC POLICY SERIES

Edward Elgar
Cheltenham, UK • Northampton, MA, USA

Published by
Edward Elgar Publishing Limited
Glensanda House
Montpellier Parade
Cheltenham
Glos GL50 1UA
UK

Edward Elgar Publishing, Inc.
136 West Street
Suite 202
Northampton
Massachusetts 01060
USA

This book has been printed on demand to keep the title in print.

A catalogue record for this book
is available from the British Library

Library of Congress Cataloguing in Publication Data
Public policy instruments: evaluating the tools of public
  administration / edited by B. Guy Peters, Frans K.M. van Nispen.
    Includes bibliographical references and index.
    1. Policy sciences—Evaluation. 2. Public administration—
  Evaluation. I. Peters, B. Guy. II. Nispen. F.K.M. van.
  III. Series
  H97.P796 1998
  320'.6—dc21
                                                      97–47513
                                                         CIP

ISBN 1 85898 744 X (cased)

Contents

Tables

Contributors

Lorene Allio (b. 1961) holds degrees in International Relations from the University of California at Berkeley and the University of Southern California. She is currently completing her doctoral studies in Political Science at Emory University. Her focus is on the political economy of reform. Having done research on Africa and Latin America, her recent research has been focused on Poland and the formation of business interest groups there. She is teaching as Adjunct Professor in International Relations at the Golden Gate University in San Francisco.

Nico A.A. Baakman (b. 1953) has studied political science and philosophy, having failed as a mechanic, at Nijmegen University. He has published widely on a variety of subjects such as the welfare state, the role of paragovernmental organizations and health care. He holds a Ph.D. for a dissertation on the limits of governance in the case of hospital building in the Netherlands, 1960–85. He is at present affiliated to the School of Public and Business Administration of the Dutch Open University in Heerlen.

René Bagchus (b. 1996) holds an MPA from the University of Leiden and a Ph.D. from the Erasmus University of Rotterdam. He is at present affiliated to the Dutch Ministry of Education, Culture and Science.

Hans Th.A. Bressers (b. 1953) is Professor of Policy Studies and Environmental Policy and Scientific Director of the Center for Clean Technology and Environmental Policy at the University of Twente. In addition, he is Acting Professor of Policy Science at the Faculty of Public Administration and Public Policy. He has published numerous articles and books, and has written chapters and reports on policy subjects: mapping, instruments, implementation, evaluation, networks and environmental policies.

Hans A. de Bruijn (b. 1962) holds a Ph.D. from the Erasmus University of Rotterdam. He is at present affiliated to the School for Social Engineering, Policy Analysis and Management of Delft University of Technology. His research focuses on policy problems and the internal management of public organizations.

Mariusz Mark Dobek (b. 1960) is Assistant Professor of Political Science at the Benedictine College, Atchison, Kansas. He has conducted extensive research on privatization in Europe. His publications include *The Political Logic of Privatization* (Westport, CT: Praeger, 1993) and most recently, contributions to the edited volume, *The Political Economy of Property Rights* (New York: Cambridge University Press, 1997).

Hans A.M. Hufen (b. 1959) studied public administration and philosophy. He has worked at the Department of Public Administration of the University of Leiden. His Ph.D. thesis concerned the choice and the application of policy instruments in Dutch technology policy. He is now a member of the Board of Directors of the B. & A. Group for Policy Research and Consulting in The Hague. His ongoing activities are centred on the relationship between the economy and environmental protection.

Roeland J. in 't Veld (b. 1942) is Dean of the Netherlands School of Government in The Hague. He is Dean of the Post-Graduate School of Social Sciences at the University of Utrecht and Professor of Organization at the University of Amsterdam. He has served as consultant to several ministers of the Dutch government and as adviser to the Council of Europe, the European Commission, the OECD and the World Bank.

Dirk Jan Kraan (b. 1947) studied public law and economics at the Erasmus University of Rotterdam. He has taught public law and public administration at the same university. He earned his Ph.D. at that university in 1990. Since 1982 he has been working in the Budget Division of the Dutch Ministry of Finance, since 1987 as head of the Bureau of Policy Review. He has published on public economics and public choice theory in various journals. His latest book is *Budgetary Decisions. A Public Choice Approach* (Cambridge: Cambridge University Press, 1996).

Stephen H. Linder (b. 1950) is Associate Professor in Management and Policy Sciences at the School of Public Health, The University of Texas at Houston. He received his Ph.D. in political science at the University of Iowa and has held faculty positions at UCLA and Tulane University. He has a long-standing interest in policy formulation, risk and institutional design and is currently working on mechanisms for enhancing dialogue in organizational settings. His recent work appeared in *Policy Sciences*, the *Journal of Health Politics, Policy and Law*, and the book *Flashpoints in Environmental Policymaking*, edited by Kamieniecki, Gonzales and Vos (Albany, NY: SUNY Press, 1997).

B. Guy Peters (b. 1944) is Maurice Falk Professor of American Government at the University of Pittsburgh and Visiting Research Fellow at the Nuffield College of the University of Oxford. He recently co-edited with Johan P. Olsen a volume on administrative reform in a comparative perspective entitled *Lessons from Experience* (Olso: Scandinavian University Press, 1996).

Arthur B. Ringeling (b. 1942) is Professor of Public Administration and Public Policy of the Erasmus University of Rotterdam and the University of Leiden. His research interests in public policy focus on policy instruments, policy evaluation, environmental policy and the institutional context of public policy processes. Former president of the Dutch Association of Public Administration (1983–89), he is active as an editor as well as a consultant.

Ernst F. ten Heuvelhof (b. 1954) is Professor at the School of Systems Engineering, Policy Analysis and Management at Delft University of Technology. His research concerns issues of governance in the field of environmental, infrastructural and physical problems.

Frans K.M. van Nispen (b. 1951) is Visiting Professor of Public Budgeting at the Institute of Public Policy of George Mason University at Fairfax, on leave from the Department of Public Administration of the Erasmus University of Rotterdam. He has mainly published on policy analysis and public budgeting. He is now working on a comparative study of the way governments deal with budget deficits.

David L. Weimer (b. 1950) is Professor of Public Policy and Political Science at the University of Rochester. His research areas are political economy and the craft of policy analysis. His recent work includes *Cost–Benefit Analysis: Concepts and Practice* (Englewood Cliffs, NJ: Prentice Hall, 1996), co-authored with Anthony Boardman, David Greenberg and Aidan Vining, and *Economy of Property Rights: Institutional Change and Credibility in the Reform of Centrally Planned Economies* (New York: Cambridge University Press, 1997). He is currently working on a book with William Gormley on 'organizational report cards'.

Kenneth B. Woodside (b. 1944) is Associate Professor in the Department of Political Studies at the University of Guelph, Ontario.

Acknowledgements

Several people have contributed at various stages to this book. We must first acknowledge Hans de Bruijn, who was one of the conveners of the symposium on policy instruments that has culminated in this study. The expertise that he brought to bear has been of great value. We owe a debt to Roel in 't Veld, who generously sponsored the symposium. We are also very grateful to Kingsley Haynes and Roger Stough for helping to complete the manuscript, and to Marjolein Kooistra who tracked down the most obscure references. Last but not least, we would like to thank all the staff at Edward Elgar for their assistance.

Guy Peters and Frans van Nispen

Prologue

B. Guy Peters and Frans K.M. van Nispen

INTRODUCTION

This volume represents one of the fruits of a symposium on policy instruments held at the Erasmus University in Rotterdam in the spring of 1992. The Department of Public Administration at Erasmus was generous enough to provide support for a small gathering of scholars interested in the question of policy instruments and their impacts on the effectiveness of public policies. This issue has enjoyed a good deal of attention in the Netherlands, and the Erasmus symposium was able to draw on that rich intellectual tradition, as well as the experiences of several other countries in interpreting the position of policy instruments in the analysis, as well as the practice, of public policy.

The symposium was designed to examine the state of the art in this one area of policy analysis. Although a range of papers was offered at the symposium, all of which are included in one form or another in this volume, we also discovered that there were some important issues that were not covered by the available papers. Since the time of the conference we have commissioned a number of additional papers, as well as updating those presented earlier. In particular, we came to understand more clearly that there were different national intellectual traditions in the study of policy instruments and we wanted to ensure that this volume reflected that range. The Dutch tradition, which to some extent is quite typical of much public policy analysis conducted in continental Europe, is well represented, but the North American tradition is now included more thoroughly than in the original seminar. Further, there are debates within those traditions themselves, and we have attempted to be as even-handed as possible when presenting the various sides of those debates.

Although sometimes seen as a somewhat arcane issue in the study of policy, examination of policy instruments also reveals a great deal about the choices that governments make when they set policy. That having been said, however, the capacity of instrument choices to ensure certain types of outcomes is sometimes overstated by the advocates of

1

one or another instrument. Thus we need to understand just what the various effects of policy choices are, and how instruments fit (or not) into the other aspects of the policy process. This book, then, attempts to assist the would-be policy maker, but, in particular, it aims to aid the policy analyst and the social scientist attempting to understand the sources and meaning of policy instruments.

We are arguing in this book that, in order to be able to make policies effectively, a policy maker must understand both the range of instruments available to him or her, and something about the differences among those instruments. Policy makers appear to have some intuitive sense that the instruments available to them are indeed different, but also do not appear to spend adequate time in making instrument choices on an informed or analytical basis. Instrument choice is often made on the basis of inertia, or tradition, or perhaps educated guesses. Policy makers in some areas have always implemented policies through certain instruments – transfer payments are customary in social welfare, for example – and do not think about alternatives. This habitual style of making policy is likely to produce safe choices in the short run, but it is unlikely to be able to adapt to changing circumstances.

Even when more consideration is given to available policy instruments, this may still not be adequate. In some such cases a single dominant criterion may be employed that then precludes additional thought about the full range of costs and benefits of the available instrument options. In recent years, for example, economic cost has been such a dominant criterion, with the degree of intrusiveness of an instrument, as perceived by the public, coming a close second. Those two criteria tend to reduce additional thought about criteria such as equity and inclusiveness that might also be important for making an informed choice about instruments.

Although we argue that instruments are important, we also point out that their role can be problematic. In the first place instruments are not always stable and may change as they are implemented over time. Whereas the instruments themselves remain objectively the same, the way in which they are perceived by the actors involved in the process, and the strategies used by the targets of the policies to escape the influence of a particular instrument, can change dramatically. Further, one size does not fit all, and there needs to be even more research on the contingent nature of instruments. The contingencies arise in the policy areas being administered and in the countries within which the instruments are used. Indeed, the existence of different national schools of instrument analysis reflects the cross-national variation in perceptions of instruments and their relative political utility and liability.

Another factor that needs additional emphasis in the literature is the political nature of policy instruments. There is a technocratic tendency in the literature to consider instrument choice as a simple exercise in selecting a technique for addressing a particular policy problem. There is an associated tendency to assume that political context does not matter and that the economics of the choices are much more significant than are the politics. In reality it may be the other way round, and the politics of instruments determine success or failure to a greater extent than do factors of direct costs or even efficiency. That is a rather bold statement, and may depend in part upon the type of evaluation being used. Still, cost may not actually prevent an instrument from working, but politics often does. Further, the final judgement of the efficacy of an instrument will always be political, whether that judgement is rendered at the ballot box or in parliament.

The pursuit of effective government through the use of the best policy instruments can also be frustrated because of the interaction of various instruments operating simultaneously. The tendency has also been to evaluate instruments as individual entities and to consider their characteristics in relative isolation. This is in marked contrast to the political context within which they must operate. The tendency has also been to consider instruments in isolation from other policies. Unfortunately for that view, the policy world is very crowded and there are already multiple instruments in place. This crowding means that any new intervention will have to contend with, and be coordinated with, a number of other programmes engaged in similar and complementary tasks. There is as yet little research on how to coordinate instruments or on the ways in which instruments interact (positively or negatively) across policies. There is a great deal of wishful thinking as a result, and also more failed programmes than there may need to be.

Finally, the study of policy instruments has focused perhaps excessively on the 'real' aspects of the instruments and has given inadequate attention to their symbolic elements. Instruments move resources and they affect people's economic behaviour. They can also be seen as having a strong symbolic element that tells the population what government is thinking (pardon the reification) and what its collective perceptions of problems and the public may be. For example, when there are shifts in social policy away from means-tested to universalistic programmes, this makes a statement about the way in which the benefits will be delivered, but it also makes a statement about the meaning of social citizenship in a country – and this may be as significant as any real benefits produced or taken away. Analysts frequently fail to make this symbolic connection, and governments frequently fail to understand the point.

In short, although this book makes a number of important contributions to the study of policy instruments, there is still a great deal of intellectual work to be done. There is a need for coordinated and systematic research on instruments and on their impacts on the relative success or failure of programmes. This research must be comparative, given the tendency to make assumptions about the universality of instruments and their effects that are often quite incorrect. Finally, the research must be broadly based, going well beyond the economic characteristics of instruments to consider their political and even cultural features, and must include the pervasive effects that instruments can have on the success or failure of policy.

CONTENTS OF THE BOOK

This remainder of this volume is divided into four parts and the chapters included have been designed to provide a range of perspectives about the existing literature on policy instruments. We begin with an overview of the alternatives, with an emphasis on the intellectual traditions that have shaped the literature. The second part of the volume examines the question of the choice of instruments by government actors, a question that has often been ignored in the literature that has focused on the characteristics of the instruments. This part emphasizes the politics of instruments, a factor that is inadequately emphasized in much of the literature. Part III provides a more dynamic conception of instruments and their relationship with the sociopolitical environment within which they function. The final section of the book provides a reassessment of the instruments literature and looks at the questions that will continue to face this perspective on public policy.

THE STATE OF THE ART (PART I)

Part I attempts to describe and analyse the state of the art in this area of inquiry, and the opening chapters provide an overview. First, the traditional approach of policy instruments is presented by Hans A. de Bruijn and Hans A.M. Hufen. They conclude that a great deal of energy has been spent on the development of typologies of instruments, but that none of these schemes is very satisfactory; indeed it is not clear to these scholars that classification is the most important issue. In addition, much attention has been given to the effectiveness of instruments, but that approach to inquiry has largely failed because of methodological barriers.

A number of alternative perceptions of instruments to that offered by the traditional approach to the study of instruments is generated by Stephen H. Linder and B. Guy Peters in Chapter 2. They identify a movement away from the *instrumentalist* school in the direction of the *constitutive* school of instruments, a movement that reflects contemporary intellectual patterns. That is, there is a movement from the advocacy of a particular instrument regardless of the situation to a view in which instruments and the rest of the policy process are considered simultaneously. Empirically, these alternative views can also be identified among different groups of both scholars and practitioners, and appear to have real influences on the choices made within government.

In the final chapter in Part I (Chapter 3) René Bagchus points to the trade-offs that exist between the degree of fit of an instrument and the circumstances in which it will be applied. Bagchus provides an interesting assessment of the development of the instruments literature and argues that it is now developing towards a more contingent view of instruments and their use. This chapter provides an argument not dissimilar to that of Linder and Peters, but does so from the continental European tradition rather than from a North American perspective.

THE QUEST FOR POLICY INSTRUMENTS (PART II)

As one part of an analysis of how policy instruments are selected, the contextual approach is elaborated by Hans A. de Bruijn and Ernst F. ten Heuvelhof (Chapter 4). They move from the application of instruments in an *intra*-organizational context to the employment of those instruments in an *inter*-organizational setting (termed organizational fit) to end up with instruments operating within networks. The authors make a plea for a contingent approach to instruments, and attempt to find ways of matching instruments with the conditions that exist within and among institutions. The nature of policy networks is especially important for understanding how instruments function and how they fit with increasingly complex political environments.

Hans Th.A. Bressers (Chapter 5) addresses the selection of policy instruments in the context of policy networks and the interaction of numerous interest groups in the policy process. In particular Bressers is concerned with how networks function during policy formulation to shape programmes and particularly to shape instrument choices. One

of the dominant themes of this volume is that instrument choice does
matter, and Bressers's chapter demonstrates the extent to which participants in the policy process believe that it matters and expend political
resources to have their favourite instruments selected.

In the following chapter Dirk Jan Kraan (Chapter 6) utilizes public
choice theory to examine the possible choices among policy instruments.
Kraan argues strongly that the effectiveness of instruments is related
to their visibility and that this visibility is a function primarily of their
codification and formalization. In addition, codification will reduce
flexibility and limit the ability of actors to adjust instruments to address
a specific situation in society. The rational political actor, therefore,
will opt for instruments that will have minimum visibility and hence will
encounter minimum political opposition. This is a convincing argument
for the importance of politics in the evaluation of instruments, and
extends the argument from the élite politics of executives and legis-
latures to the level of mass political activity.

The relation between instruments and strategies for using them is
discussed by David L. Weimer and his colleagues (Chapter 7). They
present several strategies that correspond to the demands of an inter-
organizational context and discuss how instrument choices can be
related to those strategies. The fundamental strategies they discuss can
be utilized in either the processes of policy design or those of policy
implementation, with the emphasis here on initial formulation and
design questions. These ideas about instruments are developed and to
some extent tested in the particular context of privatization in the
countries of East and Central Europe.

THE RHYTHMS AND BLUES (PART III)

The effectiveness of instruments is the subject of an essay by Roeland
J. in 't Veld (Chapter 8) who argues that at least two laws are in
operation when instruments are selected. These two laws play leapfrog
when governments make policy. On the one hand, consumers become
accustomed to instruments and, as a consequence, make instruments
obsolete over the long run (life cycle) of a policy. This, in turn, raises
the question of policy termination. On the other hand, the diminishing
effectiveness of instruments will necessitate the application of additional
instruments, resulting in policy accumulation. In Aaron Wildavsky's
words: more and more public policy is about coping with the consequences of past policies and less and less about events in society

(Wildavsky, 1979). In the end the result will be an extremely detailed system of policies, unless the system collapses under its own weight.

Kenneth B. Woodside (Chapter 9) provides a contingent approach to policy instruments. Woodside's chapter is especially important because it allows us to view the consequences of a shift from the domestic to the international realm of policy making. The international scene adds a difference in culture to the difference in interests that usually dominates policy. It turns out that the use of any specific instruments is simply not possible in international affairs, but rather there is a need to assess the interactions of national and international contexts.

A RE-EXAMINATION (PART IV)

A 'sociogenesis' of policy tools is the subject of Nico A.A Baakman's contribution (Chapter 10). He concludes that there is at present no real theory of policy instruments in the literature. To the extent that there is any theory, it is a theory of the *effects* or *effectiveness* of policy tools, however that may be defined, rather than any comprehensive conceptualization of the instruments themselves. In addition, a careful distinction should be made between scientific and practical knowledge concerning the effectiveness of those policy instruments. The blending of scientific and practical information will cause an intellectual disaster, in Baakman's view. Any one approach is not, he believes, capable of addressing both the issues of importance to practical policy makers and those of concern to academic analysts.

Finally, a critical assessment of instrumentality is made by Frans K.M. van Nispen and Arthur B. Ringeling (Chapter 11). A comparison of a policy instrument with a hammer, a pair of pincers, or a screwdriver may be appealing, but is at the same time misleading. The simple instrumental analogy neglects goals and ignores the interdependence of goals and means in policy. Besides, the selection of means is not a neutral activity for public policies. A mechanism for achieving a goal is only a label and behind that label is hidden an organizational unit consisting of human beings. Van Nispen and Ringeling argue that organizational units tend to structure problems in such a way that they can be solved by the means which have already been proved to be useful within the context of that one organization. In other words, organizations tend to address only these problems that can be solved with their available technologies. Further, an organization may define novel problems in ways that make them amenable to available technologies even if they are not really that similar to the familiar problems. A plea for a more institutional approach to instruments completes these authors' assessment of the existing literature about instruments.

SUMMARY

Governments have a wide range of options at their disposal when they decide to intervene in any policy problem. That wide scope is at once a blessing and a weakness for policy makers. On the one hand there is no shortage of ways for governments to attempt to produce for citizens the benefits they intend. On the other hand, however, the more capable practitioners quickly realize that their success will be determined, at least in part, by that very selection of instruments, and that they have many opportunities to fail. Unfortunately, the available literature provides little definitive guidance for the policy maker.

There are also numerous intellectual problems remaining in this field of inquiry. There is as yet no agreement about how 'tools', or instruments, should be classified. Likewise, there is little or no agreement on what sorts of criteria should be central to their evaluation. There is not even agreement on whether the characteristics of tools themselves or of the process of selection of tools is more important for understanding the role that instruments play in policy. Thus, although we believe that we are contributing to progress in this field of inquiry, there is still a good deal of intellectual work that needs to be done before there can be said to be a really useful theory of policy instruments.

PART I

The State of the Art in the Study of Policy
Instruments

1. The traditional approach to policy instruments

Hans A. de Bruijn and Hans A.M. Hufen

1. INTRODUCTION

During recent years, there has been a great deal of interest in policy instruments in the field of public administration. A large amount of empirical research has been performed from an instrumental perspective, while, at the same time, efforts towards theory formulation have also been presented. This chapter analyses the background of the instrumental approach and attempts to outline its development in the field of public administration. In addition, some evaluative remarks concerning this approach will be made.

The structure of the chapter is as follows. In the next section, the historical roots of researching policy instruments will be presented (Section 2). This description is followed by a section in which the term 'instrument' is described (Section 3). Research of instruments is discussed in Sections 4 and 5. Section 6 assesses the instrumental perspective. The conclusions in Section 7 round off the chapter.

2. THE ROOTS OF THE INSTRUMENTAL APPROACH

The instrumental approach can be perceived as an orientation in the social sciences, in which the issues discussed concern the way persons or public organizations purposefully influence societal processes. A number of assumptions or questions which are considered relevant underlie this orientation. The instrumental approach can be reduced to a (constitutive) metaphor which combines questions concerning the conversion of policy intentions into administrative actions (Ringeling, 1983). These questions have been quite popular in various periods and less popular in others. The persistence with which these questions resurface suggests that the instrumental orientation is not restricted to certain periods in time.[1] There is a great practical, theoretical and political–symbolic relevance to this. In this chapter, the scientific relevance of the instrumental perspective is considered the most important. This scientific relevance cannot, however, be completely separated from the practical and political–ideological relevance.

The instrumental perspective is not bound to one single academic discipline. On the contrary, it has its roots in various disciplines. The instrumental approach has long been popular in economics. Wage and price policy, as well as the level of social insurance benefits, are in this tradition conceived as instruments that aim for certain macroeconomic effects. Law contains an instrumental approach as well. At the beginning of this century, Pound presented the idea that law is an instrument of social control, and in addition to that it may be used for 'social engineering' (Schuyt, 1985). The development of public administration as an academic discipline has also given shape to the instrumental orientation.

The current popularity of the instrumental approach in various disciplines can be seen as the result of three (non-scientific) developments. First, it is striking that the instrumental approach has developed in particular in academic disciplines in which scholars have maintained strong links with the practitioners in their field. For example, people who work for university law departments often end up practising law, or vice versa. This close relationship between universities and professional practice has resulted in a strong stimulus for an increase in the amount of research that focuses on practical problems. This development also seems to hold for economists. The Dutch Ministry of Economic Affairs is sometimes fondly referred to as the recruiter of the Rotterdam School of Economics. Public administration also appears to be an academic discipline which maintains close relations with its practice.

Second, the development of the instrumental orientation is the result of a growing need for practical knowledge in government organizations. With the gradual expansion of the duties and the increasing complexity of policy implementation problems, the need for scientific and practical insights increases. Thinking in terms of goals and instruments seems, in such a situation, to be a valuable contribution to the improvement of the quality of policy processes. The instrumental approach offers such a contribution by focusing on the simple, but often difficult (to answer) questions of how the intentions of policy could be translated into operational activities.

Third, the instrumental approach has had political and ideological support for quite a long time. Disappointment with the performance of certain policy sectors in the welfare state has led to a strong need for insights into the failure of policy. At the beginning of the 1980s, the

Dutch Geelhoed commission came to the conclusion that various policy failures were caused by gaps in knowledge about policy instruments.[2] The solution to policy failure lay in the development of an instrument theory and doctrine, as well as a translation of this theory into an applicable instrumental doctrine. The recommendation of the Geelhoed commission is an appeal both for more scientific research and for support of existing political ideology. The political–ideological environment of the past decade has greatly influenced ideas about, among other things, environmental and technological policy.[3]

3. THE CONCEPT OF 'INSTRUMENT'

At first glance, the concept of 'instrument' seems simple; however, in reality it is quite difficult to describe. Research into the available literature has produced a wide variety of phenomena called 'instruments'. However, there is no sign of coherence. Financial management and control are qualified as instruments (Thain, 1985; McGuire and Stuart, 1987). Certain forms of internal management such as 'human resource policy' or 'management by objectives' are also instruments (Poister and Streib, 1989; Caudle, 1987). In relation to technological policy, 'policy experiments' are mentioned as instruments (Tassey, 1985). The control of inter-organizational relationships between government organizations also takes place with the help of instruments (Montjoy and O'Toole, 1990). In short, 'internal management' or 'internal organization', 'human resource policy', 'policy experiments' and 'network management' appear to be considered as instruments. A preliminary conclusion one can draw from this is that the concept of 'instrument' does not provide any information about the nature of a certain phenomenon, but about the fact that the phenomenon is a means for accomplishing a particular objective. Hoogerwerf's definition of an instrument is given here as a point of comparison: 'everything that an actor uses or could potentially use to aid in the attainment of one or more goals' (Hoogerwerf, 1989).

The concept of instrument can be defined more sharply by making a distinction between characterizing an instrument as an *object* and by characterizing it as an *activity*. First, an instrument can be considered as an object. This is often the case in legal literature when people speak of laws and administrative directives as instruments. They refer to the entire set of instructions and rules that together form the law or the administrative directive from government.

Instruments can also be considered as activities. Ringeling describes the concept of 'instrument' as follows: 'a collection of policy activities that show similar characteristics, focused on influencing and governing social processes' (Ringeling, 1983).[4] We shall now briefly discuss the differences between these descriptions.

An advantage of Ringeling's definition is that informal activities can also be considered as instruments. Examples of these are bribery, rhetoric, 'sweet talking' and inconsiderate behaviour. Some of these informal instruments can be reduced to an 'object' (as a rule, bribery takes place with money). However, this is not true for all of them. Informal instruments are less common in the object characterization. Using the object characterization involves the danger of reification. Certain instruments have the intrinsic character of activities. The instrument 'organization' is not so much an object as an ensemble of activities and processes (Hood, 1983). An object characterization can give an incomplete picture of the dynamic nature of instruments.

A disadvantage of Ringeling's definition is that the line between the concepts of 'policy' and 'instrument' is vague. If policy is described as 'actions in relation to a certain problem', there is scarcely any room for the concept of 'policy instrument'; only those actions which have corresponding characteristics can qualify as 'instruments'. This lack of separation between policy and policy instrument leads to the concept of 'instrument' becoming something indefinable and not always detachable from policy. The drawback of Ringeling's definition is the strong point of the object characterization: an object is, by definition, definable.

The Authors' Position

From this short discussion of the two typologies, it can be concluded that both have their strengths and weaknesses. It is not important for us to choose one rather than the other. It seems wisest to adopt the position which states that instruments can be characterized as objects. A law or government act can be regarded as an object or instrument. However, it is at the same time true that such a qualification is only valuable when considered in the abstract. For research purposes, the object characterization is not only important, but is particularly interesting in relation to the activities and actions necessary for the application of instruments. Only if abstractly defined objects, such as money, authority and information, can be transformed into activities and actions that convert intentions into policy actions, can they offer a framework for further research in the field of public administration.

Although the literature also perceives internal management, internal organization and human resource policy as 'instruments', we shall not consider these in our discussion of the literature concerning policy instruments. In this chapter we assume that the application of instruments is focused on the realization of policy output or effects. For this reason, we occasionally speak of 'external instruments'. Policy output refers to physical goods or services that are produced by the policy-implementing organization. Policy outcomes appear when the production of physical goods and services leads to the intended influence on societal processes. The central assumption of the instrumental approach is that different types of instruments individually structure policy activities as well as evoke problems and produce different effects (Salamon and Lund, 1989).

4. THE CURRENT STATUS OF RESEARCH ON INSTRUMENTS

During recent years, many public administration studies have been carried out with respect to instruments. A substantial portion of these studies have been done in the Netherlands and Germany; it is difficult to explain why the instrumental perspective has been so popular in these countries. A partial explanation could be that the Dutch and German administrative sciences have stronger roots in law than the administrative sciences in the Anglo-Saxon countries. As stated earlier, the instrumental approach, although in competition with other perspectives, is the dominant approach in law.

In the next two sections we shall describe and classify the existing research on instruments. In this section, we classify existing research into the nature of theoretical approaches, the types of instruments that are studied, the policy fields on which the research is focused, and the method of data collection used in the research.

Approaches to the Study of Instruments

Analytically, three approaches to the study of instruments can be distinguished.

1. **The classical approach** claims that the nature of instruments structures the course of policy processes (Hood, 1983; Geelhoed, 1983; Mayntz, 1983). Salamon and Lund (1989) clearly express the central idea of the classical approach: 'different tools of government action have their own distinctive dynamics, their own "political economies" that affect the context of government action'.[5] Supporters

of this approach focus extensively on the construction of a comprehensive typology of instruments. Every instrument has its subprocesses, central activities, implementation problems and effects. By carrying out empirical research for every instrument, one attempts to explain the application of instruments. This approach presumes that empirical research, after a certain period of time, leads to an instrumental theory and ultimately to an instrumental doctrine (Geelhoed, 1983). An important obstacle within this approach, and therefore also an obstacle for the development of an instrumental doctrine, is the problem of constructing a typology in which the categories are mutually exclusive (Kaufmann and Rosewitz, 1983).

2. **The instrument–context approach** attempts to explain the operation of instruments by examining both the characteristics of instruments and the variables from the context in which the instruments are applied (compare, for example, Bressers and Klok, 1987a and 1987b; Hufen, 1990; Linder and Peters, 1989a and 1989b). The distinction of this approach is that the actual implementation activities and effects are not only determined by the characteristics of instruments, but also by the context in which they are applied. For example, we can consider the following as relevant context variables: the implementing organization and the target group, and other instruments and characteristics of a policy field. In the instrument–context approach, the ideal of an all-embracing instrument doctrine significantly diminishes.

    The concept of 'context' is very difficult to define. Bressers and Klok have presented an instrumental theory in which they categorize a number of context variables into so-called 'core circumstances' (Bressers and Klok, 1987a; Klok, 1991). For a concrete elaboration of the concept of 'context', other authors often use the existing volumes of public administration theories. Insights from implementation theory, organizational management and network theory are useful sources for shaping the instrument–contextual approach.[6]

3. **Contextual approaches** go a bit further in modifying the importance of instruments. The starting-point of contextual approaches is that the instrument is only one of the many factors that determine the course of policy processes. With this notion, the 'instrumental' nature of these theories vanishes. The analysis does not concern 'instruments', but instead policy systems, policy networks, decision-making arenas or implementation processes (Wamsley and Milward, 1985; Glasbergen, 1989; Kiser and Ostrom, 1985; Hupe, 1990; Hufen,

1990). Instruments only play a modest role in policy systems, decision-making arenas and implementation processes. Theory development is therefore not so much focused on the ideas concerning instruments as on the other types of activities, on which instruments have a modest influence. With the introduction of this third approach, the instrumental approach becomes somewhat self-destructive. Contextual approaches can modify the importance of the instrument variable to such an extent that the label 'instrumental theory' is no longer applicable, since instruments are no longer sufficiently significant.

Types of Instruments

The instrumental approach to policy has urged many scientists to design a typology of instruments (Geelhoed, 1983; Hood, 1983: Mitnick, 1980; Van der Doelen, 1989). Since such a great number of typologies exists, they will not all be discussed in this chapter. Often cited is the typology of Van der Doelen, who makes a distinction between legal, economic and communicative instruments. Every group of instruments has its varieties that may limit or enlarge the possibility of influencing the behaviour of the actors involved. In Section 6, we shall make some further remarks concerning these and similar typologies.

There are many preliminary reviews concerning the three most important instrument families; studies on regulation, finance and information transfer have already been published. However, a short characterization of these instrument families should be presented in an overview chapter such as this (derived from De Bruijn and Ten Heuvelhof 1991a).

The first instrument family is legal in nature: *regulatory* instruments aim at normalizing the behaviour of social actors. The legal instrument family is varied, which sometimes makes further classification quite difficult (think, for example, of instruments such as product liability, negotiable licences and reversal of the burden of proof).

With regard to the functioning of these instruments, four crucial aspects are mentioned in the literature. First, regulatory instruments not only have an instrumental function; they also possess a normalizing and guaranteeing function. Law standardizes governmental actions and offers social actors guarantees against government interventions, which at the same time can limit the regulatory ability of these types of instruments. Second, the use of regulatory instruments requires monitoring and enforcement. Governments, however, can often not afford the monitoring and enforcement costs. Third, it is often noted that regulatory instruments have a coercive character. Coercion usually does not fit well into the interwoven relationship between government and social actors and tends to provoke resistance from actors at whom the policy is aimed. Finally, regulation has a reactive character. The formation of rules is a slow process and can therefore lag behind certain developments in society. Above all, regulation is often an instrument that is implemented after the fact. After undesirable behaviour is detected, regulation can only be used, for example, for criminal prosecution.

Influencing people's behaviour by using *financial incentives* is viewed as an alternative to influence by regulation. It is often said that the most important difference between incentives and regulation is the former's non-coercive nature. This explains the current popularity of these instruments in certain policy fields. However, this is not the case everywhere. In some areas, incentives, especially subsidies, are losing their popularity. They are becoming strongly associated with the public policy of the 1970s, a period when government, on behalf of countless social activities, simply made a grab at the public treasury.

What restrictions apply to financial instruments? In the first place, financial incentives can cause shifting mechanisms. Levies can, for example, be passed on in the price of products and subsidies can push away already existing, non-financial, behavioural incentives (moral ones, for example). In the second place, financial incentives, because of their limited coercive nature, give the targeted actors the *choice* of changing their behaviour, which is sometimes an undesirable option for government. In the third place, the use of financial incentives often requires detailed knowledge of the factors that determine the behaviour of actors on whom the policy is focused. Due to the limited coercive power of these instruments, it is very important that incentives are applied precisely. Knowledge and information concerning the targeted actors are often insufficient.

During recent years, the significance of *information transfer* has been growing. This popularity is explained by Dahme and Grünow (1983) who point out that these types of instrument fit well with the kinds of relationship that exist in a modern society. The underlying idea is that instruments that rely on the 'Obrigkeit' ('authority') of the state should be phased out. No longer coercion, but force of conviction should be the factor that provides direction to policy.

Information transfer, as a 'soft' instrument, is probably only effective if it is compatible with the frame of reference of the target group. There is also an information problem with respect to the application of these instruments. It is not always easy to comprehend the frame of reference of the target group. The problem of reaching the target groups precedes the problem that the provision of information does not always lead to change in behaviour. Contacts made by intermediary information campaign agencies with their target group seem to be an important aspect in explaining the functioning of information transfer (Van Riel, 1986). Geelhoed's remark that information transfer often only succeeds in combination with 'harder' instruments seems at least to be true in the case of government aid in technology policy (Hufen, 1990).

Policy Fields

An overview of instrument research shows us that most research is performed in the environmental and economic sectors. The contents of some of this research will be discussed shortly hereafter. Naturally, the overview cannot be complete; we shall deal primarily with empirical research that refers to the development of the theory of policy instruments.

Environmental policy

A great deal of research which deals with the application of instruments concerns the most widely applied type of instrument in this sector: regulation. Problems of enforcement, typically connected with regulation, are frequently researched. During recent years, the alarming situation with regard to the monitoring and observation of rules has often been brought up for discussion (Bressers and Klok, 1987a). Several authors defend the use of regulation as an instrument not so much for influencing behaviour, as for demanding certain standards in products (Bezemer et al., 1988). Legislation continues, nevertheless, to be a frequently used instrument of environmental policy. According to Mayntz (1983b), the conditions under which regulation could be viewed as a successful instrument are diminishing. Financing would be an alternative to regulation in some cases. In one of Bressers's studies concerning the improvement of water quality management, levies appeared to be a more effective tool than the provision of licences (Bressers, 1983).

The application of financial incentives is not equally effective in all cases. The rules relating to compensation for extra investments made by companies in environmentally friendly provisions had limited effects, and sometimes consequences other than intended (Grimberg et al., 1988). The implementing agency appeared in one third of the cases not even to have asked whether the subsidized investments were indeed 'extra'. The instrument was also used for various other unofficial purposes. Additional research showed that formal goals of environmental policy were being increasingly realized. In the period between 1984 and 1989, for example, there was a significant reduction in the use of PCBs (polychlorinated biphenyls). Closer research showed, however, that the specific financial incentive was of little importance for 59 per cent of the applicants (Vermeulen and Goes, 1989). In addition to the financial incentive, both the environmentally friendly attitude of business and the enthusiastic attitude of the civil servants at the operational level, appeared to be of at least equal importance. The policy aimed at decreasing environmentally damaging exhaust fumes was successful from an instrumental point of view, as far as it encouraged the production of environmentally friendly automobiles. The reduction in lead emissions did not take place, however, since the number of kilometres driven increased (Klok, 1987).

Since financing is obviously not equally effective in all cases, discussions about environmental policy frequently urge the introduction of new types of instruments (Bezemer et al., 1988). Mention is made, among other things, of using contracts as instruments. Contracts can here be regarded as 'written agreements between two or more actors'. The policy maker exchanges a part of the policy objectives for the practical applicability of the instrument. The target group, in turn, benefits from the fact that unattainable policy goals are exchanged for attainable options. In practice, the realization of contracts often meets with problems. Furthermore, it appears that in half the cases, the goals stated in the contract are not achieved (Klok, 1989b). Thus, new instruments have their negative sides as well. For this reason, Baggot (1986) makes the modifying remark that the value of contracts lies especially in the possibility of making agreements with powerful, otherwise almost unreachable, members of a target group (see also Klok, 1989a).

Energy conservation policy
Many studies about instruments are also to be found in the field of energy conservation policy. These studies generally support the development of policy. Since information transfer has been the most applied instrument during the first fifteen years of energy conservation policy, it is understandable that the effectiveness of certain variants of information transfer have been most intensely researched (Onderzoekers Kombinatie Utrecht, 1989). In many cases, such research was quantitative, studying the effects of informing large target groups. The outcome of a large-scale information campaign of energy-conserving behaviour appeared to be modest. At the time of writing, different types of information programmes are being increasingly combined with

other instruments (Centrum voor Energiebesparing, 1991). Various studies investigating the functioning of subsidy regulations which have conservation as their goal are available. Research concerning regulations in this field is scarce, since this type of instrument is rarely applied in this sector (Van der Doelen, 1989; see, however, Arentsen, 1991).

Studies of instruments are focused on the various target groups of the policy. The following can be distinguished: agriculture, industrial utility construction, other construction, family housing, traffic and transportation. The research also follows the policy practice in this respect (Piers Consultancy, 1991). Most studies concern households and the construction of homes. In his doctoral thesis, Van der Doelen (1989) researched the implementation of instruments which focused on energy conservation in industry.

Economic policy
De Haan et al. (1986) use the instrumental approach to policy as a framework for a descriptive analysis of the tools of Dutch socio-economic policy. The approach also offers Dercksen (1986) a framework for his doctoral thesis, which describes the application of instruments in relation to industrial policy in the Netherlands during the 1950s. Among other things, he analyses the way in which instruments are applied in the field of productivity stimulation, trade and export, and technological innovation. The application of instruments is seen as a result of interactions between organizations in the existing 'industry–political configuration' (Dercksen, 1986). The influence of non-public organizations is, for obvious reasons, also stressed in other studies of economic policy. The development process in this field demonstrates that government, in regulating economic processes, has designed a great number of conference consulting circuits, in which employers, employees and researchers participate in the decision-making process. In a review concerning the application of wages and prices as instruments of government policy, it is emphasized, and rightly so, that it is not so much the government, but more the interaction between the employers, employees and government that explains the course of policy processes (Rood, 1985).

In recent years, the provision of subsidies to businesses, especially by the Dutch Ministry of Economic Affairs, has been extensively researched. Damen (1987) studied relief measures and came to the conclusion that legislation on these is extremely limited and that the organization of their implementation is very unclear. Based on an evaluation that used legal criteria, the instrument was weighed and found insufficient. Vermeend (1983) concluded that the effectiveness of the fiscal instruments of government, at least, leaves much to be desired. The government has grossly overestimated the influencing ability of this instrument, especially with regard to the fiscal instruments used in Holland during the 1970s and 1980s. Most investment decisions are, according to Vermeend, based on the returns that companies expect. More important than the investment-stimulating effect of fiscal instruments is the effect of cutting costs. The political evaluation of financial support for the shipbuilding industry was damning. The effectiveness of fiscal investment facilities was severely criticized (Vermeend, 1983). Van der Doelen (1989) has pointed out that, during the procurement of energy subsidies by companies, the so-called gift-effect arises. Companies obtain grants when they would have undertaken the subsidized activities in any case, regardless of the grant.

In an examination of the establishment of the maximum subsidies in general housing, Klijn (1990) states that government is compelled by necessity to make sub-optimal decisions. Government strikes a balance between inefficiency and ineffectiveness. By providing high subsidies, the government can ensure that a relatively large number of companies participate in the process of realizing its goals. At the same time, there is a danger that the government might make conditions too attractive, possibly leading to inefficiency. By providing low amounts of subsidies the government runs the risk that a relatively small number of companies will cooperate. Supporting only a small number of companies, however, is not effective. In his analysis of economic studies, De Bruijn (1990) concludes that the lack of knowledge of potentially subsidized activities is the bottleneck in the process of providing financial support. In his dissertation, Noorderhaven (1990) focuses on another problem concerning the application of economic subsidies. He examined the problems that arose during the negotiations between government and business with regard to reviewing requests and apportioning subsidies. He pays special attention to gaps in and overlaps of responsibilities between the party that gives the subsidy and the party that receives it. He also demonstrates how these contacts determine the effectiveness of the instrument. Another study examines more closely the causes which underlie the continuous failure of the Dutch Ministry of Economic Affairs to reach medium- and small-sized businesses (Hufen and Schuilenburg, 1990).

Quantitative and Qualitative Research

The instrumental perspective is not characterized by an independent methodology. Quantitative and qualitative research methods are used concurrently. The analysis concerning the application of instruments relating to water quality management contains a qualitative analysis of the determination of water quality (Bressers, 1983). Van der Doelen's research on energy conservation is intentionally quantitative in design (Van der Doelen, 1989). He processed his survey data on the effects of energy conservation measures by businesses using quantitative methods. The environmental research project carried out by Vermeulen and Goes (1989) also has a quantitative aspect. However, the researchers who use quantitative methods of data collection are not dogmatic advocates of this method of gathering and processing data (Bressers, 1989). In the case of qualitative methods of data collection, case studies appear to be popular (De Bruijn, 1990; Hufen, 1990).

5. RESEARCHING INSTRUMENTS: THEORETICAL DEVELOPMENTS

In the preceding section, existing research of instruments was classified on the basis of four criteria (approaches, types, policy fields, quantitative and qualitative research). A discussion of the research leads one to the conclusion that there is apparently no central question but, instead, a series of interconnected questions. Partly due to the influence of previous research, the central question within current research shifts towards instruments. The theoretical approaches influence this shift as well. We shall now attempt to describe several themes that currently seem to be of importance.

Practice of Policy Implementation

Evaluating the effectiveness of instruments is one of the most important issues in the classical approach, and remains central in recent studies (Van Dijk, 1986; Kuks, 1987). Currently, questions about the effects of policy implementation are less of an exclusive concern; attention is also focused on the practice of policy implementation.[7] Here, central issues include which actors participate in the application of instruments, what degree of influence these actors have on various sub-processes and how cooperation between participants is realized, and so on. The description of the application of instruments supplements the review of effects. The evaluation of effects is considered interesting. However, research is increasingly focused on the policy implementation process and not on the effects. From a theoretical point of view, this shift reflects the growing interest in the contextual approach. In this approach, the relevance of variables 'surrounding' the instruments is used as an explanation of the stages in their implementation.

Combinations of Instruments

In other respects, the classical approach is on its way back. Supporters of this approach, such as Geelhoed, claim that instruments should always be researched independently of each other. An instrumental theory must be 'pure', that is, every type must be individually studied. This 'purity' should also be the rule for the practice of policy implementation. In other words, during the application of instruments in practice, one should use either one type of instrument or the other. A combined application is, in his opinion, one of the causes of policy failure. The analytical distinction between types of instruments is difficult to maintain in research on the practice of policy (Hood, 1983; Van der Doelen, 1989). The apportionment of subsidies is preceded by a phase in which the provision of information stimulates applications (Hufen, 1990; Vermeulen, 1988). Apparently, the simultaneous and harmonized application of two instruments, in this case financial incentives and information transfer, are sometimes desirable during the implementation of policy. It seems, too, that a very sharp analytical distinction between instruments is also untenable and sometimes even counterproductive in practice (Hufen, 1990). Some researchers go so far as to advocate research into combinations of instruments, which would avoid the one-sided perspective of a mono-instrumental approach (Elmore, 1987; Van Woerkom, 1988).

New Instruments

During recent years, appeals have been made for the application of 'new instruments'. Hupe (1990) speaks of post-modern instruments; De Bruijn and Ten Heuvelhof (1991a) speak of 'second generation instruments' (see also Mayntz, 1983b). These appeals are commonly a continuation of a critical analysis of 'old' and even obsolete instruments. Traditional regulation is regarded as old-fashioned (Mayntz, 1983). A solid power base of government, which is assumed when the instrument is chosen, is often lacking. An effective application of instruments could even be obstructed by 'authoritarian' legislation or financing. De Bruijn and Ten Heuvelhof (1991a) identify five families of new instruments. They distinguish multi-faceted instruments, incentives, indicators, instruments focused on persons and communicative instruments. Policy practice also calls for the application of a new type of instrument (Klok, 1989a). Contracts are in some cases a new instrument in environmental policy. In economic policy, the introduction of Programme-like Business-oriented Technology Stimulation (PBTS) is considered to be a new type of instrument. The 'new' element of 'new' instruments is not always evident. It appears, for example, from Noorderhaven's thesis, that the old system of issuing subsidies can be seen as the design and performance of a contract (Noorderhaven, 1990).

In addition to the emphasis on new instruments, attention is also focused on new strategies for their application. To give several examples: licences should be applied so as to conform more with the market (Bressers, 1985); a strategy of 'policy implementation by learning' would be applicable to the use of instruments (Hufen, 1990); one-sided legal instruments could be used by applying a strategy of multi-sided policy implementation (Kocken, 1966a). In addition to these strategies, De Bruijn and Ten Heuvelhof (1991a) also mention fine-tuning, network management, network constituting and serendipity.

Instruments and Coincidence

Behind the classical approach lies the hidden assumption that social processes are in some way controllable. This assumption is less evident in the instrument–context approach and the contextual approaches. 'Policy', 'problems' and 'instruments', nevertheless, also provide a framework for an analysis of these approaches. For this reason, the notion could arise that only 'policy', 'problems' and 'instruments' are of relevance, whereas unanticipated circumstances can also be of great importance. This is demonstrated by O'Toole (1990) in his analysis of the control of water quality management. Because of accidental circumstances, the privatization of the construction of water treatment plants appeared to lead to unexpected positive outcomes. In his general review of 'focused influencing' and instruments in particular, Rosenthal (1988) highlights the impact of unanticipated circumstances. The provision of economic subsidies can be viewed as a process of trial and error, in which the policy maker attempts to 'get lucky' (De Bruijn, 1990).

Naturally, the significance of coincidental events can be considered in the instrumental analysis. However, the instrumental approach sometimes carries the risk of focusing too strongly on the notions of 'instrument', 'policy' and 'problem', so that the possible influence of coincidence disappears from the picture (see Eijsbouts, 1989).

Policy Networks and Instruments

Policy instruments are not 'self-implementing'. Their application demands organizational efforts, often not restricted to the activities of the implementing organization. Recent studies of the application of instruments have also taken into consideration the influence of actors in an implementation network. Klijn (1990) points to the influence of the culture of the construction sector and the parliamentary pressure put on officials who grant subsidies in that sector. Koolhaas (1990) mentions the influence of powerful members of the target group and mutual dependences between implementors and actors in the implementing environment. Hufen (1990) points to the influence of actors outside the implementation area on the assignment of subsidies in technology policy (see also Arentsen, 1991). Various studies have demonstrated that the characteristics of policy networks are helpful starting-points for attempting to clarify the way in which instruments function. In conjunction with this, attempts have been made to explain and identify the consequences of a particular network for the application of instruments (De Bruijn and Ten Heuvelhof, 1991b). Interest in the organizational aspects of the use of instruments becomes evident with questions concerning the separation between policy formulation and implementation as well as with the question concerning the applicability of new instruments. In recent years, both questions have often arisen, both in practice as well in the science of public administration.

Dynamics and the Concept of 'Instrument'

The concept of 'instrument' appears relatively constant. The practice of policy, however, shows that this is partly inaccurate. For many years, instruments appeared to have been applied in achieving many different goals, in many different ways (Hufen, 1990). Therefore, there is no longer any reason to speak of one fixed instrument. Bressers advocates paying more attention to the variability of instruments in research. The functioning of instruments should be studied in connection with the previous choice of instruments and their subsequent 'influence' (Bressers, 1989). The 'influence' of instruments could be seen as an anticipation of changes, the reaction to policy results and the reactions of the target group to the policy. The cybernetic approach seems to provide a structure to take the variability of instruments into consideration. Another helpful theoretical concept is offered by the view of the application of instruments as a learning process (Hufen, 1990).

6. EVALUATION OF THE INSTRUMENTAL PERSPECTIVE

It has become clear that research conducted from an instrumental point of view is prolific and varied. However, the instrumental perspective also has its limitations. As with any theory, some questions and themes are highlighted, while others are intentionally ignored. This means that the instrumental perspective on the one hand clarifies, but on the other hand neglects certain important elements. Hereafter, we shall try to identify some advantages and disadvantages of the instrumental perspective.

Disadvantages of the Instrumental Approach

Gaps in the typology
The formulation of a typology was initially seen as an early contribution to the development of an instrumental theory. The large number of currently existing classifications emphasizes the serious interest in establishing a theory. At the time of writing, Van der Doelen's typology seems to be generally accepted. However, the typology is not uncontroversial; it seems that a convincing classification that can serve as a basic structure for the development of a theory does not exist. Various problems impede the development of the 'ultimate' classification. A problem of typologies is that the categories are not exhaustive. Many typologies, for example, disregard the importance of informal instruments. However, informal instruments are a significant tool for influencing the course of policy processes in the practice of public administration (Ringeling, 1983, 1988). Furthermore, most typologies do not appear to be mutually exclusive. A 'grey' area of instruments exists. It is unclear which category the instruments in the 'grey' area belong to. Another objection is that instruments are seen as static objects. An actor applies an instrument as a carpenter his hammer. After a certain amount of time it 'fits like a glove'. Minor changes of the instrument are taken for granted, yet the initial point of view remains static.[8] The failure to construct an indisputable typology means that the theoretical possibilities are much smaller than the supporters of the classical approach would like us to believe.

Theoretical one-sidedness
From a theoretical point of view, the existing research on instruments is one-sided. The theory development has been strongly focused on environmental and economic policy fields. Furthermore, existing theories are narrowly focused on the application of instruments, whereas the history of instrument choice and realization often also contains an explanation of their functioning.[9] According to some, the existing instrument theories have an insufficient appreciation of the complexity of the environment in which instruments are applied (Toonen, 1979). It is claimed that some theories fail to acknowledge the complexity, so that they pay insufficient attention to it. This criticism is not valid in so far as practically all theory developments concerning policy instruments pay attention to the context of the application. However, there will most likely always be discussion about whether the extent of such attention is sufficient.

A number of public administration authors will argue that the theory development of policy instruments places the emphasis on instruments, whereas these are only one of the many variables in the policy or implementation process (Toonen, 1979). For this reason, there is always too little stress on complexity. As a general proposition, this is a very bold point of view. The idea, however, that the instrumental approach is more fertile in one policy field than in another is, naturally, a valid one. The aforementioned criticisms are certainly true for some policy fields, but not for others.

Reification
Using the concept of 'instrument' carries the risk that the analysis diverges greatly from the perceptible reality, since policy activities may possibly be reified. As soon as the 'object' character of policy is too heavily emphasized, it becomes unclear which concrete activities or behavioural patterns are important. The danger that the applied concepts, which are only intellectual ideas, and cannot be clearly transcribed into reality, might be given substance, is called reification. This problem can be avoided by continuously clarifying the sub-processes of activities that fall under the functioning of the instrument. However, it remains unavoidable that the instrumental perspective only pays attention to certain concepts and themes, while disregarding others.

More theory means more restricted practical applicability
The instrumental perspective raises in many people the expectation of applicability. It is commonly believed that knowledge of instruments provides the opportunity for change. However, the instrumental per-

spective can reduce the notion of reality to terms of cause–effect relationships and even to thinking in terms of goals and means. Instruments are then the manipulatable variables that can ensure the accomplishment of goals. However, instruments usually do not appear to be the most important explanation for actual changes in social processes. This is reflected in the aforementioned theoretical development. The classical approach gradually abandons the field for the other two approaches. This development strengthens the theoretical dimensions of instrumental research, but at the same time weakens its practical applicability. The more the functioning of instruments is explained by a rich variety of contextual variables, the less attention is paid to instrumental variables. The outcome can be that the increase of knowledge of instruments provides more insight into the policy implementation process, but not into the possibilities of controlling that process. The 'short cut' from the instrumental theory to control seems to be blocked. An instrumental theory, built for the most part on contextual variables that cannot be manipulated, offers at best more insight, but only little direction for purposeful change.

Advantages of the Instrumental Perspective

Correspondence with the practice of policy
The instrumental approach corresponds closely to the practice of policy. In the practice of government and policy, one commonly thinks in terms of instruments. For this reason, the instrumental orientation could play an important role in bridging the gap between the theory and practice of policy implementation. Theoretical insights are then related to concepts and constructions that are commonly used in practice.

Enlightenment
The instrumental approach sometimes possesses an exposure or 'enlightenment' function. The instrumental approach emphasizes the 'repertoire character of government actions' (Van de Graaf and Hoppe, 1990, p. 96).

When choosing a policy instrument, questions concerning the way in which policy intentions can be translated into concrete actions have to be dealt with. Choosing an instrument is therefore an activity that reveals policy rhetoric. By asking questions about the functioning of instruments, it could appear that the change of policy means little, because the same instruments are used both before and after the change. Policy visions can successfully be attacked if it appears to be impossible to translate these visions into instruments. Contrasting policy visions sometimes appear to be made applicable by the use of the same instruments and are therefore identical at the instrumental level. Finally, policy intentions sometimes appear to be so complex at the instrumental level that they cannot be achieved.

Arrangement and comparison

The instrumental perspective perceives policy as being constructed from a series of instruments. This perspective produces a recognizable arrangement of policy processes. The recognizability consists, in particular, of answering the obvious question concerning the way government should attempt purposively to influence social processes. The arrangement of administrative reality from an instrumental perspective offers attractive possibilities for description and explanation. In his doctoral thesis, Dercksen (1986) demonstrates the way in which instruments provide a conceptual framework for the description of developments in a certain policy field. One step beyond this is the idea that the instrumental perspective contains concepts for comparison of organizational activities, groups of organizations or nations (Hood, 1983).

A relevant variable

A final important advantage of the instrumental approach is that it offers insight into a variable that could be of importance in many policy processes. Despite the fact that contextual variables can push the significance of an instrument in the background, the attention on the instrument itself cannot be lacking in many analyses.

This is the case, first, because the influence of contextual variables could be insufficient to abolish the significance of the instrumental variable. Knowledge and theory development of instruments are naturally important in such a situation.

Second, the nature of an instrument can influence the way in which contextual variables apply their power. The same contextual variables can have different effects with different instruments. In addition to this, instruments partly constitute their own context. The application of instrument A will involve other actors in the implementation arena than would have been the case with the application of instrument B.

This latter phenomenon means that the relationship between instrument and context is a reciprocal one. There is interaction between instrument and context. The criticism of reification, sometimes levelled at the instrumental approach, reflects a different meaning. For a social scientist, objects (instruments) are not as relevant as human activities.

At the same time, however, the progress of these activities can only be properly understood if one realizes that these activities are derived from and influenced by a set of instruments. 'Objects' are then described and analysed in relation to human beings.

7. CONCLUSION

The roots of the instrumental approach are deep. This conceptual orientation is found in law, economics and political science, as well as in public administration. The approach even seems to have flourished in the field of public administration during recent years. However, the success of this approach is probably also threatening, since the realm of intellectual ideas concerning the instrumental perspective has been widened considerably in two ways. First, it appears that an increasing amount of attention is being paid to the context in which instruments are applied; the same goes for non-instrumental variables. Second, by translating instruments as objects into instruments as activities, the door is opened for a variety of other theories. Research on instruments demonstrates elements of network theories, implementation theories and learning theories. This both widens and weakens the significance of the instrumental approach. It appears to be of crucial importance continuously to return from theoretical reflection to concrete key processes or central activities. If that is done, the approach can keep fulfilling an important function: critical reflection on the practical problems of policy implementation. Furthermore, it is clear that, from a theoretical perspective, the classical approach has lost a great deal of its power, but, for the time being, there is still plenty of meat on its bones.

NOTES

1. According to Schuyt, the revival of the instrumental approach is, in view of strong American legal–philosophical criticism of the instrumental perspective at the beginning of this century, incomprehensible (Schuyt, 1985, pp. 113–24).
2. The Geelhoed commission advised government about deregulation and privatization in 1983. It was during this time that the 'Grote Operaties' (large-scale operations) began, aimed at reducing the public deficit. The instrumental approach is very appropriate to these activities.
3. It is striking that the policy intentions described in the policy reports of these fields are written in the language of the instrumental orientation: 'instruments', 'objectives', 'effectiveness', 'efficiency','implementation', etc.
4. Ringeling drops this definition in later publications, but instead speaks of 'a means' (Ringeling, 1988, p. 1).

5. Compare Ringeling's description and particularly 'similar characteristics' (Ringeling, 1983).
6. Hufen uses implementation theory; Klijn, Koolhaas and De Bruijn use a network perspective.
7. Evaluation research shows a similar development (Kraan-Jetten and Simonis, 1987).
8. For this reason, the concept of 'static object' is introduced (Bressers and Klok, 1987b).
9. Ringeling and Bressers advocate the study of the choice of instruments (Bressers and Ringeling, 1989, pp. 3–24; Klok, 1989; Hufen, 1990).

2. The study of policy instruments: four schools of thought[1]

Stephen H. Linder and B. Guy Peters

1. INTRODUCTION

One of the academic hallmarks of the second half of the twentieth century has been the slow but steady diffusion of economic language and concepts throughout the social sciences, including political science. For some political scientists, this process has enriched the discipline, creating new hybrid approaches, such as public choice, and inviting new patterns of collaboration; for others, it has eroded the philosophical basis of political inquiry and displaced substantive notions of politics with instrumental ones. By the end of World War II, economic values and instrumental rationality had already attained a special prominence in non-academic circles, most notably among governmental policy makers, with economics singled out among the social sciences for institutionalized access to the White House. More importantly, for academics and policy makers alike, economic thinking eventually transformed the meaning of government action. In place of constitutional or functional significance, government action assumed the form of remedial interventions in economic and social life, effectively rehabilitating the classic liberal notion of a carefully delimited public sphere. This time, however, the delimiting was to be accomplished not so much by popular will or constitutional guarantees as by the technical assessments of experts. Both the framing and justification of action-as-intervention relied on technical criteria and appealed to scientific rather than political authority. Consequently, those intending to study public policy, or to improve it, were compelled to speak and reason in the vernacular of interventions and instrumental rationality, and, to a large extent, still do so.

An important corollary of identifying government action with forms of intervention was that diverse policies could be represented analytically as artificial and substitutable instruments, subject to technical scrutiny in their own right. Government-as-intervener would rely on a

wide range of instruments, each with distinctive performance characteristics, to accomplish the purposes expressed in its policies. For the
political scientist, knowledge of these instruments and their attributes
could reveal something of government's implicit purposes while, at the
same time, hinting at the prospects for their accomplishment. Nevertheless, scepticism about instrument study endures, in large part, as a legacy
of mistrust for its origins in a technical rationality that eschewed political
practice and displaced the ideals of political community. In its current
incarnation, however, instrument study has largely outgrown these
origins, and has come to encompass the pragmatist's claims against
objective reason (Anderson, 1987), as well as the radical planner's
designs for discursive community (Fischer, 1990).

The next section offers a brief sketch of the development of instrument study as a research area. We then identify four distinct schools of
thought within this area and trace their implications for modelling the
assessment and choice of instruments. Models in this instance may be
of both a prescriptive and empirical sort, since the motivation of those
in instrument study often extends beyond passive observation to making
claims about superior instruments and improved methods of assessment.
Movement between the prescriptive and the empirical places instrument
study in esteemed company, ranging from realist theories of political
participation to incrementalism and development administration, disciplinary injunctions on separating 'facts' from 'values' notwithstanding.

2. THUMBNAIL GENEALOGY

The groundwork for instrument study in political science was fashioned
by Dahl and Lindblom in the early 1950s in a monograph (Dahl and
Lindblom, 1953) on the politico-economic techniques employed by the
modern state. Their contribution involved a fusion of the Anglo-
American, structural–functional analysis on the scope and purpose of
government activity with the continental, economic-planning work on
the comparative performance of different interventions (Tinbergen,
1956; Chenery, 1964). In the decade that followed, Dahl was to contribute to the largest typological inventory of instruments yet assembled,
but it was largely in the idiom of the continental tradition (Kirschen et
al., 1964). Lindblom's attention turned to resolving the tension between
market and social rationality endemic to planning theory since the 1920s
(Braybrooke and Lindblom, 1963). The fusion of function and technique
that they introduced would not reappear for another generation or so,
this time under the guise of policy design (Miller, 1984; Linder and

Peters, 1984). In the meantime, the study of policy instruments by political scientists followed two separate paths.

One path, supported by the continental tradition, took root in Canadian studies of instruments that emphasized political attributes, such as relative coerciveness. Order among these attributes, grounded in political culture or ideological commitments, then served as a basis for ordering instruments and predicting their use (Phidd and Doern, 1978; Woodside, 1986). Recent efforts focus on national policy styles. Richardson (1983), for example, focuses on the use of bargaining or imposition as modes of government intervention. In the USA, the tradition's economic-planning emphasis blended with public finance and rational-choice theory to supplant its instrument focus with problems of optimal organization. Research springing from this hybrid form became identified with institutional design (Hult, 1987).

An alternative path, following the structural–functional tradition, supported inductive exercises in identifying core, public policy functions from inventories of instruments. Typologies proliferated without much convergence on either basic functions or essential instruments. These efforts continue, based, in part, on the assumption that a set of elemental functions and their instrument counterparts can serve as building blocks for a theory of modern governance (Hood, 1983). Lowi's work linking core functions to distinctive political processes (Lowi, 1972) provided a bridge between the dominant process focus of the nascent policy field in the USA and ongoing case studies of selected instruments. As implementation work later came into prominence among process studies, instruments earned a place as administrative means, a key parameter among the determinants of programmatic success (Pressman and Wildavsky, 1973). With the recent shift in the literature to a formulation emphasis, instruments are treated more as intermediate product than as means (Linder and Peters, 1989a; Ingram and Schneider, 1990). Thus, approaches to fashioning better instruments are currently at issue, as are efforts to understand the process of assessing and choosing among them.

For many political scientists, experience along these two paths has recast the original equation of instruments and technical rationality in favour of a more particularistic view that places context and values at the heart of instrument assessment. The field of instrument study, however, is far from a consensus on the question of relative emphasis. We might expect different views of the policy-making process to colour the treatment of instruments and the roles attributed to context and values. Similarly, we might expect commitments to different analytical approaches to influence prescriptions about instruments and about their proper fashioning. In either case, recognizing the diversity of premises and their consequences for both behavioural and prescriptive modelling provides a useful frame of reference for capturing how far instrument study has come, and for speculating on the directions in which it ought to go.

3. FOUR DISTINCT APPROACHES

Choices about the instruments of intervention are typically made without benefit of systematic, comparative assessments. Whether bound by the constraints of time, as in the case of the policy maker, or by disciplinary norms, as is the policy researcher, some instruments are simply deemed better than others by virtue of training, experience or precedent and are embraced accordingly. Detailed comparisons across the range of 'tools' available to government, or careful scrutiny of their differential characteristics are given, at best, only perfunctory acknowledgement along the lines of obligatory calls for more research. As a result, the prevailing differences in approaches to instrument study and choice tend to reflect differences over basic assumptions and premises that normally remain in the background, rather than the more conventional methodological disputes over model specification and analytical emphasis. Thus, our differentiation among schools of instrument study highlights background factors and commitments over more obvious differences in methods or instrument claims. These background differences, in turn, will be linked to the framing of instrument choices and their advocacy.

Although we emphasize differences that exist among distinct schools of instruments research, there are also some important similarities in much of the work on this topic. First, most discussions of instrument choice focus on the (presumed) objective merits of the instrument, rather than on the heuristics and decision-making routines that officials or analysts employ to choose among instruments. Cognitive heuristics are generally mediated by perceptions of the instruments; hence, any 'objective' features of instrument performance are accommodated only indirectly. Second, much of the discussion centres on a relatively facile distinction between market-based tools and tools associated with the authority and financial resources of governments – authority and treasure in Hood's terms (Salamon and Lund, 1989). Comparisons tend to be limited to these two, generic alternatives, making strategic use of the terms of partisan debate on the appropriate scope of government. Third, the measurable economic effects of instruments seem to receive a disproportionate share of the attention, at the expense of social and political effects. Finally, two important micro-level links are largely omitted: how does a given instrument emerge as a favoured choice – is it creative synthesis, substitution from habit, or a winnowing down? – and how is it eventually equipped with the programmatic details that transform it into public policy?

Instrumentalists

The first school of instrument study can be characterized as 'instrumentalist'. These scholars, as well as perhaps a majority of policy makers, endorse a select few instruments to which they ascribe all power (see, for example, Anderson, 1977). In other words, the policy claim coming from these scholars is: we know a particular tool, and understand its inner workings; its effectiveness is either proven or highly plausible; and we expect it, or a limited set of variations on it, to be effective in most foreseeable circumstances. Here, the proper tool can turn policy failure into success. While the sanctioned tool may not be the best in every sense for a given circumstance, it is felt to be less prone to failure from unexpected contingencies; it is robust, in the statistician's parlance, and versatile, performing reliably in most situations for most purposes. Analysis, then, should attend to the traits and characteristics of instruments, with the aim to identify, refine and extend a small set of 'universal' instruments to a wide range of applications and to document optimal performance under varying constraints. There is no attempt to contextualize the role of the instrument, whether by problem area or by policy-making situation, but rather to establish utility across contexts. The instrumentalist perspective appeals principally to technical rationality. There is little room for 'politics' in instrument assessment. Nor is there allowance made for diversity of opinion on the character of optimality. Much of the discussion centres on applying trusted instruments in new ways and offering refinements to extend their applicability.

The instrumentalist's commitment to a limited repertoire of policy instruments comes from several sources. One is professional or disciplinary. It appears that the disciplines of economics and law tend towards rather strong commitments to certain instruments. Naturally, these are the instruments that are derived most directly from the basic methodologies of those disciplines. Lawyers tend to be committed to instruments grounded in legal process, such as regulations and contracts, while economists tend towards market-based instruments, such as tax incentives, that complement the operation of the prevailing price system. Socialization in the norms of the profession effectively builds a

'trained incapacity' to think otherwise about the instruments available
to government.

A second source of the instrumentalist position is ideology. As policy
issues became more ideological in the 1980s, there was a tendency for
academics and policy makers to select their tools according to their
political correctness for the several ideological camps. In particular,
Conservatives tended toward privatized means to solve public problems
that they attributed in large part to the shortcomings of public bureaucracy (Savas, 1987). An apparent opening on the left now has Democrats
in the USA returning to advocate more direct government involvement in solving problems, for example, national health insurance, public
works activity, protectionism.

Finally, instrumentalists may formulate their biases for or against
particular instruments based simply on power considerations. Within
government, for example, the members of tax-writing organizations and
their staffs may tend to rely on tax instruments as the most appropriate
means of solving social problems. This choice obviously enhances their
centrality within the policy process. Power considerations such as these
may also account for the choices made by different academic analysts:
if legal instruments are used, lawyers will have greater leverage over
the policy process, and so on.

Proceduralists

At the other end of a scale of commitment to particular instruments
are individuals whom we classify as 'proceduralists'. These analysts
eschew commitment to any instruments outside the context of a particular, concrete problem. They assume that there are important
differences among tools but that no one tool or family of tools can have
universal applicability. Further, proper choice is not the product of a
discrete calculation but rather a tentative resolution of a dynamic
process of adaptation (Browne and Wildavsky, 1983). Proper tools, then,
almost by definition, are a function of the particular decision-making
situation in which a given policy problem or set of problems is situated.
Not surprisingly, proceduralists place greater emphasis on the process
of iterative tool development than on the characteristics of tools in
isolation. The implicit (or sometimes explicit) assumption is that bad
instruments can be made to work, just as good ones can be made to
fail, depending on the particulars of their application. Therefore, there
is no *a priori* right or wrong choice among instruments, nor, on the
whole, do instruments' intrinsic properties matter a great deal. Rather,
it all depends on the outcome of a pluralistic, problem-focused process.

The proceduralist effectively negates most of the instrumentalist's claims. The positions of politics and instruments are reversed; politics becomes central and instruments peripheral. Tool choice is no longer the core concern; at best, it is derivative and, at worst, artifactual. Instrument study becomes an investigation, not of instruments *per se*, but of cases where particular instruments emerge as the by-product of *in situ* processes. Each case offers a lesson in feasibility and preparedness for those anticipating similar situations in the future. To the extent that instruments are at issue, they are best recast ahead of time to accommodate the political forces anticipated in each situation.

The proceduralists place substantial emphasis on the role of implementation and embed instrument study in the implementation rather than formulation phases of the policy process. The prevailing assumption is that any instrument selected will, in reality, be shaped more by the complex process of making it operate than by any *ex ante* blueprint or conceptual design. In terms of its origins, the proceduralist approach has both European and North American variants. In particular, the 'bottom up' school of implementation studies (Hjern and Hull, 1982), and the network approaches more characteristic of European political science (In 't Veld et al., 1991), are proceduralist largely out of opposition to instrumentalist claims that politics, even of an administrative sort, simply does not count for much when it comes to the performance of instruments. The American version reacts more to the threat of centralized planning implicit in a formulation emphasis and in depictions of policy instruments as direct rather than indirect means of achieving any of central government's ends.

Contingentists

This school's approach corresponds most closely to a traditional, social-planning view that instruments should be chosen according to how well their performance characteristics satisfy the requirements of a particular problem setting (Bobrow and Dryzek, 1987; Dunn, 1988). Once the demands of the 'job' are clear, it is a straightforward matter to locate a match or best-fitting tool from among those that appear relevant. Instrument study then is occupied both with the structuring and articulation of situational demands as problem-solving requirements, and with methods of rational assignment intended to ensure that the most appropriate tool is selected. Performance, in this view, is contingent, not so much on the character of the tool itself, as the instrumentalists would have it, or on the context of its application, as the proceduralists assume, but rather on the *ex ante* goodness of fit between tool and context.

A focus on fit comes out of basic systems logic that ties form to function and attributes performance to their complementary alignment. A systems orientation pervades the structural–functional tradition in political science and finds reinforcement in the engineering perspective common to both planning and policy analysis. Here, the context sets the conditions for assessment, but it is not the dynamic and particularistic context of the proceduralists. It is instead a highly structured and reified affair, expressed principally in typological terms as a given mixture of requirements. Further, the requirements themselves tend to be treated as objectively verifiable conditions, as though they were physical properties universally accessible to the trained observer.

The contingentist view of instruments similarly aspires to objectivity. For purposes of assessment, instruments are treated as bundles of performance characteristics, a view shared by the instrumentalists. Once the problem has been structured and the characteristics of plausible instruments established, however, few degrees of freedom are left for fashioning a solution. The match between problem and instrument that constitutes the contingentist's solution is typically found or 'discovered' through deduction rather than being devised inductively. Further, to the extent that politics enters into the contingentist's account, it enters mainly as yet another feature of context, perhaps posing additional requirements.

Given their attachment to systems concepts, contingentists are likely to include policy analysts who approach instrument assessment as a problem-driven task and admit objectivist notions of performance and requirements. Thus, the appropriateness of instruments can be expected to vary widely across contexts, even though views of either one – instruments or contexts – are not expected to vary much, at least not in a systematic way, from one 'objective' analyst to another. Indeed, the definition of the contexts may be expected to be more variable than the presumed operating characteristics of the instruments that might be applied within them.

Constitutivists

The 'constitutivists' go further than the contingentists in arguing that as well as understanding the particulars of the context for which a given tool will be adapted, there is a need to attend to that tool's subjective meaning. Subjective meaning here refers not only to non-instrumental aspects, such as symbolic and ethical import, but also to the instrumental features whose interpretation and significance are mediated by values and perceptions. In contrast to our characterization of policy analysts, in this school of thought there is no objective reality about tools and their characteristics that is perhaps only imperfectly knowable and to which certain experts can claim privileged access. Rather, tools represent one form of socially constructed practice whose meaning and legitimacy are constituted and reconstituted over time (Steinberger, 1980; Forester, 1985).

Instruments may well be 'fitted' to problems as the contingentists claim but there is no pretence of rational assignment based on objective features. For the constitutivist, the understanding of both tools and problems is a subjective process shaped by social or professional interaction as much as by contemplation. In a sense, then, meaning must be established and sometimes negotiated as an antecedent to any matching of tool and problem. For those engaged in instrument assessment, pursuit of meaning may entail a self-reflexive assessment of values and biases (interestingly, a process stressed in the more Freudian of Lasswell's writings, his positivist reputation notwithstanding).

For those inclined to Deweyan ideals, the construction of meaning, especially when relevant to public purposes, must be grounded in the community that constitutes the contingentist's context for the problem. Once faith in experts' claims to objectivity and truth are shaken, the focus of assessment can shift to democratic and communal sources. Here, the radical planner's efforts to develop community-based assessments become relevant. For the true constitutivist, however, attending to community goals and purposes is not enough. One must also consider the meanings evoked by particular constructions of tool and problem and seek to transform or renegotiate these as part of the assessment. This approach to assessment shares some elements with critical theory. It can also subordinate instrumental rationality to more classical forms, such as practical reason, and, in the ideal, seek their embodiment in a dialogic community.

Distinguishing the constitutivists from the other schools of instrument study does more than simply welcome more radical factions into the fold; it opens the door to the workings of subjective factors in instrument assessment. On the one hand, it raises suspicions about claims to authoritative problem definition and rejects the myth of the neutral instrument. On the other hand, it admits as relevant the beliefs and perceptions of the professional engaged in instrument research. From a constitutivist perspective, we can expect judgements about instruments and interpretations of context to vary somewhat according to their source. But the variation will be far from idiosyncratic; it should reflect differences in values and perceptions that are, in part, linked to more easily observed social factors, such as professional training and partisanship. This comports more with our intuitions about the practice of instrument assessment than does the objectivism of the contingentists and instrumentalists or the relativism of the proceduralists. We expect the conservative policy analyst with extensive training in neoclassical economics to construct different 'matches' than would the reformist political scientist with roots in transformative politics. This adds texture to the canvas of instrument study, taking us well beyond the early beginnings in functional typologies, and adds subtlety to the rudimentary market versus non-market dichotomy that gave instrument study its initial parameters.

4. CONCEPTUAL FRAMES AND GOVERNMENT'S INSTRUMENT CHOICES

We have presented the four views of instruments as schools of thought, that is, as coherent points of view held by academics and policy researchers that roughly parallel methodological differences and contending models of policy making. The implications for how we study instruments – what factors are important and how judgements are made – should be clear. A summary appears in Table 2.1.

The first column arrays the four views by their conception of the key factor in the 'success' of policy instruments. The second column addresses the way instruments should be assessed, according to each view. And finally, the connection to partisan or pluralist politics is considered in the third column. Since this last was not given as much attention in the preceding narrative as were the 'key factors' and 'modes of assessment', some brief comments are in order. The term 'design', appearing in the third column, connotes the systematic assessment of alternative instruments.

For the instrumentalist, for example, the assessment of instruments is a technical matter guided by expertise rather than bargaining or political commitments: design effectively precludes politics. For the contingentist, in contrast, design shapes politics, as different patterns of competition and partisanship are engendered by the type of instrument chosen, consistent with Lowi's construction of the policy-making universe. Since the proceduralist eschews design, at least in the sense used here, it represents the antithesis of the instrumentalist view, displacing technical analysis with political accommodation. The constitutivist view is distinctive in that design and politics are depicted as mutually constitutive.

Neither one precludes the other, nor determines it, in a mechanistic sense. Instead, the politics–design dichotomy itself is abandoned in favour of an interactive notion of design as competing political constructions of instruments. Here, the objectivist notions of 'problems' and 'instruments-as-solutions' are replaced with the interpretivist's sensitivity to non-instrumental meanings.

Table 2.1   Schools of thought in instrument study

Schools	Key factor	Modes of assessment	Relation to politics
Instrumentalist	Instrument attributes	Optimality under constraint	Design precludes politics
Proceduralist	Adaptation	Evolving accommodation	Politics precludes design
Contingentist	Goodness of fit	Matching tool to task	Design shapes politics
Constitutivist	Evoked meaning	Interpreting contested meaning	Politics as design

The more important implication for public policy, however, may well be whether the differences among schools matter for the kinds of policy devices government actually uses. Do each of the schools present a sufficiently distinctive ordering of instruments, or a way of reasoning about them, to allow an *a priori* bias towards the access of any particular school to the government's decision makers? Privileged access by a given school, favourably predisposed toward certain instruments, then, might be a reliable predictor of the prominence of those instruments in policy. And if so, is the government's portfolio of instruments more a reflection of its alignment with a particular school than of cautious or calculated deliberation over instruments' performance?

Consider how such an 'instrument bias' might work. At one extreme, a 'proceduralist' government is likely to avoid elaborate analytical exercises in instrument comparison and design in favour of commitment to a few ensembles of context–problem–instrument. These ensembles of patchwork and adaptation should both sustain a working political coalition and have sufficient symbolic resonance to elide performance issues. At the opposite extreme, the 'instrumentalist' government settles on a few select instruments, that comport with their ideology or aspirations, because of performance claims. In the proceduralist instance, a bargaining style of pluralist politics precludes instrument design; in the instrumentalist case, it is an unswerving commitment resting on some prior technical analysis.

On a more general level, the proceduralist is particularistic, while the instrumentalist is universalist. And yet, the expected right–left ideological distinctions do not readily apply. We find attachment to a few instruments, with technical justifications befitting an instrumentalist, in Thatcher-era Britain; but the regime was committed to instruments of public divestiture, effectively emptying government's portfolio of existing instruments. Similarly, instances of a proceduralist view with a left-leaning ideology can be found among progressive urban governments in North America. Accordingly, while there may be a bias in the way instruments are viewed, we do not necessarily know ahead of time whether the set of instruments favoured by a certain bias will be a left, right, or centrist one, ideologically.

A more intriguing implication of this bias appears, however, once the other two schools are brought into the picture. Like the instrumentalist, the contingentist is linked to rationalistic modes of assessment; here, the contingencies of an instrument's application are given more weight than the traits of the instrument in the abstract. Still, analysis is central to the deliberations over instrument choice. For the constitutivist, the relative significance of instruments is based on the construction of their meaning. When the constructions are contested, the resolution process may begin to resemble the proceduralists' emphasis on adaptation. The relevant distinction, then, for governments affiliated with one school or another is probably not ideology so much as technology. Instrumentalist and contingentist governments are far more inclined towards technocratic modes of policy making, while the constitutivist and proceduralist schools incline government towards participatory or pluralist modes, respectively. These speculations clearly warrant further research.

5. CONCLUSIONS

This description of four alternative schools of thought about policy instruments and their linkage to the context within which they operate is to some extent a brief historical depiction of the evolution of the field. Although elements of all these four types are found in the empirical analysis we are conducting, there appears to be an intellectual movement toward the constitutivist end of the spectrum. This movement reflects in part the intellectual patterns of the times, more accepting of institutional and phenomenological explanations than the more positivist past. It also reflects a growing understanding that instrument selection is not a simple mechanical exercise of matching well-defined problems and equally well-defined solutions. Rather, it is fundamentally an intellectual process of constructing a reality and then attempting to work within it.

This treatment of the four schools also reflects something of the development of our own thinking about policy instruments and the task of policy design. Not only does it reflect our greater acceptance of the constitutivist argument, but it reflects the tension between the academic analysis of designs and involvement in the real-world process of designing. Both of these are worthy exercises and both are necessary for the development and improvement of policy, but they have different requirements and different purposes that must be carefully distinguished if our work is to be of use to either camp.

Finally, this chapter also represents the need for greater empirical work in the area of policy instruments. There is a great deal of work already completed in the (presumed) objective characteristics of certain instruments, but there is less on their political and perceptual nature. We are already embarked upon such an exercise, but we urge other scholars to join us in attempting to understand how government chooses what it will do, and how it will seek to do it.

NOTE

1. Portions of this chapter are drawn from our article 'The study of policy instruments', *Policy Currents* (vol. 2, 1992, no. 2, pp. 1–7).

3. The trade-off between appropriateness and fit of policy instruments

René Bagchus

1. THE CHOICE OF POLICY INSTRUMENTS[1]

In the 1980s and early 1990s a substantial amount of scientific research discussed policy instruments (De Jong and Korsten, 1993, p. 2). The study of policy instruments often constitutes one of many variables for analysis. In many cases the research question is a variation of the following: to what extent has the implementation of a particular policy instrument contributed to effectiveness? These studies discuss only marginally, or not at all, the selection of policy instruments. However, implementation and performance are only two of the many building blocks which comprise the theory of instruments. A third aspect is the choice of instruments (Bressers and Klok, 1987a, p. 76), which becomes more important as knowledge of implementation and performance increases. Gradually it becomes apparent that in certain contextual situations some policy instruments are more effective than others. In some cases, the policy instruments employed are labelled as ineffective, and it seems logical to switch to other instruments. Conditions for this switch-over offer some insight into why and how specific policy instruments are chosen.

The limited scientific interest in the choice of policy instruments is even more remarkable, considering the divergent views on this subject. Bressers and Klok (1987b) write the following:

> Increasingly the awareness emerges . . . that a larger variety of instruments is possible. These instruments together form a kind of toolbox, from which one can make a rational choice, taking into careful consideration the demands of the desired effects and the circumstances. (p. 78)

Ringeling argues in his inaugural lecture (1983) on the same subject:

A free choice of policy instruments is not possible. A service or department has gained experience with a specific instrument. The proposals of such a unit as to how the problem should be solved and which instruments should be used are a reflection of the experience. This restricts the possibilities of authorities to choose from the different policy instruments. (p. 10)

A greater contrast does not seem conceivable. Whereas Bressers and Klok emphasize the possibilities of the choice of policy instruments, Ringeling emphasizes the restrictions involved in choosing policy instruments (see also Linder and Peters, Chapter 2, this volume).

The tension between these two approaches constitutes the theoretical foundation of this chapter. Three theoretical approaches to the choice of policy instruments will be examined: traditional, refined, and an institutional approach regarding the 'choice' of policy instruments. This last approach will be discussed at greater length. In Section 5, the approaches will be illustrated in the light of the choice of policy instruments in the education sector. In the final section conclusions and several implications of the examined approaches will be discussed.

2. AN INSTRUMENTAL HEGEMONY?

In this section two instrumental approaches to the choice of policy instruments will be reviewed. We have named these approaches the traditional and refined instrumental approach. The research published over the last few years on the choice of policy instruments can often be classified under one of these two categories. Both will be discussed in this section. In Section 3 an alternative approach to the choice of policy instruments will be formulated on the basis of a number of critical comments. The different approaches will be discussed in the light of the following five aspects:

- the features of policy instruments;
- the relationship between environment and policy instrument;
- the relationship between policy instrument and issue;
- the way policy instruments are realized or designed;
- the appraisal of policy instruments and the meaning ascribed to instruments by the decision makers who use them.

The Traditional Instrumental Approach

The traditional instrumental approach views the choice of policy instruments in the light of a strict goal–means rationality (Geelhoed, 1983;
Hood, 1983; De Haan et al., 1986; Needham, 1982). Policy instruments
are regarded as neutral and are valued as such. In this respect, policy
instruments do not have intrinsic features of their own. These are
derived from the objective to which they are directed. The traditional
instrumental approach pays little or no attention to the context in which
the policy instrument is designed or is applied. The focus is on the
policy instrument and context is absent. Regarding the relationship
between context and policy instrument, the traditional instrumental
approach argues that policy instruments are a means of direction from
the centre.

Furthermore, in the traditional approach the centre decides on the
hierarchy of objectives. The goal–means rationality is also the basis for
choosing policy instruments; it determines their usability. This means
that the objectives are determined independently of the policy instruments and prior to the selection of instruments. As a result, the choice
of policy instruments can be regarded as the operationalization of these
objectives. The objectives are external to the policy instruments. Only
after they have been determined can the means be related to the goals
(Schuyt, 1985, p. 114–18). Within the traditional instrumental approach
the number of alternative policy instruments is unlimited and only
dependent on set objectives. Consistent with the objectives, the choice
pertains to an evaluation of alternative policy instruments and their
consequences. The realization of instruments and the meaning ascribed
to them is in the traditional approach distinctly consequential (Schuyt,
1985, p. 115). This means that policy instruments are valued in accordance with their effects. These effects, in their turn, are related to the
predetermined objectives.

The Reaction to the Traditional Approach: Refined Instrumentation

This chapter began by stating that in the 1980s much research discussed
policy instruments. An important part of these studies is aimed at
the elaboration and differentiation of what we have called traditional
instrumentalism. Therefore we have called this approach refined instrumentalism (Bressers and Klok, 1987b; Hufen, 1990; Linder and Peters,
1989b; De Bruijn, 1990; De Bruijn and Ten Heuvelhof, 1991a). First of
all, the refined instrumental approach differentiates the ways in which
policy instruments are regarded. It refines the traditional approach to

the extent that the latter takes policy instruments into consideration without paying attention to underlying values and norms. The refined instrumental approach studies in depth the tension between instruments, on the one hand, and more universal values, morals and ethical principles, on the other. This means that, according to the refined approach, policy instruments have designated intrinsic features – outside of their context – that lead to the development of instrument typologies (Van der Doelen, 1989).

According to traditional instrumentalism, no relationship exists between context and policy instrument. The refined approach, however, emphasizes this relationship. The target audience of the policy instrument also emerges. As a result, the refined approach puts somewhat in perspective direction from the centre. By introducing interest in social dynamics – the context (De Bruijn and Ten Heuvelhof, 1991a, p. 7) – the mechanical use of policy instruments becomes refined. It is obvious that many other actors are involved in the policy process, influencing the selection, implementation and performance of policy instruments. This also puts into perspective the relevance of the policy instrument compared to the final objective (De Bruijn and Hufen, 1992, pp. 74–5).

A third aspect which clarifies the difference between traditional and refined instrumentalism is the way in which policy instruments are chosen. According to the refined approach, context exists apart from the goal–means relationship. In refined instrumentalism the choice of a policy instrument is regarded as the 'pushing and pulling' between actors with conflicting interests (Hufen, 1990, p. 207–9). Self-interest plays a major role in the process. A fourth, related difference concerns the way in which the choice of policy instruments is made. Earlier it was stated that according to the refined approach a context exists separate from the goal–means relationship. The context plays a major part in selection, application and continuation of policy instruments. In accordance with the 'pushing and pulling' of actors with interests, an actor chooses between available alternative policy instruments by evaluating the possible consequences. In contrast, traditional instrumentalism places no limitations on the number of alternatives so long as they meet the set objectives. In refined instrumentalism the actor evaluates only those alternative policy instruments from which he then chooses according to his own judgement.

A fifth aspect deals with the appreciation and evaluation of policy instruments. According to the traditional approach, appraisal is mainly related to the degree to which the objective is achieved. Refined instrumentalism puts this in perspective, stressing, instead, that the effects caused by policy instruments cannot solely be explained by the policy instruments themselves, but also, to a large extent, by the context in which the policy instrument is used.

An Optimal Fit: Four Conditions

Contingent reasoning links much research within refined instrumentalism. Policy design not only requires knowledge of alternative policy instruments, but also knowledge of the circumstances in which these alternatives have been selected and applied. Clearly, dependent on context, certain policy instruments are more effective than others. This gives rise to questions such as: 'In what circumstances do which policy instruments lead to effective intervention?' or 'Which alternative policy instruments are not effective in certain circumstances?' In brief, design is aimed at policy instruments which 'fit' particular situations. A policy instrument is effective when a 'fit' exists among conditions. In refined instrumentalism four conditions play a central role in designing effective policy instruments:

- the characteristics of the instrument;
- the policy issue (Elmore, 1987, p. 175),
- contextual factors; and
- the characteristics of the target audience.

According to this theory, a policy instrument is effective when there is an optimal fit between, on the one hand, the characteristics of the policy instrument, and, on the other hand, the characteristics of the context, objectives and target audience. In this case, the instrument is called an effective policy instrument, and all four conditions (Hupe, 1990, p. 232) are satisfied.

A Useful Toolbox?

The preceding sub-sections outline the conditions which play a role in the selection of policy instruments. Two problem areas can be identified. First, a connection needs to be made between the conditions and the policy instruments. Second, a connection needs to be made between the characteristics and the achievements of the instrument. Establishing these connections is not without problems, and these are discussed briefly in this section.

The first problem is that a connection needs to be made between the effectiveness of policy instruments and the conditions. It is necessary to determine which conditions must be met in deciding which policy instrument is most effective in particular circumstances. However, the conditions give different messages which call for different reactions. In addition, the conditions' dynamics must be taken into account. Over time the conditions may follow a different course, and at varying speeds. They are dynamic partly due to the activities of the actors. The 'objective' facts of the context or target audience do not automatically influence the selection of policy instruments. Such facts are noted and interpreted by individuals who all wish to safeguard their own interest, and all have their own opinions about which strategies and tactics should be pursued. The messages of the conditions are seldom fixed and unalterable, which makes it very difficult to agree on their character and meaning. Often they are not fixed because they are influenced by people who 'use' them or react to them. This means that in analysing them one should bear in mind the attitudes, values and morals of the people involved.

The second problem in contingent reasoning – and in the refined instrumental approach – concerns the relation between the characteristics of the policy instrument and its achievements. In contingent reasoning the emphasis is on the idea of being 'congruent' (Schreyögg, 1980, 1982; Donaldson, 1982). Even if we can create a fit between the instrument and the effectiveness of that instrument, we still need to determine whether one influences the other, and, if so, which. Thus, it is unclear in which direction the different contingencies operate. Besides that, the success of policy instruments is only measured by their degree of effectiveness. This is one-sided, to say the least. Furthermore, many more factors are involved in design than conditions listed. This makes it difficult – if not impossible – to relate achievements to the characteristics of the policy instrument.

One of the consequences of using a contingency approach is that the design of policy instruments has evolved from a creative and interactive process with few rules to a searching process with obvious, deterministic restrictions. The designer needs to understand the context. From this knowledge springs automatically – like a *deus ex machina* – the single effective policy instrument. Even though many studies have been published on refined instrumentalism, so far a full synthesis of the relationship between the conditions has not materialized. Despite some coherence, manageable rules still elude designers. As a result, designing policy instruments on the basis of these views becomes a serious predicament. Selecting policy instruments according to the refined instrumental approach is a matter of continual equilibrating between unmanageable complexity and oversimplification. This means that little attention is given to the role of people or the significant position of the government.

Consequently, concepts such as action, dynamics, attitudes, values and morals remains unexplored. A new approach which takes these aspects into account needs to be found. An institutional approach to the choice of policy instruments will be a first step.

3. THE INSTITUTIONAL APPROACH

The two perspectives – traditional and refined instrumentalism – discussed in the preceding section can be considered dominant: an instrumental hegemony exists. The last sub-section shows that many criticisms can be made of these approaches. In this section the institutional perspective – in reaction to an instrumental approach – will be discussed. In this view, the emergence of policy instruments is considered as an institutional process. This clarifies the main difference between this approach and the previous approaches. They speak of an institutionalized context, but not of institutionalized policy instruments, whereas the approach discussed in this section examines both. This distinction, which may appear trivial, has consequences when the choice of policy instruments is studied more closely. This institutional approach takes into account the standard criticisms – lack of attention to people, to the significant role of the government, to action, to dynamics, to values and morals – of both traditional and refined instrumentalism. The meaning of the institutional perspective can be summed up in the following twin concepts: present–past, design–evolution and result–process.

From Present to Past

First, the meaning of an institutional perspective can be denoted by the twin concept present–past. Refined instrumentalism explains that actors adjust themselves to incentives from within the environment. Thus the selection of policy instruments creates an optimal fit between instrument and circumstances. As the institutional structures change, the environmental incentives and consequently the selection of policy instruments change as well. It is believed that this adjustment happens without delay. In selecting policy instruments, the history and context in which they occur play no part at all. The selection of policy instruments is mainly explained by variables which are active at that particular moment (Bressers, 1993, p. 309). However, the institutional approach takes the past into careful consideration. According to Krasner (1988), the main feature of an institutional perspective is that choices made in the past restrict the availability of future options. This means that the number of alternative policy instruments is restricted as a result of a historic exclusion of alternatives and 'sunk cost'. This exclusion of policy instruments can be either material or psychological. In an institutional approach the emergence of a policy instrument is not only explained in terms of preferences and possibilities of actors who are active in the here and now. The preferences and possibilities of particular policy instruments and the nature of the existing ones can only be understood as part of a historic development. The choice of policy instruments is not just an adjustment to the present situation; the past also has a continuing effect. An institutional approach can offer an explanation of the fact that policy instruments are established over a period of time, even in those situations when they are not considered to be functional (Thelen and Steinmo, 1992, p. 2).

From Design to Evolution

Designing effective policy instruments on the basis of conditions is the main feature of refined instrumentalism. It has also become clear that, according to this view, four conditions – the characteristics of context, policy instrument, policy issue and target group – are central to selecting policy instruments. The institutional approach questions intentional behaviour of the actors and the possibility of designing effective policy instruments. According to this view, the choice of policy instruments can be explained partly by historical process and represents an incremental development which is, to a small degree, determined and controlled by the actors involved (Brunsson and Olsen, 1993, pp. 1–5).

From Result to Process

Earlier it was explained that refined instrumentalism considers the selection of policy instruments from a static point of view which is highly functional. Both the traditional and refined approach are strongly result-oriented. Policy instruments are appraised by their degree of effectiveness. The institutional view questions this orientation of actors in choosing policy instruments. The emphasis is no longer just on the result of policy instruments but more on the process of their emergence. Thus, the dominant criterion of effectiveness can be questioned. March and Olsen (1984, pp. 734–9) state that in selecting among alternatives actors are not guided by effectiveness; they are guided by the logic of appropriateness – appropriate behaviour according to conventions, routines and particular ways of thinking and acting. In a context in which actors

fulfil particular roles, they are continually aware of the roles they are
expected to play. The way in which they are expected to act is determined by the role which they impose on themselves, or is imposed by
others within the community. The foregoing implies that in an institutional view the emphasis lies no longer on the effectiveness of policy
instruments, but on the process of formation (Toonen, 1993, p. 258).

4. THE INSTITUTIONAL APPROACH FURTHER ELABORATED

In the previous section three twin concepts were presented, allowing us
to establish the meaning of an institutional perspective on the formation
of policy instruments. This section will elaborate on a number of consequences of this perspective, using the following theoretical notions:
policy community, existing social relationships, instruments paradigm,
institutionalization in depth and breadth, and the specific position of
the government within the policy community. For each of these
aspects the consequences of choosing policy instruments will be discussed.

The Policy Community

Actors in civil administration do not operate in a vacuum. They belong
to a context characterized by a number of specific actors (Wright, 1988).
This context is – in this research – called a policy community. A policy
community is the aggregate of actors pertaining to a particular policy
area (Bekke et al., 1994, p. 15). By definition, a community exceeds the
boundaries of organizations. Jordan (1990) remarks on the notion of
'policy community':

> The policy community idea therefore seems to rest firmly on the notion that
> the particular policy of the moment is processed in a context in which there
> is a recognition that there are, and will be in the future, other issues which
> also need to be dealt with. In a policy community a specific item of business
> is transacted in a context where the participants already have mutual needs,
> expectations, experiences. (p. 326)

A policy community, therefore, can be regarded as a specific kind of
policy network. Due to the large amount of general knowledge and
personal relationships, extensive communication within the community
becomes possible. The actors have, in the course of time, established
particular interaction patterns in which certain experiences, values,

morals and paradigms are exchanged. Another feature of a policy community is the high degree of mutual dependence among the actors. Furthermore, routines play a role within the policy community. The behaviour of actors within the community is usually determined by conventions. The same applies to the choice of policy instruments. In addition, ideas are developed in the community which identify the problems and determine the norms and values regarding solutions and appropriate policy instruments. Within this context policy instruments are formed. The next sub-sections deal with the consequences of this process.

Existing Social Relationships within the Policy Community

Policy communities are characterized by long-standing social relationships between actors. Granovetter (1985) describes how behaviour in a specific social context is influenced by continuing social relationships. Actors do not decide and behave like atoms functioning outside a social context. Heclo and Wildavsky (1974) state:

> There is no escaping the tension between policy and community, between adapting actions and maintaining relationships, between decision and between governing now and preserving the possibility of governing later. (p. 15)

Behaviour and decision making of these actors is embedded in a context of social relationships, the policy community. These social relationships play, in their turn, a role in the actions of the actors, and, consequently, the choice of policy instruments. Apart from the degree of goal attainment, the appraisal of policy instruments also depends on the way in which the features of policy instruments support and sustain these continuous relationships within the policy community. None of the actors has any interest in damaging these relationships, especially when a mutual dependence exists between the formation and implementation of future policy. Therefore, optimal goal attainment with a policy instrument which jeopardizes carefully constructed relationships is, for many actors, not a realistic option. This implies that policy instruments are labelled appropriate when they are a continuation of, or support, existing positive social relationships among actors. The continuation of these relationships has become an end in itself.

The Instruments Paradigm

Actors function in a specific policy community in which a framework
of ideas and routines prevails. This framework not only determines the
objectives of the policy, but also the policy instruments which are used
to achieve them. Analogous to 'Gestalt', this framework is shared by
most members of the policy community, and is embedded in an 'instruments language' by which the policy makers communicate. This
framework is considered to be self-evident. By analogy with the policy
paradigm (Hall, 1993), this is called the instruments paradigm. It is
concerned with the aggregate of ideas, conventions, rules, values and
morals which not only specify the objectives, but also the policy instruments to achieve them. In this sense, it is similar to Kuhn's scientific
paradigm (Koningsveld, 1984). An instruments paradigm means that
actors have definite ideas about the appropriate instruments for a particular situation. These convictions and matching instruments are rarely
questioned. An instruments paradigm and its policy community are
closely intertwined. The recruitment of the members of a policy community takes place on the basis of a dominant instruments paradigm.
When the instruments paradigm is mainly of a legal nature, this leads
to an expansion of legal departments and the hiring of employees with
legal knowledge. The instruments paradigm thus lodges itself in the
policy community. This intertwining of instruments paradigm and policy
community takes us to the next issue.

**The Institutionalization of Policy Instruments: in Depth and in
Breadth**

We call this intertwining 'institutionalization'. We can distinguish
between institutionalization in depth and in breadth. The depth of
institutionalization refers to the degree to which policy instruments
define the conduct of the members of a policy community. This involves
measuring the internalization (Croskery, 1995, pp. 107–9) of a policy
instrument and the degree to which it has lodged itself in the behaviour
patterns and routines of the members of the policy community. Concerning the depth of institutionalization, it should be noted that actors
do not 'know' of alternative policy instruments. They simply do not
form part of the repertoire, as a result of an evaluation.

The breadth of institutionalization refers to the degree to which
policy instruments are intertwined with the context. This can involve
other policy instruments, but also the organization which uses the instrument and the technology that comes with it. A policy instrument can

be institutionalized to a greater or lesser degree. The depth and breadth of institutionalization reinforce each other. Obviously, the degree of institutionalization affects the choice of policy instruments. Summing up, the choice is restricted, either because actors do not 'know' of alternative instruments or the costs of changing the instrument are too high, involving a whole range of other changes.

The Government within the Policy Community

One of the most important members of the policy community is the government. Although the government is not an absolute ruler it still has a distinct position, role and responsibility within a community. It owes its distinct position to its duties, the structure of networks in which it operates, and the rules which apply within those networks (Ringeling, 1990, p. 64). The unique role of the government becomes apparent when we consider that actions by governmental organizations are character-ized by an orientation towards precision, legality, legal protection, democratic justification and legitimacy (Bekke, 1990, p. 16). In addition, values such as stability, sincerity and reliability are important. It is obvious that this distinct position affects the choice of policy instru-ments. Sincerity, for example, refers to the degree to which actors understand the formation of policy instruments and their motives in applying them. Precision alludes to the possibility for actors to influence choices. Reliability is shown by the attitude of the actors during the process. Legitimacy refers to the support given to the formed policy instrument by the actors involved. As a result, the appraisal of policy instruments is not just linked to the extent to which a policy instrument achieves the desired goals, but also to the way in which a policy instru-ment is created. This can be called double legitimacy.

Besides, according to a more normative principle, the government is considered to be hierarchically superior to the other members of the community (De Bruijn and Ten Heuvelhof, 1991a, p. 171). This principle is, for that matter, no less normative than the principle that the govern-ment is a member like any other member, as specified by refined instrumentalism. This superior role is often imposed by the members of the policy community. Furthermore, this superiority partly stems from the fact that the government is restricted by legislation and has to act accordingly.

Three Approaches

The foregoing makes it clear that the terms given to the three approaches – traditional, refined and institutional – are not just labels or word-play. Behind the labels lie different views and approaches regarding the choice of policy instruments. The traditional approach emphasizes the goal–means relationship, refined instrumentalism emphasizes the context–instrument relationship, and the institutional approach emphasizes the process–instrument relationship. In the next section these theoretical notions will be illustrated by some empirical facts.

5. THE EDUCATIONAL SECTOR AND POLICY INSTRUMENTS: FIT OR APPROPRIATENESS?

A Sector and an Instrument

The preceding theoretical notions have been used in empirical research in the education sector. The education sector has been chosen for a specific reason. Looking at the use of policy instruments, the first thing we notice is a restricted governance repertoire, a repertoire which is, first and foremost, dominated by a combination of legal and financial instruments. Second, we note that within this limited repertoire remarkably often a specific instrument, the circular, is used. The subject of this empirical research is focused on this instrument. The circular can be described as:

> a communication of a general nature, written by federal government, obligatory or permissive, in whatever form and under whatever name, which is aimed at and sent to a number of administrative bodies, a number of persons in private and public law, or a group of natural persons outside of federal government, with which this government maintains a functional or financial relationship. (Vereniging van Nederlandse Gemeenten, 1985, p. 13)

The use of this instrument gives rise to two observations. On the one hand, it seems to have great disadvantages. For example, it imposes a serious implementation burden on educational institutions and, in addition, leads to numerous coordination problems at a central level. As a result, the use of this instrument provokes protest from target groups. The doubts concerning this policy instrument have led to several attempts to restrict its use, all of which have failed. On the other hand, this policy instrument has been in use for a very long time and is used very frequently. These seeming contradictions prompt the following question: what determines the choice of this policy instrument, the circular, in the area of education policy? To answer this question, we examine four case studies in the education sector and present our findings in the following sub-sections. The same aspects as in Section 2 will be discussed: context and instrument, the nature of the instrument, instrument and issue, the appraisal of instrument and the choice of instruments. It should be noted that these can only be described in broad outline.

Context and Policy Instrument

From the research it appears that the context in which the actors involved in choosing circulars can be described as a policy community. The interaction within the policy community is characterized by long-standing relationships; the community itself is characterized by a relative closeness. This will be illustrated by the following example. In this case, negotiations within the policy community continued, despite the fact that these had been formally broken off by the education minister. The members of the policy community believe this setback to be no more than a ritual step in the negotiations. As a result of the personal relationships the negotiations continued in the policy community. From the research the unique role of the Department of Education within the policy community becomes apparent. This specific role is connected with the financial and legal resources at its disposal. The legal resources are linked with article 23 of the Constitution, in which private and public education are considered equal from a financial point of view. The prevailing interpretation of article 23 implies that, in principle, each new area of education policy is arranged centrally and on a legal basis with sufficient guarantees for equal treatment. A second resource is financial. Institutions depend on the Department of Education for funds, so that the Department is uniquely responsible. Thus when the funding is stopped, this is at the expense of the employees of the educational institutions. Furthermore, it appears from the case studies that within policy communities an instruments paradigm is at work. This paradigm is of a legal nature. Alternative, non-legal policy instruments play no role. To a large extent, the instruments paradigm is determined by the history of the policy sector: public and private schools were given financial equality in the Constitution. This means that government expenditures for public education must also be made for private education. The educational legislation includes requirements that private education must meet to be eligible for funding. Now, 75 years later, the school funding controversy and its outcome – the equal financial treatment of public and private education – still affects the choice of policy instruments.

The case studies prove that various values prevail in the policy community. One of the dominant values is the striving for equal treatment and guarantees for the target groups. In order to ensure equality of rights and optimal legal security, the circular is often chosen as policy instrument. This instrument enables the policy makers to develop the issue of equality of rights in full detail. Apart from the above-mentioned substantial values, the way in which the proceedings are held also plays a role in the choice of policy instruments. When a circular is established in closed session, without the involvement of the 'right' actors, this will lead to rejection. This is particularly important in relation to proceedings in the educational policy communities. Thus, it appears that the appropriateness of policy instruments is a significant factor. The choice cannot be explained merely by the range of interests as they have developed over a particular period of time. The actors operate in a community in which overall agreement exists on which are the 'right' problems and instruments, and in which good behaviour is rewarded. The choice of policy instruments is more than just 'pushing and pulling' and design on the basis of knowledge of the environment. It is foremost a question of answering to the 'right' values.

The Nature of the Instrument

The case studies suggest that it is wrong, and pointless, to speak of 'the' characteristics of 'the' circular. The characteristics of this policy instrument are determined by the context in which it evolves and is applied. It only derives its meaning through interaction with the different actors. Several characteristics go to form one circular, but one characteristic shared by all case studies is that the measures taken are always temporary. Because of this, the circular takes on a strategic function. Its temporary nature allows actors to react to the changing circumstances, without having to fix their own actions for a longer period of time. This makes it easier, for instance, to react to future cutbacks. Further, by means of this instrument Parliament can be bypassed so that forming policy will not be delayed. Since Parliament is considered a serious handicap in pursuance of the policy process, this becomes an interesting option for the actors within the policy community. Furthermore, the circular plays a major role in controlling conflicts as it, so to speak, immunizes them. This is possible because the circular enables actors to operate flexibly and to reach compromises.

This is relevant in a policy community in which conflicts are considered damaging. The case studies also show that circulars can take on symbolic meanings. For example, one of the case studies shows that a relatively small budget is allotted to deal with a major social problem. In this case a law is not feasible; it is considered to be politically wise to do 'something'. This 'something' becomes a circular. It gives a signal to the actors involved that the government is taking the matter seriously and is prepared to do something about it, without having to commit itself for a long period of time.

When policy instruments have taken on the characteristics of the context, and no longer have any intrinsic values of their own, it is better to speak of 'appropriate' policy instruments. A 'fit' – as in the refined approach – suggests, at the least, that some characteristics of the policy instrument are stable and cannot be changed. However, this is not the case. Policy instruments do not merely adjust to their environment; they take on the characteristics of the context. They also blend into the environment and become a part of it. They merge, as it were, with the environment.

Instrument and Issue

The above-mentioned relationship raises the question as to which way this relationship is heading. Is it a temporal causative relationship: does defining the issue precede the instrument, or the other way round? This study has found evidence for the former. Issues are defined simultaneously or prior to establishing the policy instrument. The following will explain what this means for the circular. In the light of the creation of policy instruments, issues are depoliticized and redefined as quantifiable problems. Specialist knowledge within the policy community makes this possible and necessary. Depoliticization is necessary to avoid conflicts. The case studies demonstrate that the problems are temporary; there exists a temporary state in which the circular plays a role. After all, the circular is a temporary instrument; other issues will arise. The nature of the issue varies from case to case. Despite that, the circular is 'chosen' in these cases. This implies that policy instruments are created independently of the nature of the issue. This suggests a strong link between policy instrument and context. The creation of policy instruments can better be understood as a goal-oriented process rather than the solution of a problem. Therefore it is better to speak of an appropriate instrument rather than of one designed to fit the circumstances.

The Appraisal of Policy Instruments

Although a range of circulars is used, this does not mean that the actors who were involved in the process regard this policy instrument as the most effective. Apparently, other factors are involved which cause the instrument to be regarded as the 'right' one. The case studies demonstrate that circulars are not just appraised by their impact and effectiveness. It appears that a circular is also evaluated by the way in which it originated, for example, whether the actors involved in the policy community consider the process to have been correctly concluded. In this case, a correctly concluded process means that the 'right' actors have been involved at the 'right' moments. Importantly, they have been able to contribute to the process, in content and on a governance level. This means that the establishment of, in this case, a circular has been concluded in a manner that allows some openness, as well as a degree of legitimacy. This is related to the 'right' intentions of the actors and the agreement between them. The impact of the policy instruments becomes less important than the process of their establishment. When a policy instrument in the policy community is considered to be congruent – an optimal fit between instrument and conditions – the target group will not necessarily agree. Often they apply different criteria. As the research shows, circulars have a bad image, depending not so much on the performance of the instrument as on what it symbolizes. The circular symbolizes an intervening government which centrally directs the actions of educational institutions and, as a result, restricts their freedom. This determines to a high degree the image of the instrument, irrespective of its actual performance.

Obviously, the establishment of policy instruments is not solely concerned with the decision process and the design of a fit between policy instrument and a given number of conditions. It is also concerned with the fact that a circular is a carrier of meanings, morals, values, and ideas which are shared by the members of the policy community. Moreover, the actors involved are driven by the logic of appropriateness, in which conventions and rules play a major role as part of existing routines. The logic of calculated self-interest fades into the background.

The Choice of Policy Instruments

Only a limited number of alternative policy instruments feature in the different case studies. These alternatives have primarily a ritual function, in the sense that the outside world needs to be given the impression that the alternatives and results have been 'rationally' evaluated. It also becomes clear that the choice of policy instruments is restricted by earlier choices. The choice of policy instruments is thus path-dependent. To begin with, a temporary instrument – the circular – is applied to solve a temporary problem. However, the problem turns out to be more persistent. Because a circular has been chosen in the past, it is more difficult to switch to another instrument. In the meantime, experience has been gained with this instrument and the target group relies on it. To deviate from the 'right' path will require extra effort and cost. After a period of time the choice of the circular has become routine, and the alternatives are no longer evaluated. Frequent use of this instrument will also result in a far-reaching degree of institutionalization, in depth and breadth. Circulars become internalized: the policy instrument has become part of the executive routines and actions of a limited number of civil servants. Alternative policy instruments are not considered at all. As long as the alternatives do not become available, the circular will remain 'the' instrument, and the only conceivable instrument. Furthermore, the empirical study shows that institutionalization in breadth occurs. In most cases the circular is heavily intertwined with other policy instruments or with actions relating to the implementation.

On the basis of the foregoing, it can be concluded that the choice of policy instruments is partly determined by intentionally finding a fit between the different contingencies out of calculated self-interest. Other factors such as path-dependence, routine and institutionalization are equally important.

6.   CONCLUSIONS AND IMPLICATIONS

The 'choice' of policy instruments has been studied from an institutional point of view. The use of this perspective has given rise to questions about the degree to which actors are able to design an effective policy instrument on the basis of contingency rules. The designing of policy instruments represents an incremental and historic development which is directed and controlled, only to a limited extent, by the actors involved (Brunsson and Olsen, 1993, pp. 1–5). An institutional view of the establishment of policy instruments will help to eliminate the misconception that policy instruments can be chosen just like the tools in a toolkit and that they can simply be designed on the basis of contingency rules. The institutional view has made it clear that it is not merely the effectiveness of a policy instrument that is relevant in the choice. The 'right' process of establishing policy instruments plays a significant role in the appraisal of the final result – the policy instrument. In this process policy instruments need to mirror the values and morals which prevail within a policy community. The term 'appropriateness' emphasizes all this and refers to 'the right governance actions given the values and morals within a context'. This context has been described as a policy community. In this specific context the striving for effectiveness is no longer the most important consideration, but rather, being able to conform to certain values, morals, conventions and rules in the policy community. In a policy community actors are not just led by the logic of calculated self-interest. Such a context requires appropriate behaviour, which is determined by prevailing conventions, values, morals, habits and rules. The next sub-sections will briefly discuss a number of implications, using the same line of argumentation as in Section 4.

The Institutionalization of Policy Instruments: from Present to Past

Earlier in this section a distinction was made between institutionalization in depth and in breadth. In depth means the degree to which a policy instrument is part of the behaviour patterns and conventions of a civil servant and refers to the degree to which the actions of the actors involved are determined by the policy instruments. Institutionalization in breadth refers to the degree to which policy instruments are intertwined with their context. From this study it becomes apparent that policy instruments are not only physically, but also mentally intertwined. We have called this the internalization of the policy instrument. Policy makers are partly controlled by the instruments at their disposal, described in this study as institutionalization in depth. This means that the choice of policy instruments is not a free choice; nor is it merely a process of pushing and pulling, motivated by calculated self-interest. Policy makers gain experience with a policy instrument and invest in it mentally. Therefore, to alter the policy instrumentation not only calls for an expansion of the toolbox, but also for a cultural change.

Administrative Routines: from Design to Evolution

The case studies show that an important aspect of choosing circulars is the continuation of old administrative routines. When new concepts of governance and new instruments paradigms are introduced, ways of thinking and acting, set patterns of governance and instruments paradigms, do not disappear straight away. For years, generations of civil servants have been working with concepts in which a strong, centrally controlling and ambitious government formed an important element.

These concepts have been partly internalized, mentally set and, as a result, have become part of the current routines. It is not easy to give up these concepts. The set routines put a check on the introduction of 'new' policy instruments and 'new' governance strategies. First of all, the meaning of 'new' instruments can be questioned. The main components of these new instruments have originated in old paradigms. This means that the old governance paradigms still have influence. New instruments also become part of the 'old' governance paradigms and the corresponding interaction patterns. In that case, there is a danger that old interaction patterns will undermine the practical meaning of 'new' governance routines. In the end it is not the instruments, but the players, which are relevant.

Process Values and Objective Values

In the appraisal of policy instruments, it has been determined that many actors have an ambivalent attitude towards the instrument. Circulars are not usually regarded as the most effective policy instrument to achieve the set objectives. In other words, there is not a fit between instrument and circumstances. Nevertheless, this instrument is frequently used. First of all, this is due to the contribution of the instrument to the continuation of the policy process. It enables actors to reach compromises in sub-areas and consequently to minimize conflicts. In this way, continual interaction is guaranteed between the actors who are dependent on each other. Besides, the positive appraisal is due to the 'right' establishment of the instrument. This means that the 'right' actors have been able to exert their influence at the 'right' moment. When both the dominant values within the policy community are mirrored in the process and in the results of the process, this can be called an appropriate policy instrument. Using objective and process values side by side is the only logical and possible way of appraising policy instruments. Effectiveness is not achieved merely by interest in process standards, and neither does interest in objective standards alone result in 'appropriate' policy instruments. By navigating between these competing values, the 'right' policy instrument can be effected.

Beyond Choice?

The preceding sections raise questions concerning the interpretation of choice. This final sub-section will present three alternative interpretations on the basis of the findings of this research. The first stresses obligation and responsibility, so that the establishment of policy instruments is seen in this light. Sections 3 and 4 explained that actors within a specific community are not only led to select the most effective alternative instrument, they are led by 'appropriate' behaviour. As a result, choice is replaced by obligation. The establishment of a policy instrument is not the result of an evaluation of alternatives – a choice – but of an obligation, or a sense of responsibility. The felt or imposed obligation and the sense of responsibility are related to the significant position of the government in the policy community.

The second interpretation sees the establishment of policy instruments as a striving for legitimacy. The striving for legitimacy by an organization is expressed by its actions – in this case the choice of policy instruments – corresponding to the values and morals which exist in the policy community to which the actors belong. The legitimacy is part of the congruence between the characteristics of the policy instrument and the social values and morals, which are expressed by the actions of the different actors within the policy community. This interpretation does not emphasize the output of a specific process, but rather, the process itself. Thus, a value such as effectiveness disappears into the background.

The third interpretation views the establishment of policy instruments as a ritual, for example, a ritual of change and renewal, expressed in vivid language so as to satisfy the members of the policy community. This vivid instrumental language symbolizes the energy and dynamics of the proposed governmental interventions.

NOTE

1. This chapter is a short account of a dissertation study entitled *Gepaste instrumenten, de totstandkoming van beleidsinstrumenten als plicht, ritueel en zoektocht naar legitmiteit* (Appropriate instruments: the generation of policy instruments as obligation, as ritual and as search for legitimacy).

PART II

The Quest for Policy Instruments

4. A contextual approach to policy instruments

Hans A. de Bruijn and Ernst F. ten Heuvelhof

1. INTRODUCTION

In this chapter we elaborate on the context in which instruments are applied. The substantial attention devoted to this notion in instrument theory was noted in Chapter 3. First, at a somewhat abstract level, we shall demonstrate how such a context can be characterized in modern societies; theoretical insights on networks will be used (Section 2). In Section 3, we indicate how the operation of instruments can be analysed on three levels. These levels are described in Sections 4, 5 and 6 and discuss the meaning of a network-like context for the introduction of instruments for each level.

2. CHARACTERISTICS OF NETWORKS

A policy network is the aggregate of actors (both administrators and target group) who are involved in a certain policy problem. As a rule, policy networks possess a number of characteristics that can be summarized as follows (De Bruijn and Ten Heuvelhof, 1993, pp. 85–109; De Bruijn and Ten Heuvelhof, 1995b, pp. 161–79).

A first characteristic of a network is *pluriformity*. Pluriformity is dominant in networks at various levels and in various ways. Large organizations consist of sub-organizations which differ substantially from one another and are open to a variety of influences. The network as a whole can also be pluriform. The power of various actors in a network can vary, such as the degree to which they are open to their environment. A consequence of this pluriform nature of networks is that the degree to which actors are sensitive to guidance signals can vary greatly: a different signal may be appropriate for each different actor.

Second, actors in networks are also characterized by *isolation*. They possess a certain amount of autonomy and are thus relatively isolated in relation to their environment. They each have their own frame of reference and are sensitive only to those signals that fit into that frame. Thus, they are typically self-contained or only 'tuned in' to actors with a comparable frame of reference. For an actor with administrative ambitions, this means that instruments need to be tuned in to his/her frame of reference. Thus, the use of legislation and regulation in a network will have little chance of success when the norms underlying these rules are not acknowledged by an actor who is directed by his/her own norms.

A third characteristic of networks is the presence of *interdependences* between actors. These can be expressed by several variables (finance, competences, political support, space, and so on), and can be simple or very complex. Thus relations can be asymmetric and asynchronous – asymmetric because actor A is dependent upon actor B, B upon C and C upon A (simple bilateral relationships are not always possible) and asynchronous because these dependences are not all simultaneously present. At various times, actors will realize that they are dependent upon one another, so that simple exchanges are not always effective.

The characteristics mentioned above tend to intensify each other. An 'objective' analysis of interdependences may reveal that cooperation between certain actors can be worthwhile for the actors involved. In the perception of the actors, the complexity of interdependences can be so great that they will close themselves off to it.

The combination of these characteristics of pluriformity, isolation and interdependences implies that networks are constantly changing. Thus, a change in the degree of isolation may influence the interdependences in a network, while these in turn may influence the pluriformity of a network. As a result, networks are almost always highly dynamic. The power positions of actors may change; new actors may enter the network; others may exit. Developments in the environment of a network can alter the mutual relations. Also significant is the situation in which two networks encounter one another or when a network divides. The dynamics of these and comparable developments can be viewed as a fourth characteristic of networks or as the logical consequence of the three characteristics mentioned. For a policy maker, such dynamics will require the use of instruments that have a certain flexibility.

The structural characteristics of networks offer both threats and opportunities for governance. These are summarized in Table 4.1

Table 4.1   Governance and network structures

	Pluriformity	Isolation	Interdependence
Threats to	Intra-organizational: the target unit in the organization is not able to influence the rest of the organization	Guidance signals may be frustrated by the isolation of the target group	The target group uses dependences
	Inter-organizational: actors are sensitive to varying guidance signals		Because of interdependences, many unintended and unforeseen effects Delay
Opportunities for	Chance that at least some of the actors in the network are sensitive to guidance signals; other actors can be influenced by these actors	Isolation implies autonomy; autonomy of the target group is necessary for effective governing	Breaking through isolation
	Pluriformity may result in vulnerability and thus sensitivity to guidance signals	Prevents disintegrative function of many guidance signals	Steering actor uses interdependences
		Isolated actors are very sensitive to guidance signals that fit their own frame of reference	

and will be discussed briefly. A more detailed discussion can be found elsewhere (Bruijn and Ten Heuvelhof, 1991a). A pluriform organization can be difficult to govern because not all sections of this organization are equally sensitive to the same guidance signal from outside. For example, the environmental affairs unit of a company will usually be sensitive to environmental regulations. It remains to be seen, however, whether this unit is able to influence the line managers of the production process.

An inter-organizational network with a high degree of pluriformity will only be partially sensitive to generic guidance signals. Governance in the retail trade is more difficult because of the many differences between retail companies, and there are natural limits for fine-tuning. On the other hand, pluriformity often implies that at least part of the network is sensitive to a particular signal. This offers opportunities for influence, especially when that part of a network is able to influence other actors. For example, within a pluriform target group, certain actors can be influenced. The guidance signal may be proliferated further if these actors are market leaders (other actors will follow) or when a network has low tolerance for variety, so that imitation might occur. Opportunities for influence also arise when pluriformity results in a certain degree of fragmentation.

Isolation can also be a cause of failure for a steering actor. An actor who is isolated from his environment or from another actor is difficult to influence, but three opportunities exist. Isolation implies that an actor possesses a certain amount of autonomy. Such autonomy could be beneficial to governance: once an isolated actor is receptive to a guidance signal, he/she often profits from the force and potential of autonomy. Furthermore, isolation ensures a certain amount of protection for the organization: it will be insensitive to a large number of guidance signals and thus less vulnerable to distracting signals from the environment. Finally, an actor might be isolated because of his own frame of reference. There are, however, guidance signals that can fit this frame of reference, and a policy maker will be sensitive to these.

Interdependences will make governance more difficult since the administrator depends on the target group. Each actor will attempt to use these interdependences for his own profit. A consequence of the sum of such behaviours is that many unforeseen events may occur in a network. Furthermore, the sum of interdependent relations will hinder attempts to govern. The opportunities of interdependences are limitless; like actors who are the target, an administrator can use these opportunities to break through the isolation of the target group.

3.   LEVELS OF GOVERNANCE

In this section we shall examine the different levels of governance: operational, tactical and strategic.

Operational: Targeted Application of Instruments

The operational use of instruments is the most straightforward, and the targeted use of instruments is characteristic of the application: 'instruments cannot be neatly separated from goals' (Majone, 1989, p. 117). An administrator has a goal. To realize that goal, he/she will steer another actor and, to that end, uses an instrument. The operational administrator strives for the use of an instrument which fits the nature of the problem at hand. In this instance, governance is direct: the instrument is directly targeted at influencing the behaviour of the steered actor. The majority of such interventions can be placed in this category. Important issues that can be addressed at the operational level are characteristics of the instruments, choice and use of instruments, mixture of instruments, expected outcomes, and implementation problems that need to be overcome.

Context variables such as the characteristics of the network can influence the choice, application and effectiveness of instruments. The attention at this level, however, is focused on the nature of the instruments and the question of whether the instruments fit a particular context. The structure of a network is an accepted fact. The primary question at the operational level is which instruments are suitable for use in network-like contexts. We can mention, *inter alia*, covenants and financial incentives which belong to the so-called second-generation instruments (De Bruijn and Ten Heuvelhof, 1991a).

Tactical: Smart Governance

While the nature of the instruments remains an issue at the tactical level, attention is focused here particularly on the various ways an instrument can be applied, that is, the same type of instrument can be used in various ways. The application must correspond to the policy-marketing context.

In tactical governance, the administrator forms a perception of the network and subsequently attempts to use his instruments in a 'smart' manner to exploit the characteristics of the network. The tactical use of instruments increases the opportunities for governance, and this provides interesting insights into the use of various instruments.

Strategic: Network Management

Network management is rarely limited to the question of how instruments can be used most intelligently given the structural characteristics of the network. It can also include changing the structure of a network by transforming interdependences, isolation and pluriformity and thus creating governance opportunities. Strategic policy making gives credence to the advice to adapt 'institutional constraints' prior to the use of instruments so that new conditions are created for their use.

Network management differs in at least two respects from operational and tactical governance. First, it is often a type of metagovernance. Network management results in alterations of the network structure which subsequently provide opportunities for the effective use of instruments at the operational or tactical level. Network management thus provides the framework within which operational and tactical governance can be shaped. A simple example: a strongly fragmented target group may be steered by enhancing the degree of organization. By creating an intermediary organization, for example, the policy maker may have produced a contact point so that agreements can be made with the target group. Enhancing the degree of organization is a type of meta-governance: the pluriformity of the target group is decreased (strategic) so that opportunities are created for reaching agreements with the target group (operational or tactical).

Network management is not only a type of meta-governance: the realization of the goals of the administrator can also be the direct outcome of network management. When a government attempts to reduce the pluriformity of a target group through the creation of an intermediary organization, not only is pluriformity almost always reduced (meta-governance), but in the longer run, relatively autonomous forms of behavioural change may occur.

Second, strategic policy-making tolerates goal displacement. Like operational and tactical governance, it is targeted (changing the network structure in order to create opportunities for the policy maker to realize his own goals). Targeting at the strategic level is of a different nature from that at the operational or tactical level. The multiple interdependences in a network, as well as its dynamics, imply that the consequences of strategic governance are only predictable to a limited extent. A policy maker who attempts to transform bilateral interdependences into multilateral interdependences in order to create more possibilities for exchange will have limited certainty about what effects he creates. It is possible that a target actor will isolate him/herself because of increased complexity and thus reduce the opportunities for governance. Interdependences may then be altered (an intended effect of strategic governance), but the isolation of certain actors has also increased (an unintended effect). This implies that a high degree of tolerance for goal displacement is necessary at the strategic level. Every modification in the structure of a network may generate unexpected changes and threats to policy making. Without tolerance for goal displacement, opportunities cannot be used and threats cannot be neutralized.

The three levels of governance have been summarized in Table 4.2, which highlights the main characteristics of each level.

Table 4.2   Three levels of governance

Types of governance	Characteristics
Operational: use of instruments	• Targeted • Contingent on structure and process • Accepting of network structure
Tactical: 'smart' use of instruments	• Targeted • Contingent on structure and process • Exploitative of network structure
Network: changing the network structure and thus the decision-making processes (strategic)	• Target-seeking • Typically meta-governance • Changing structure and process • Distinction between structure and process loses meaning

The level of governance may have important consequences for the method and/or the selection of instruments, as we shall see in the next section.

4.   OPERATIONAL: SECOND-GENERATION INSTRUMENTS

In this section, we focus our attention on the operational level. The central question in this section is: which instruments are suitable for policy making in a network-like context where pluriformity, isolation and interdependence are manifest?

It is generally the case that generic instruments which are used bilaterally and hierarchically have little effect in a network. Target groups possess power to block (interdependences); they are sensitive to guidance signals in different ways (pluriformity); and they can use their isolation to frustrate those signals. For these reasons, many types of regulation will be ineffective. Three groups of instruments can be mentioned which are useful in networks.

Communication Instruments

Many organizations which are to be regulated have a reticent nature. They recognize guidance signals only when they correspond to their own frame of reference. Every signal from the outside has to permeate a 'perception filter', so it would be wise to try to influence the composition of this filter. The most important means for exerting this kind of influence seems to lie in the exchange of knowledge and information, that is, communication instruments (Kotler and Andreason, 1987; Meltsner and Bellevita, 1983, p. 42; Van Riel, 1986). Communication instruments can restrict as well as broaden knowledge. Restricted exchange of knowledge is directed at influencing the will. Full exchange of knowledge is directed at expanding the knowledge of the target group. When instruments are applied in the latter way, the target group maintains the freedom to process the information. Both forms of information exchange can be used but the more cautious the target group, the more difficult it will be for restrictive instruments (influencing the will) to have any effect.

Communication instruments can also be multilateral, that is, policy makers and target group exchange information which can result in mutual benefit. As seen from the perspective of the 'perception filter', communication instruments can be very effective. They are not just a transfer of knowledge, but rather they influence the 'perception filter' of organizations and increase the susceptibility of organizations to other guidance signals and/or instruments. Thus, communication instruments are somewhat weak. They are seldom applied alone, but are usually used in combination with other instruments.

Multilateral Instruments

Many regulative instruments are bilateral. The administrator imposes an obligation on the target group. Formally the latter has minimal or no defence. In cases where the target group is powerful, the use of multilateral instruments is advisable (Van Ommeren and De Ru, 1993; Pröpper and Herweijer, 1993). By applying multilateral instruments, the powerful position of the target group is acknowledged. Both parties bargain about mutual commitments.

Multilateral instruments can also be used in different parts of the organization, which acknowledges the pluriformity of the target group. Examples of multilateral instruments are treaties, policy agreements and the gentleman's agreement. Multilateral instruments also play a significant role in modern arrangements such as public–private partnerships.

Incentives

Communication instruments are directed at changing the 'perception filter' of the target group. Instruments can also be used so as to take the composition of this filter into account in advance. Guidance signals can be shaped in such a way that the target organization recognizes the signals and allows them to enter.

A well-known approach in this regard is governance through incentives (De Bruijn and Ten Heuvelhof, 1991a, p. 113–25). An incentive is a financial behavioural stimulus of a limited compulsive nature (De Bruijn and Ten Heuvelhof, 1991a, p. 114). They can be positive (subsidies) as well as negative (taxes), and the target group is, in large part, free to decide whether to react to the incentive. The guidance signal will pass through the 'perception filter' of the target group since thinking in terms of profits and losses is a common feature among many organizations (public and private). Thus, the incentive takes into account the objections of organizations to be governed. By using the incentive, the administrator harmonizes his/her policy to the power position, objections, and pluriformity of the target group, and thus changes the financial circumstances within which the target group must operate. The hope is that the target group will, in turn, decide to alter its behaviour (in the way the government has indicated). The changes in the circumstances have to be such that they are recognizable to the target group.

5. TACTICS

The question addressed in this section, shifting our attention now to the tactical level of governance is: what tactics are suitable in a network-like context, and how might these lead to broadening the governance opportunities of instruments? The way in which instruments are applied at the tactical level is important since one instrument can be used in different ways. The instrument of regulation, for instance, can be used bilaterally or multilaterally; how it is applied is the result of negotiation between policy maker and target. An instrument such as regulation has little effect in a tactic of bilateral governance (see Section 4). When regulation is the result of negotiations, there are more opportunities for governance in the network, or to put it differently, when attention is given to tactics, the governance opportunities of certain instruments are increased.

By way of illustration, we refer below to a number of tactical uses of instruments and the resulting increase of governance opportunities. 'Dumb' tactics are possible as well, and these will lead to limited steering opportunities. Examples of these will also be given (De Bruijn and Ten Heuvelhof, 1995a).

Bilateral and Multilateral Governance

Instruments can be used bilaterally. In the case of regulation, for instance, an administrator formulates rules based on his own authority and imposes them on the target group. Multilateral governance implies that a policy maker negotiates with the target group about the rules to be formulated and the monitoring of these rules. A set of instruments which is bilateral by nature can be applied multilaterally. An analysis at the operational level about the use of regulation in networks may lead to the conclusion that this instrument is inappropriate in a network-like situation (Jenkins, 1980, p. 215). The bilateral imposition of rules can be frustrated by the interdependences, isolation and pluriformity of a network. Attention to the various tactics that can be used when employing rules will also provide opportunities for this instrument in a network.

The reverse, however, can also be the case. By nature, a covenant or agreement is a multilateral instrument: it is a document that has been undersigned by two or more equal parties. It can, however, be used bilaterally. This occurs when a policy maker drafts the covenant and forces it on the negotiating partner. In a complex network, this tactic will often prove ineffective and will limit governance opportunities. A tactic of multilateral steering in complex networks will often constitute a structure-contingent type of governance. In this instance, a policy maker identifies the pluriformity, isolation and interdependences in the network and decides to negotiate with the most important actors, thereby respecting the network structure.

Direct and Indirect Governance

The direct use of instruments where an administrator directly imposes norms is well known, and again we take regulations as an example. An indirect use of regulations means that norms are imposed on a third actor who is then able to influence the behaviour of the target group. In this manner, government can, for example, require the use of an environmental trademark (direct governance), and subsequently influence the behaviour of companies through the preferences of consumers (indirect governance). This is an example of structure-contingent steering where the structural characteristics of the network are employed (in this case, the dependences between consumers and companies).

Generic Governance and Fine-tuning

Generic governance implies non-differentiation in respect of the target group while a tactic of fine-tuning implies differentiation. When pluriformity is the dominant characteristic of networks, guidance signals should be adjusted to the variety within the target group via fine-tuning. In this way, governance may acquire a structure-contingent nature. Fine-tuning can also be process-contingent. A policy maker will then attempt to attune problems and solutions to one another so as to increase the chances for linkage or to render decisions more precise.

Slow and Fast Governance

Finally, the speed at which instruments can be used should be mentioned. It is clear that such temporal tactics can be a type of process-contingent governance. Decision-making processes are often left unfinished because problems and solutions are not available at the same time. Actors will abandon their problems and solutions when it is convenient for them, and they do not always pay attention to opportunities for linkage. A tactic of slowing down or speeding up may help to link problems with solutions.

Such a tactic can also be related to the structure of a network. Since networks are always dynamic, a policy maker can slow down attempts to steer at times when the configuration of pluriformity, isolation and interdependence is unfavourable. Once a favourable configuration exists, the pace of governance will be increased.

6. STRATEGIES: THE USE OF INSTRUMENTS AS NETWORK MANAGEMENT

In this final section, we consider the possibilities of changing the characteristics of a network through the use of instruments.

Pluriformity

Reforming the target group
Instruments can be used so that they have important consequences for the pluriformity of the target group. As a a rule, a pluriform target group requires the use of a differentiated set of instruments and/or a tactic of fine-tuning.

Some of these instruments will not be sufficiently differentiated for the pluriformity of a target group (operational or tactical level), but will have an important secondary effect in that the pluriformity changes (strategic level). These instruments will not affect the members of the target group to the same degree. They may relate to everybody but, given differences in the members, the effects may vary. As a consequence, some will gain relative to others and some will lose, and the pluriformity of the network will change. A distinction, for instance, may develop between a limited number of strong members and a relatively large number of weak ones. These and other processes have been analysed in respect of negotiations about the use of regulations (Kochen, 1966; Ekkers, 1984) and the provision of subsidies (De Bruijn, 1993).

Reducing pluriformity: barriers to entry
Other instruments function as 'barriers to entry' and, as a result, reduce the pluriformity in a network. The stipulation of a minimum number of pupils for a school and a minimum number of citizens for a municipality will have a direct impact on the pluriformity of a network: it will decrease.

Instruments that influence actors in a network can operate directly or indirectly. The most direct use occurs when an administrator creates a new actor. Such a regulation can confer certain competences and responsibilities on the new actor such as power over cash flow, and so on. Utility companies have been created in this way. Also, the current trend of distancing civil service from government can be seen as an example of network management under the category of 'adding new actors to the network'.

In the indirect version, the policy maker creates rules that allow the creation of new actors. Such rules describe the conditions that the new actor should meet. They specify 'barriers to entry' and 'conditions for entry'. The rules may also create the possibility that actors other than the policy maker create new actors. On the basis of such rules, housing corporations have been created in the Netherlands (Gerrichauzen, 1990, p. 20). The law stipulates what conditions a corporation must meet before it can operate, but other actors will have to take the initiative to create a housing corporation.

Reducing pluriformity: incentive for cooperation

Instruments can be designed to encourage actors to cooperate and thus reduce the pluriformity of the network. Through financial incentives, the target group can be pressed into cooperation. The number of actors and/or the differences between actors involved may decrease. The isolation of actors in respect of one another will also decrease.

Isolation

Access to the target group

Instruments may help an administrator gain access to a target group. This is especially so in the case of preferential instruments. Often a target group is interested in the fact that such an instrument has been applied, and will open up to the administrator. For example, while a subsidy is sometimes used at the operational level, it is also used by the donor to appease the recipient or to gain access to the recipient (Vermeulen, 1993).

Such access can be gained because a policy maker will set conditions on the application of preferential instruments: formal conditions and sometimes extra informal conditions. Formal conditions: the applicant for a subsidy will have to provide full information about the variables that are regarded as important by the donor. In subsequent government interventions, this information is available to the administrator, which implies a change in degree of isolation compared to the first intervention. Informal conditions: an administrator can use a preferential instrument freely with regard to topic A, on the condition that the target group will not resist the use of a limiting instrument with respect to topic B, and the isolation of the target group is reduced. At the operational level, the effectiveness of instrument A can be regarded as negative, but when the strategic level is taken into consideration, this view may change.

The obligation to openness
With regard to isolation, examples abound of instruments which oblige
the actor to make certain information public. The Act on Openness of
Administration ('Wet Openbaarheid van Bestuur') applies to many
public organizations and obliges them to make their information open
to the public. For the private sector, we can point to the legal obligation to publish annual reports, safety reports, environmental reports
and so on. Companies are not always keen to publish reports on their
financial performance or their polluting emissions of their own free will
(Stone, 1975). Publication will lead to public discussion or may
encourage the company to reflect on its behaviour.

Changing the frame of reference
Many instruments exist that are not aimed at changing behaviour but
at changing the perception of problems, changing values and norms,
and even at transforming the 'belief systems' of organizations
(Donaldson and Lorsch, 1983). This is often the case with communicative instruments. Such instruments can be directed at both content
and process. Dutch environmental policy is aimed at internalizing the
values behind such a policy within the population and the target group.
The idea is that after internalization, it will be easier to use instruments
at the operational level in order to change behaviour; in this case
behaviour becomes more environmentally friendly. The massive amount
of information used in order to create a basis for large infrastructural
projects is also of this type. Other instruments are then only aimed at
realizing process values, such as instruments that are aimed at 'keeping
perceptions in motion' (Termeer, 1993).

Interdependence

An instrument constitutes a network
The use of instruments at the operational level will influence the interdependence between actors. Often this is self-evident: the use of an
instrument will create new relations and also new interdependences. It
may even constitute a network of interdependences (De Bruijn, 1990).
Policy makers and target groups become dependent upon one another,
but the network may also include new actors or even parts of existing
networks in other policy areas.
    It is important here that the use of instruments not only constitutes
interdependences, but may also give rise to centrifugal and centripetal
forces. When a policy maker imposes across-the-board cutbacks, the
chances are that the entire network will be mobilized against him/her.

Centrifugal forces then develop. If cutbacks are imposed on one or a few actors, centripetal forces may be generated. Those who are not confronted with cutbacks will not support those who are affected by them, and the policy maker will meet with less resistance from the network. The network is then reconstituted by the way in which the cutback instruments are being used. This may be a short-term effect, but it can also be for a longer term.

A telling illustration of centripetal forces is the Gramm-Rudman-Hollings Amendment used by the US federal government to reduce the budget deficit annually. If the government does not succeed in achieving the annual decrease in a certain year, the regulation obliges government to make across-the-board cutbacks on a number of specified budget items. As a consequence of this rule, there is an annual round of negotiations between the 'advocates' of the budget items. The law has made them dependent on one another (Van Nispen and Rijntalder, 1990; Hahm et al., 1992).

Naturally, all sorts of middle positions are possible between centrifugal and centripetal forces. In negotiations with the Dutch Ministry of Education, the universities have regularly divided into a block of technical and a block of general universities. Such a break with a negotiating partner provides the minister with opportunities. Instruments can then be used to make the break more visible or, at least, to make the position of the representative of the universities (the Union of Cooperating Dutch Universities) more difficult.

Moreover, interdependences thus created can remain in force even after the instrument has been used. Policy makers and target groups have been dependent on one another for some time. When the policy maker wishes to intervene again after a period of time, it may be attractive to reactivate previous relations since the actors are aware of each others' interests and may exploit this. The initial relationship is thus institutionalized so that a transfer of effects from the operational to the strategic level is a fact.

Coercion to self-organization

In many contexts, a target group is defined as a 'black box.' An administrator who only uses indicators is not interested in internal processes, but only in their outcome. Covenants or rules may indicate what obligations a target group must meet without detailing how they are to be met. The 'glass jar' concept in environmental policy is a well-known example (Bressers, 1985). The target group as a whole is faced with a certain goal to be met, a 'glass jar' is imposed upon the target group, while the way in which they are going to meet it (how they distribute costs and benefits) is left to themselves (under the glass jar). This idea can be codified in a juridical regulation (De Bruijn and Ten Heuvelhof, 1991b).

In the application of this and other black box approaches, actors can become dependent on one another where they had previously been independent. These new interdependences are important effects of operational policy making. They may give reason to a target group to organize itself so that the network structure is changed.

Suppression of types of cooperation
Interdependences may be a reason for actors to cooperate. Such cooperation may be beneficial to these actors, but it can have a negative effect on others. Network management may imply that a policy maker encourages relations between certain actors. The best known example is anti-cartel legislation. There are great incentives for cooperation between companies who have a competitive relationship.

By cooperating, they can establish certain advantageous pricing arrangements. Governments can use anti-cartel measures to suppress such agreements which are viewed as detrimental to the free market and to free competition. These rules suppress certain types of cooperation.

7. CONCLUSION

Networks provide opportunities for policy making. By distinguishing among operational, tactical and network management, such opportunities can be expanded.

5. The choice of policy instruments in policy networks

Hans Th.A. Bressers

1. INTRODUCTION

Policy networks operate in both policy formation processes and policy implementation processes. But the networks are not identical in each case. The reason for this is that some actors have better access, different objectives, more information or more power in respect of one process than the other. This chapter focuses on how policy networks function in the process of policy formation. Within this process we concentrate on the choice of policy instruments. As will be demonstrated, policy instruments can be viewed as various combinations of institutional rules deliberately designed to influence certain action arenas (Ostrom, 1986).

Much research into the application of policy instruments and their impact on the target group is aimed at providing information which can help the government in its efforts to reduce or limit social problems. Unfortunately, however, policy instruments are rarely selected on the basis of implementability and effectiveness. Different policy fields tend to show a preference for their own 'favourite' types of policy instruments and use these repeatedly regardless of their actual contribution to reducing the problems in specific fields. This limits the government's learning capacity, particularly when major new challenges present themselves which cannot be solved by minor policy adjustments. Wider-ranging policy adjustments usually also necessitate changes in the circumstances governing the selection of policy instruments. In this light, it is important to study the factors which influence the policy formation process.

For various reasons, the development and results of policy formation processes are difficult to predict exclusively on the basis of the characteristics of individual actors (Bressers and Ringeling, 1989, pp. 16–20). All sorts of structural and cultural aspects can influence the choice of instruments. It is therefore more useful to look at the policy field as a whole, focusing on such aspects as traditions, trends (including meta-policies, which are often even less specific than policy fields), international requirements and the presence of structures and experience required to implement the instrument (Bressers, Pullen and Schuddeboom, 1990, pp. 46–50).

This chapter aims to establish how the choice of instruments is influenced by the characteristics of the network of actors involved in a policy problem. This imposes some restrictions on the explanatory factors (Hufen, 1990, p. 208). It is assumed, however, that the influence of network characteristics is sufficiently great to explain an empirically recognizable part of the selected instruments. The central problem in this chapter is: in what way do characteristics of policy networks influence the probability that various types of instruments will be selected during the policy formation process? The answer to this question is sought by means of a theoretical exploration based on deduction from a central assumption. The findings are then illustrated by several examples from Dutch policy practice. The main emphasis is on identifying characteristics of instruments and networks relevant to the central problem and on exploring the mutual relationships between these characteristics. These characteristics can be regarded as a set of institutional rules.

In Section 2 a typology of policy networks is developed, in which two network characteristics play a central role. Section 3 then deals with some relevant characteristics of various types of policy instruments. Section 4 establishes the relationships between the instrument characteristics and the network characteristics. In Section 5 these are discussed, making a distinction between the various types of policy network. Section 6 contains a summary.

2.   TYPOLOGY OF POLICY NETWORKS

Following Hufen and Ringeling (1990, p. 6), the term 'policy network' is defined here as a social system in which actors develop comparatively durable patterns of interaction and communication aimed at policy problems or policy programmes. This definition implies that the identification of a concrete network must be preceded by demarcating a certain policy problem or policy programme and that this demarcation also determines the limits of the network (Zijlstra, 1982, pp. 67–9).

Policy networks can be typified in many different ways (Bressers, O'Toole and Richardson, 1994). Arentsen (1991, pp. 106–11), for instance, highlights the division and coordination of tasks. De Bruijn and Ten Heuvelhof (1991a, pp. 28–41) mention various network characteristics relevant to the 'barriers, opportunities and normative aspects' of policy efforts to control behaviour. They characterize the network as: pluralistic, closed and interdependent. These aspects jointly make up the dimensions of the network's 'complexity'. Arentsen as well as De Bruijn and Ten Heuvelhof relate these characteristics mainly to policy implementation. This chapter assumes certain characteristics regarding the interactions between the actors in the network (Rosenthal et al., 1984, pp. 156–9).

One obvious characteristic of the network is the intensity of this interaction. Another factor that influences interaction is the way in which the objectives, information and sources of power are distributed among the actors (Bressers, 1983, pp. 193–4). The intensity of the interaction between the actors (individuals, groups and organizations) in the network is referred to as 'interconnectedness'. Here interaction not only refers to the contacts in the relevant policy formation process and the habits that have developed in this connection over time, but also to the relationships between these actors outside the actual policy formation process (Zijlstra, 1982, pp. 83–95). Apart from the possibility that these same actors also encounter each other in other processes (Arentsen and Bressers, 1992, pp. 110–13 and 116–19), the origination of these relationships also depends on the presence of intermediary groups or organizations designed to improve contacts in the network and encourage staff sharing (employees who work simultaneously at different organizations in the network) or staff transfers (employees who move from one network organization to the next) (DiMaggio and Powell, 1983, p. 148).

Koppenjan, Ringeling and Te Velde (1987, pp. 245–50) use the term 'sector formation' as one way of typifying policy fields. Sector formation is the degree to which '[semi-]private organizations take part in policy formation by means of formal consultative structures or by being members of committees or advisory bodies'. This can be understood as one of the possible indicators of the degree of 'interconnectedness', in the meaning used by us. Their assumption is that strong sector formation will result in less decisive formal relationships and a consultative, rather than authoritative, policy style.

The second central characteristic of a policy network concerns the distribution of objectives between the actors within it. These objectives can either be conflicting or compatible. Objectives are in conflict where the realization of one actor's objective impedes the realization of the other actor's objective. Within every network, the various actors will have compatible and conflicting objectives. For this reason, a more general variable must be chosen to typify the network. The variable we have selected for this purpose is 'cohesion'. The degree of cohesion in a policy network is described here as the extent to which individuals, groups and organizations sympathize with each other's objectives in so far as these are relevant to the policy field. This sympathy generally stems from shared values and a shared view of reality. This, therefore, is not a specific but a general consensus. If there is an extremely high degree of cohesion, the actors are inclined to place the border-line between 'us' and 'them' on the periphery rather than in the middle of the network.

Up to a certain point, interconnectedness can be seen as a 'structural' characteristic and cohesion as its 'cultural' counterpart (Godfroij, 1981, pp. 101–3). It is also possible to refer to 'institutional' and 'ideological' structures (Smith as quoted by Termeer, 1993, pp. 20–21). These structures, incidentally, are given more complex definitions than interconnectedness and cohesion. Smith asserts that the institutional and ideological structures protect each other against corrosion. A positive relationship can also be assumed between the intensity of the mutual interaction (interconnectedness) and the degree of general consensus (cohesion). There is, however, no reason to assume that the two characteristics necessarily go together. In typifying the development of 'social–cognitive configurations', Termeer herself uses a distinction between a social aspect (interaction structures and interaction rules) and a cognitive aspect (definitions of reality) (Termeer, 1993, pp. 30–35, 44–5). With the empirical analysis the structures of interaction are generally operationalized in terms of the intensity of the mutual interaction, while the interaction rules are discussed largely in terms of the degree to which mutual cohesion is displayed (see, for example, Termeer, 1993, pp. 82–4). In this sense, both interconnectedness and cohesion can be regarded as social characteristics of the network. Though in the approach of Ostrom (1986) every characteristic of the 'action arena' tends to be regarded as 'institutional', we prefer to acknowledge the influence of institutional rules on network characteristics, without suggesting that they are identical.

The third characteristic concerns the distribution of information in the network. Naturally, equality (or lack of equality) in terms of the quantity, quality and perception of information available to the individual actors (resulting in 'definitions of reality') is important, but so is the degree to which the network as a whole is informed. This is closely related to the level of professionalization (Koppenjan, Ringeling and Te Velde, 1987, p. 76). Some networks function as a community of experts (Arentsen, 1991).

The fourth characteristic concerns the distribution of power between the actors in the network. There may be a perfect balance of power or, alternatively, one actor may dominate one of the (groups of) actors.

The central assumption in this chapter is that, in general, the more an instrument's characteristics help to maintain the existing characteristics of the network, the more likely it is to be selected during the policy formation process. This assumption is developed further below.

The notion that 'self-replication' is an important characteristic of social systems, and not only of living organisms, is currently attracting a great deal of interest. The work of Luhmann (1984) has played an important role in this context (see also Van Twist and Schaap, 1991), where the emphasis is placed on cognition and communication. Logically speaking, however, other characteristics of social systems could lead equally well to self-reproduction. As early as the mid-1970s, Majone (1976) developed this idea in connection with the relationship between the distribution of power and selection of instruments. He asserts that the selection of different policy instruments has little or no impact on a policy's success, as instruments can only be used during the implementation process in so far as the balance of power allows it. He argues that even if it were possible to develop instruments which could be implemented in spite of powerful opposition, these opponents would prevent the selection of such an instrument during the policy formation process. As a result, the selected instruments never pose a serious threat to the existing balance of power.

This reasoning, of course, is not always fully applicable. After all, the balance of power is not static and it is precisely the tactical manipulation of differences in power with different policy processes or at different times that can eventually lead to a shift in the balance of power. The process is characterized by interaction (Schrama, 1991, pp. 25–64; Godfroij, 1981, pp. 36–40). This, however, is no reason to reject Majone's assumption outright. The development and results of a policy process can change the circumstances in which that policy process takes place several years later. But the fact remains that it is first and foremost the current circumstances which determine the outcome of a process (Arentsen and Bressers, 1992). It is for instance perfectly plausible that the greater the government's power in the policy network, the more capable it will be of selecting instruments which give it (or its allies) the power required to implement the policy.

Applying the same idea of self-replication to the degree to which the network as a whole is informed, we arrive at the hypothesis that the more the network takes on the character of a 'community of experts', the greater the chance that instruments are selected whose implementation depends partly or even wholly on a high level of knowledge. This

can be a deliberate 'strategic choice' of the actors involved, for example
to seal the network off from 'outsiders'. But it also may occur quite
unintentionally, simply because the high level of knowledge required to
apply the instruments is considered to be 'normal'. Mintzberg, incidentally, also sees the origination of a strategic choice as 'formation' rather
than as 'formulation' (Mintzberg, 1979, p. 443), indicating that it need
not be a deliberate choice on the part of a certain actor, but rather a
pattern that arises as the process evolves.

In this chapter we shall not treat the network characteristics in
relation to the distribution of information and power any further.
Instead we shall concentrate on exploring the relationship between the
two aforementioned network characteristics, that is, interconnectedness
and cohesion, and the choice of instruments. Like power and knowledge,
strong interconnectedness and cohesion create, all other things being
equal, advantages for the participants as well as opportunities to keep
this situation intact. Intensive contacts and general consensus in the
network make for an orderly and predictable environment and,
according to Richardson and Jordan (1979, p. 115), order and predict-
ability are among the main motives for the participating parties to form
networks.

Naturally, any attempt to analyse networks exclusively in terms of
interconnectedness and cohesion represents a further narrowing down
of the explanatory factors. In our view, however, this restriction is
supported by O'Toole and Hanf (1990, p. 27) who claim that the use of
a large number of variables in research into the relationship between
inter-organizational relationships and policy processes impedes the
development of theories and the accumulation of knowledge. Though
obviously a larger number of variables can – greatly – increase the
model's explanatory power, we believe that for a theoretical exploration
within the brief scope of this chapter it is preferable to start with the
simplest model possible.

A further simplification is achieved by drawing a distinction between
only two degrees of interconnectedness and two degrees of cohesion.
The result is a typology comprising four types of networks. Naturally,
the various variables will in practice result in many intermediate situations. The reason for still using a typology is that the relationship
between one network characteristic and the choice of instruments often
partly depends on the position in respect of the other network characteristic (Ostrom, 1986, p. 470). In this sense, the expectations developed
in the sections below can be seen as a form of contingency theory
(O'Toole, 1990, pp. 121–35).

Table 5.1   Four types of policy networks with tentative examples

| | Interconnectedness | |
Cohesion	Strong	Weak
Strong	Agriculture	Economic affairs
Weak	Environmental management, 1990s	Environmental protection, 1970s

By way of clarification, Table 5.1 gives examples in each cell. Here, as in the rest of this chapter, emphasis is placed, on the one hand, on the interconnectedness and cohesion between actors on the government side and, on the other, on the actors in the 'field' where the 'target group' and its representatives occupy an important place. This by no means implies that these two groups are necessarily or even probably homogeneous and coherent. But it does imply that the important government organizations, like ministries (whose names have been used to designate the sectors), fulfil a special role among the actors in the network (Ringeling, 1990). The examples are tentative as no systematic study into the characterization of the policy fields has been made. They do not form the basis of the exploration of the relationship between network characteristics and instrument characteristics which are discussed in the next section, but are only used by way of illustration.

The term 'green front' is sometimes used in the Dutch agricultural sector to indicate the close relationships between the target groups, the government bodies and various other organizations, including the processing industry, a bank and a university. The interconnectedness is so strong that comparisons are sometimes made with the cooperation between the Japanese government and Japanese industry (Siemons, 1992). Compared with the agricultural sector, the relationship between the Ministry of Economic Affairs and Dutch industry is characterized by a weaker degree of interconnectedness (for instance, the description of the choice of technology policy instruments by Hufen, 1990). In both cases, however, there is a strong degree of cohesion. Both ministries are inclined to stand up for their 'own' target groups in order to promote what are perceived to be the long-term interests of the group as a whole.

As regards the environmental policy in the 1970s, the situation can be typified as a combination of relatively weak interconnectedness and weak cohesion between the policy makers and the target groups (that is, the various categories of polluters). Many environmental officials at the ministry saw industry as their 'natural enemy'. In the course of the 1980s, however, the distance between policy makers and target group has narrowed in the environmental sector. This was thanks to the fact that the then Environment Minister, Mr Winsemius, and his successors have encouraged an approach based on cooperation with the target group. The main result was a strong growth in the number of mutual contacts. In fact, the ministry has now even appointed special target group managers to maintain these contacts. Target group consultation is currently a prominent item on the environmental policy agenda. A strengthening of the degree of cohesion is, however, impeded by the nature of the policy problem, which inevitably involves a conflict of interests. Unfortunately, pollution prevention does not always pay. As a result, in the course of the 1990s the environmental policy network has shifted towards a situation still characterized by weak cohesion, but with strengthening interconnectedness.

3. CHARACTERISTICS OF POLICY INSTRUMENTS AS INSTITUTIONAL RULES

Policy instruments have been classified in various ways (Van der Doelen, 1989, pp. 45–80). In order to relate the probability of the selection of one or several of these types of instruments to specific characteristics of the policy network, it is necessary to distinguish characteristics of instruments which can be logically related to the distinctive characteristics of the network. This section seeks to trace the relevant instrument characteristics. In this connection, 'network constitution' as a policy instrument is left out of consideration as this concerns both the dependent and independent variable of the relationship explored here. Network constitution, incidentally, can play a role in deliberately increasing the probability of selection and application of new policy instruments (see the remarks above on environmental policy). Below we shall discuss a number of aspects of policy instruments from which relevant characteristics can be derived.

In his literature survey, Van der Doelen (1989) mentions several variants on each of his three control models (communicative, economic and judicial). These variants are: controlling and constituting, general and individual, and limitative and expansive. In his typology of instruments, he emphasizes the latter distinction. We refer to 'expansion' when the provision of resources makes the totality of behavioural alternatives more attractive and to 'limitation' when the reverse is the case (Bressers and Huzen, 1984, pp. 54–5; Honigh, 1985, p. 38). Further clarification along these lines is given by referring to expansion when, on balance, resources (money, information, powers, and so on) are made available to the members of the target group and to limitation when, on balance, resources are withdrawn from the target group (Klok, 1992). This therefore concerns the provision or withdrawal of resources.

As a further indicator of the expansive or limitative character of policy instruments, Van der Doelen also mentions the presence or absence of a formal freedom of choice for the members of the target group as to whether the instrument is applied (Van der Doelen, 1989, pp. 77–8). Some instruments, like certain forms of information and subsidies that are available on request, have an 'optional nature'. In other words, the members of the target group are free to choose whether or not the instrument is applied to them. The application of such instruments, incidentally, often also leads to bilateral legal relationships.

With some instruments the bilateral or multilateral nature not only appears in the application, but is built into the actual design of the instrument. This is the case with covenants and other agreements.

As regards the difference between instruments from the 'economic' and 'judicial' control model, it has been noted that these labels might give the wrong impression. Legal instruments are often accompanied by financial sanctions, while economic instruments are anchored in legal regulations. So rather than making a strict distinction between the various types of instruments, it is more realistic to refer to a continuum in which a wide range of instruments occupy intermediate positions (Bressers and Klok, 1987b, pp. 92–4). The distinction between 'economic' instruments (incentives) and 'legal' instruments (directives) is often based on the question of to what extent a normative appeal is made to the law-abidingness of the target group ('thou shalt' or 'thou shalt not' regulations make such an appeal; financial incentives do not). In addition, many characteristics attributed to incentives or directives rest on the degree to which the scale of intensity of a certain target group behaviour is in proportion to the scale or intensity of the government reaction to that behaviour. From an ideal typological point of view, incentives are more commensurate with behaviour than regulations, particularly as the latter often draw only a single normative borderline. In the case of regulations, a more or less tailor-made instrument commensurate with the behaviour is often only realized during the policy implementation stage and not in the earlier policy formation stage.

Apart from the selection of policy instruments, the process of policy formation also usually involves the choice of implementing organization. In this connection, the role of the policy makers in the policy implementation process is important. Do the government actors participating in the policy formation process also assign themselves or closely affiliated organizations an important task in the policy implementation process? Or are they happy to leave policy implementation to more remote organizations, for example at lower government levels? If so, do they keep a finger on the pulse? Strictly speaking, these considerations do not involve a specific instrument characteristic. But the choice is an important factor in determining whether and how the instruments work in practice (Honigh, 1985, pp. 40–42). For this reason, this choice is also included in the analysis.

The instrument characteristics discussed relate to the degree to which the instrument involves a 'normative appeal', 'proportionality', the 'provision or withdrawal of resources', the 'freedom to opt for or against application', 'bi- or multilaterality', and the 'role of the policy makers in policy implementation'. These characteristics, with the possible exception of the first, can be considered as institutional rules, predominantly for subsequent processes. They are discussed in the next section.

4. RELATIONSHIPS BETWEEN NETWORK AND INSTRUMENT CHARACTERISTICS

This section explores the relationships between the above-mentioned characteristics of policy instruments and the two network characteristics, cohesion and interconnectedness. Our guiding principle is the central assumption that the more an instrument's characteristics help to maintain the existing characteristics of the network, the more likely it is to be selected during the policy formation process. Other explanatory factors or mechanisms are deliberately excluded from the analysis. To elaborate the central assumption, however, regular – though necessarily brief – references will be made to aspects of the policy formation process which are important to the reproduction of network characteristics in the selection of instruments.

The two network characteristics, interconnectedness and cohesion, are seen as interrelated aspects in the analysis, that is, it is assumed that the influence of one network characteristic may depend partly on the other. In certain cases, therefore, it is not correct to make a straightforward link between each of the two network characteristics and the specific instrument characteristics in the form of expectations indicating that 'the more (network characteristic), the greater the probability that instruments will be selected which (instrument characteristic)'. The analysis in this section is ordered according to the dependent variables

– the instrument characteristics – which are each discussed separately. The expectations formed in this connection will be summarized by type of policy network as hypotheses in Section 5.

Normative Appeal to the Target Group

With some instruments, such as regulations and persuasive public information, the government makes a normative appeal in order to encourage the target group to choose or reject a certain type of behaviour. The legitimacy of the government is thus used to steer and control policy (Bressers and Klok, 1987b, p. 92). This is not the case with other instruments.

If there is strong 'cohesion', the main concern of the authorities is to support the target group in its efforts to achieve its own aims. The selection of instruments that make a normative appeal to the law-abidingness of the target group is then less likely. Where minor policy adjustments are involved, the authorities generally aim their measures at detailed aspects of behaviour rather than at the behavioural pattern as a whole. Therefore, even where the government acts against the target group's preferences, a high degree of cohesion will limit the deployment of normative instruments, stressing their authority over the target group members. After all, the use of such mandatory regulations would soon undermine the existing cohesion.

One exception, however, concerns behaviour that is detrimental to the interests of the entire group. In a situation characterized by strong cohesion, the government actors and target group actors feel part of the same group. If individual behaviour threatens to harm the general interest, the deployment of normative instruments will help to keep the character of the network intact, thereby confirming the group values and reinforcing the legitimacy of choosing mandatory regulations (dos and don'ts). One example is the behaviour of companies which secure competitive advantages by unfair means.

Proportionality of Target Group Behaviour and Government Reaction

The demands that must be met to achieve proportionality between the target group's behaviour and the government's reaction during the policy formation and policy implementation processes differ markedly between general and individual instruments. General instruments, such as price subsidies and excise duties, require little specific knowledge of or contact between representatives of government and target groups. Individualized instruments, however, are a different matter. To design and implement such instruments, it is necessary to collect detailed information on the target group's situation. If the degree of interconnectedness is strong, there are more opportunities, all other things being equal, for government bodies to learn about variations in the target group's behaviour.

On the other hand, though strong interconnectedness enables the selection of better-proportioned, individualized instruments, it does not yet provide the motive for doing so. Clearly, the best way of maintaining strong cohesion is to take account of the circumstances of the target group members. Individually applied instruments which are designed to be commensurate with the target group's behaviour are ideal for this purpose. This type of instrument is therefore most frequently used in situations where strong interconnectedness and strong cohesion are combined. Where the interaction is less intense (strong cohesion, weak interconnectedness), this type of instrument may also be desirable. In this case, however, intermediary structures will be necessary to apply the instruments, thus making implementation less straightforward.

With the more general type of proportional instruments, these considerations do not apply. Such incentives are not aimed at the behaviour of individual members of the target group. In fact, with general measures, the individual members are often not even aware of the existence of the policy incentive (for example a price measure). Where cohesion is weak, however, the government may be inclined to opt for more normative-type measures. In this case, 'invisible' control by means of general incentives would be a less obvious choice.

Providing or Withdrawing Resources to/from the Target Group

The application of some policy instruments entails that the target group receives funds, powers, rights, know-how or other resources in exchange for observing a certain desired behaviour. Alternatively, resources may be withdrawn from the target group to counter undesired behaviour.

If cohesion is strong, the authorities will by definition be positively inclined towards the target group's main aims. In such situations, government will obviously seek to influence behaviour by means of a 'reward' rather than a 'penalty'. After all, the withdrawal of resources would obstruct the target group in its efforts to achieve its objectives. A high degree of cohesion will be preserved by providing rather than withdrawing resources.

Strong interconnectedness between representatives of the government and the target group modifies this relationship to a certain extent. By its very nature (provision or withdrawal of resources), the instrument gives rise to a more important objective for the target group and its representatives than for the policy makers. After all, the authorities mostly will not incur any expenses for providing the resources (for example know-how or powers). In the case of subsidies, the government can use this to justify a higher budget (which, from an office policy angle, even offers certain advantages). Therefore, particularly in the case of strong interconnectedness, government organizations will be mainly guided by the consideration that good relations with the target group will be extremely beneficial to the working climate for the government's representatives. As a consequence, the frequent contacts involved in situations of strong interconnectedness will reinforce the tendency to reward the target group with additional resources rather than withdraw resources. In the latter case, the strong degree of interconnectedness would be undermined.

Target Group's Freedom to Opt For or Against Application

Van der Doelen (1989) sees the freedom of the target group's members to opt for or against the application of certain policy instruments as an indicator of the expansive character of these instruments. This, however, is not to imply that he sees this freedom as a characteristic of all 'expansive' instruments. For each of the three control models (economic, judicial and communicative), he distinguishes between examples of expansive instruments with and without freedom of choice (Van der Doelen, 1989, p. 77). There is a difference with the preceding instrument characteristic, even though a certain interrelatedness is probable.

Typically, the target group will be free to opt for or against application in situations where the government's objectives are broadly similar to those of the target group or, to use our terms, if there is a high degree of interconnectedness. Where the aim is to stimulate the target group to undertake actions which they themselves perceive as significant (for example technological innovations in industry), the parties involved in the policy formation process will often regard mandatory enforcement as unnecessarily heavy-handed. Such strong-arm tactics could impair the degree of cohesion. However, if the target group is free to opt for or against application, irrespective of the envisaged aim, there will almost by definition be no conflicting objectives between government and target group. The danger of undermining the cohesion is small, as each member of the target group can simply ignore the policy whenever that suits his/her individual circumstances. Freedom to opt for or against application can therefore be seen as a 'safety valve' which protects the general consensus in the network.

Instruments involving freedom of choice also avoid the need for close monitoring of the target group. After all, any target group members who want to apply the instrument will generally come forward voluntarily. It was noted earlier that strong interconnectedness makes it easier to collect information on the target group. Offering the target group freedom of choice can therefore be seen as a way of dealing with a low degree of interconnectedness. In this case, therefore, strong cohesion will be reinforced by weak interconnectedness.

Bilaterality or Multilaterality

Agreements such as covenants involve intensive negotiations between the representatives of government and the target group, not only during implementation but also in the formation process (Klok, 1989a).

The example of covenants, incidentally, shows that it is not necessarily correct to see 'bilaterality or multilaterality' as a characteristic that always coincides with 'freedom to opt for or against application'. Covenants, like regulations, are aimed at limiting the target group's freedom of choice in the policy implementation stage. For this reason, these instruments are suitable for situations involving weak cohesion. In the case of strong cohesion, intensive negotiations will not be necessary if the policy makers opt for instruments involving the provision of additional resources and the freedom to opt for or against application.

A high degree of interconnectedness provides a 'natural' setting for bilateral instruments requiring many contacts between the government's policy makers and (representatives of) the target group. Moreover, the use of such instruments ensures the continuation of intensive interaction.

Role of Policy Makers in Policy Implementation

Given the central assumption that the network characteristics will generally reproduce themselves, strong interconnectedness in the policy network will promote the implementation of policies by organizations which also participate in the policy formation network. This helps to maintain the intensive mutual contacts while, on the other hand, the existence of these contacts also encourages the policy-making parties to use them in the application of policy instruments.

Even in the case of strong cohesion, policy makers will be reluctant to entrust the full responsibility for implementation to lower authorities or other institutions outside the network, particularly if their attitude towards the target group is less positive or unknown. If the target group is opposed to application, policy makers will want to keep implementation in their own hands to ensure that the entire process is managed carefully. In the more probable case that the instrument consists in the provision of additional resources, application by an organization within the network will help to reinforce cohesion. In both cases, this provides good reasons during the policy formation process to entrust implementation to organizations within the network which also participated in the policy formation process.

These two influences will have a mutually reinforcing effect. In a situation of strong interconnectedness and strong cohesion, the policies will be implemented almost exclusively by organizations from within the network. As noted above, where strong cohesion is combined with weak interconnectedness, it is sometimes necessary to set up intermediary structures to permit implementation. Only in the situation of both weak cohesion and weak interconnectedness will policy implementation take place, without pressure from outside the network, in a decentralized manner and with little direct supervision from the policy makers (that is the ministry responsible).

5. FOUR TYPES OF NETWORK AND THE RELATED CHOICE OF INSTRUMENTS

In the previous section, the various instrument characteristics were used as the starting-point in the search for the relationship with the characteristics of the policy network. In this section, the procedure is reversed: an inventory is made of the findings from Section 4, making a distinction by type of policy network. To this end, four hypotheses are formulated. For each of the four situations, an attempt is made to indicate which types of policy instruments have a higher-than-average chance of being selected during the policy formation process. The examples from Section 2 are used by way of illustration.

Section 4 leads to the following hypotheses. In each hypothesis the variables correspond to the order in which they were introduced in Section 4.

A. The more a policy network is characterized by strong cohesion and strong interconnectedness, the more the selected instruments will be characterized by:

1. absence of a normative appeal to the target group, except in

the case of behaviour that is damaging to the target group as a whole;

2. proportionality between the target group's behaviour and the envisaged government reaction; this also applies to individually applied instruments;
3. net provision of additional resources to the target group;
4. freedom for the target group to opt for or against application of the instrument;
5. bilateral or multilateral arrangements;
6. implementation by policy makers themselves or by affiliated organizations.

B. The more a policy network is characterized by strong cohesion and weak interconnectedness, the more the selected instruments will be characterized by:

1. absence of a normative appeal to the target group, except in the case of behaviour that is damaging to the target group as a whole;
2. proportionality between the target group's behaviour and the envisaged government reaction; this relationship is only weak due to the fact that with individually applied instruments intermediaries often have to be engaged to achieve proportionality;
3. provision of additional resources to the target group;
4. a high degree of freedom for the target group to opt for or against application of the instrument;
5. absence of bilateral arrangements;
6. implementation by policy makers themselves or by intermediary organizations.

C. The more a policy network is characterized by weak cohesion and weak interconnectedness, the more the selected instruments will be characterized by:

1. a normative appeal to the target group;
2. absence of proportionality between the target group's behaviour and the envisaged government reaction;
3. withdrawal of resources from the target group;
4. a low degree of freedom for the target group to opt for or against application of the instrument;
5. absence of bilateral arrangements;
6. implementation by parties other than the policy makers.

D. The more a policy network is characterized by weak cohesion and strong interconnectedness, the more the selected instruments will be characterized by:

1. a normative appeal to the target group;
2. proportionality between the target group's behaviour and the envisaged government reaction, provided instruments are individually applied;
3. limited withdrawal of resources from the target group;
4. absence of freedom for the target group to opt for or against application of the instrument;
5. many bilateral or multilateral arrangements;
6. implementation by policy makers themselves or by affiliated organizations.

The above hypotheses indicate, for the four types of policy networks, which characteristics of policy instruments increase their probability of being selected. Below we shall establish, for each of the policy networks, which policy instruments best satisfy these characteristics. It should be emphasized that our aim is not to determine which policy instruments are the 'best' in the various situations (Glasbergen, 1989, pp. 20–22). If any instrument could be termed the best, then it would probably be the greatest possible openness towards the other policy instruments. Openness, after all, increases the likelihood of instruments being selected on the basis of implementability and effectiveness. Remember also that this chapter contains only a partial analysis, that is, it is restricted to a few explanatory factors and one central assumption. The inclusion of other assumptions or factors would naturally lead to more detailed conclusions than those set out below. Such a widening of the scope of analysis, however, cannot be performed systematically here. The examples only serve as an illustration and are not intended for purposes of corroboration or verification.

For easier comprehension, the conclusion is summarized before we proceed to individual discussions by type of policy network. In the case of policy networks with both weak mutual interconnectedness and weak cohesion, regulations can be expected to be selected relatively frequently. With weak interconnectedness but strong cohesion, an emphasis on investment and research subsidies and written information is expected. Strong interconnectedness but weak cohesion stimulates the use of agreements and other instruments requiring the active cooperation of the target group, while simultaneously reinforcing a personal sense of responsibility for the policy field. A combination of strong interconnectedness and strong cohesion will lead to a pragmatic choice of instruments. The emphasis here will be on subsidies and personal information (education and advice), but there is also room for all other types of instruments necessary to 'set one's own house in order'.

Strong Cohesion and Strong Interconnectedness

Hypothesis A presents a policy network with strong cohesion and strong interconnectedness as a situation in which few types of instruments are excluded. This hypothesis can be developed as follows. When the group interest is involved, direct regulation is certain to be applied. There is also, however, a clear tendency to provide the target group with additional resources. The emphasis is on supportive instruments, such as research, information and subsidies. Implementation is entrusted as little as possible to other authorities. The net addition of resources may, incidentally, consist, on the one hand, of resources being withdrawn (for example by imposing levies) and, on the other, of these same levies or other larger flows of resources being pumped back into the target group for alternative purposes. 'More complex' instruments, requiring an extensive exchange of information between government and individual members of the target group, need not necessarily be avoided. The participants' strong sense of belonging to a group which prevails in this type of network makes it possible – to a much greater extent than with the other three types of instrument – to consider the selection of instruments as a 'technicality' which must be approached pragmatically. In these circumstances, the instrumentation of the policy is largely a question of 'keeping one's own house in order'.

As an example of such a network, Section 3 mentioned the 'green front', the policy field for agriculture. And, indeed, a wide range of instruments is used in this field. The most important elements here will be subsidies, research and information, but regulations, levies and price measures are also used where the interests of the group as a whole are at stake, such as with the surplus manure policy (Termeer, 1993, pp. 101–2, 134, 178–81, 237–8). In addition, information is often provided through direct contact, that is, not merely in written documentation and mass-media communications, but mainly in the form of targeted advice and education.

Strong Cohesion and Weak Interconnectedness

The inventory of instrument characteristics with this type of network in hypothesis B points, among other things, towards instruments which provide the target group with additional resources and avoid a normative appeal to the target group. In this case, intermediary organizations will generally be engaged to implement the policy. Investment subsidies and research subsidies, as well as written and mass-media information, fit in with this picture. Price measures can also be useful, provided that these are seen as positive incentives.

In Section 3 the relationship between the Ministry of Economic Affairs and industry was given as an example of such a network. Notwithstanding the many developments identified by Hufen (1990, pp. 51–76) in relation to the technology policy instruments, these still remain within the limits of the instrument characteristics indicated above for this type of network. One example of a positive price incentive was the successful attempt to keep electricity prices low for large-scale users in the Netherlands. It should be noted, incidentally, that this success for economic policy had negative consequences for energy-saving policy.

Weak Cohesion and Weak Interconnectedness

Hypothesis C, which relates to a policy network with weak interconnectedness and weak cohesion, points to a strong limitation of the instruments applied. The emphasis will be on regulations. In the policy formation stage, no real attempt is made to achieve proportionality between behaviour and government reaction. As the responsibility for implementing the policy is often passed on to other authorities, it is possible to opt for licensing systems which necessitate individualized implementation (that is, by others).

This description links up fairly well with the environmental policy that took shape in the 1970s. We therefore look at some exceptions. The licensing system formulated in the Nuclear Energy Act (mainly to provide protection against radiation in industrial and medical applications) was actually implemented by the ministries themselves. This, however, concerned a special policy network surrounding the application of ionizing sources, which happens to be characterized by a strong degree of interconnectedness and cohesion. This regulation fulfils the same kind of role for this network as the surplus manure regulations do in the agricultural field, that is, to protect the group's overall interests and the good reputation of the target group (Arentsen and Bressers, 1992, p. 108). Another example concerns the Dutch water quality levies. Apart from being formally intended as compensation for cleansing effluents, these were also initiated by another ministry, namely the Ministry of Transport and Public Works. The sphere of public works also involves a network characterized by strong interconnectedness and cohesion. In fact, the target group consists of the members of the water boards! At a later stage, other regulatory levies were rejected on the basis of arguments which would have served equally well to block the (successful) water quality levies (Bressers, 1987, pp. 118–20).

Weak Cohesion and Strong Interconnectedness

Where a policy network has weak cohesion and strong interconnectedness, hypothesis D asserts the relevant instruments are based on bilateral or multilateral arrangements and simultaneously make a normative appeal to the target group. The joint effect is that emphasis is placed on the target group's own responsibility during consultation meetings. In appealing to this personal sense of responsibility, policy makers try to secure the commitment of the target group. This commitment can then be officially laid down in agreements (such as covenants). The ministry supervises compliance with these covenants and thus continues to play an active role. The target group's own sense of responsibility can also be reinforced by imposing certain obligations, such as liability insurance or research, reporting and information requirements.

In this package of policy instruments it is not difficult to detect the wave of 'new' instruments which have started to play an increasing role in environmental policy over the past few years. According to our hypotheses, these instruments now stand a better chance of succeeding than in the 1970s, thanks to the intensification of contacts between the ministry and the target group over the past ten years. This intensification, incidentally, is the result of a deliberate long-term policy pursued by the Environment Ministers Winsemius, Nijpels and Alders. The actual structure of the policy network can therefore be made the focus of the policy in order to create the right conditions for successful operational policy in the long term. De Bruijn and Ten Heuvelhof (1991a, pp. 67–9) call this network management'. Often, however, the character of the network will change without the need for government to take action.

6.   SUMMARY

This chapter has centred on the following question: in what way do characteristics of policy networks influence the probability of different types of instruments being selected during the policy formation process? To answer this question, a distinction was first made between some characteristics which could be important for the typology of policy networks. Two of these were analysed more closely: the degree of interconnectedness (the intensity of the interaction in the network) and the degree of cohesion (the sympathy of the actors in the network for one another's objectives). On the basis of this, four types of policy networks were distinguished.

Subsequently, a distinction was made in Section 3 between six characteristics of policy instruments, most of which can be considered as institutional rules for subsequent processes. The relevant instrument characteristics are: absence/presence of normative appeal to the target group; the degree of proportionality between target group behaviour and the government's reaction; the provision or withdrawal of resources to/from the target group; the degree of freedom of the target group to opt for or against application of the policy instruments: bilateral or multilateral instruments; and the role of the policy makers in policy implementation. In Section 4 these were related to the characteristics of the policy network. The central assumption here was that in general the more an instrument's characteristics serve to maintain the existing characteristics of the network, the greater its chance of being selected.

This led us to conclude that the instrument chosen for policy networks with both weak interconnectedness and weak cohesion will often take the form of regulations. With weak interconnectedness combined with strong cohesion, the emphasis will be placed on investment and research subsidies as well as on written information. Strong interconnected linked with weak cohesion will stimulate the use of agreements and other instruments which require the active cooperation of the target group, while simultaneously stimulating its personal sense of responsibility for the policy field. A combination of strong interconnectedness and strong cohesion will serve to promote a pragmatic choice of instruments; the main elements here will be subsidies and personal information (education and advice), but there will also be room for all other types of instruments considered necessary to 'keep one's own house in order'.

6. A public choice approach to the selection of policy instruments

Dirk Jan Kraan

---

1. INTRODUCTION

In the economic literature policy instrumentation is usually discussed from a normative perspective. In particular, the analytical apparatus of welfare theory is well equipped to evaluate the advantages and disadvantages of alternative instruments to attain a given policy objective. To that purpose the objective must be stated in terms of changes in economic outcomes, especially in the quantities of production and consumption. The fundamental criterion of evaluation is allocative efficiency. In cases where a given policy objective can be attained by alternative instruments, for instance either by a subsidy or by regulation, it is usually possible for the welfare-theoretic analyst to offer advice about the merits of the alternatives in the light of this criterion.

However, in practice we often observe that policy makers do not ask for advice on the basis of welfare-theoretical analysis, or, if unsolicited advice is given, that they decide for the inferior alternative from a welfare-theoretical point of view. The reason for this state of affairs is not that policy makers are irrational or immoral, but rather that they have interests and associated criteria that are inconsistent with allocative efficiency. This does not mean that policy makers never decide in favour of the most efficient solution. Sometimes they do. In order to understand when and why they do, a positive, rather than normative analysis is called for. Such an analysis is not only of interest for a better understanding of the policy-making process, but also for a more effective use of welfare-theoretical advice. This chapter aims to provide such a positive analysis. To that purpose it makes use of public choice theory, which is the dominant positive economic theory of government.

In a positive, as opposed to normative, analysis of policy instrumentation, the interests of the policy makers take centre stage. In the present chapter two such interests will be considered, namely: (1) the interest of politicians in discriminatory fiscal benefits, and (2) the

106

interest of agency administrators in the agency budget. It will be argued that each of these interests has an influence in choice situations where alternatives for policy instrumentation are available. Four types of choice situations will be looked at in particular, namely: (1) regulation versus regulatory tax, (2) regulatory tax versus subsidy, (3) subsidy versus tax expenditure, and (4) fee versus earmarked tax.

Section 2 sketches the role of the above-mentioned interests in the behaviour of politicians and agency administrators and briefly reviews the literature on these themes. Section 3 treats each choice situation from the normative perspective of welfare theory as well as from the positive perspective of political and bureaucratic interests. This analysis clarifies the contrasts between both perspectives. Section 4 states the conclusions.

2. POLITICAL AND BUREAUCRATIC INTERESTS

In the public choice literature there are two strands of thought concerning the motivation of politicians. In one approach the objective of the politician is conceived as electoral success or, more specifically, as the maximization of electoral votes or of electoral plurality. In the other, the objective of the politician is conceived as the implementation of preferred policies. The first view has its roots in the work of Downs (1957), Tullock (1967) and Davis, Hinich and Ordeshook (1970) on electoral competition. The second has its roots in the work of Buchanan on fiscal illusion (1967) and in the work of Wittman on electoral competition by politicians with policy preferences (1973, 1977, 1990). At the conceptual level the contrast between the views seems to be rather fundamental: according to the first, politicians consider policy implementation as a means to winning elections; according to the second, they consider winning elections as a means to policy implementation. In practice the difference is less important: in many circumstances the need to win elections puts severe constraints on the freedom to pursue preferred policies. In the extreme case of: (a) complete information on the part of electors and politicians about the tax costs and benefits of publicly provided services, (b) a first-past-the-post electoral system, and (c) existence of a vote-maximizing electoral equilibrium, the political margin of freedom vanishes completely. To the extent that information is less complete, the electoral system is more proportional, and the distribution of voter 'ideal points' in the policy space is less balanced, the opportunity for politicians to exploit fiscal illusion and to pursue policy preferences increases, but the resulting room for manoeuvre will depend on the nature of the policies. In particular, politicians cannot afford to alienate the parts of the electorate by which they are traditionally supported. Moreover, they will be anxious to gain popularity among other parts of the electorate where they expect to win new support.

The empirical literature on political motivation presents substantial evidence in support of the assumption that politicians are primarily motivated by policy preferences, but shows also that the margins for deviation from electoral objectives are often very small.[1]

For the selection of policy instruments the preceding argument implies, among other things, that politicians favour alternatives that lead to discriminatory fiscal benefits. Examples are tax expenditures and subsidies. The implementation of a discriminatory tax decrease or expenditure increase makes it possible to strengthen the hold on existing electoral supporters and to gain new ones. Moreover, it is relatively easy to win approval for it by a parliamentary majority. Of course, a tax decrease or expenditure increase has to be funded and will often be resisted by politicians whose electoral supporters do not gain, but even if a policy instrument is only supported by a minority, this minority can often get its way by the formation of a logrolling coalition with minorities on other issues.

On the other hand, politicians are averse to alternatives that lead to discriminatory fiscal sacrifices. An example is a regulatory tax. This instrument is aimed at the reduction of specific harmful behaviour. Usually a discriminatory tax increase is highly unpopular among the people who have to pay it. It tends to destroy electoral support among the affected citizens. Furthermore, it is hard to implement. Of course, a tax increase raises revenue and may be supported by non-affected citizens, but even if a parliamentary majority is willing to approve it, the minority can defend itself by the formation of a logrolling coalition with minorities on other issues. In practice this implies that discriminatory tax increases for minorities can only come about by complicated package deals that involve compensation for the affected minorities.

In this chapter the selection of policy instruments will be analysed on the basis of the assumption that politicians want to maximize benefits from discriminatory expenditure and to minimize sacrifices from discriminatory taxation for potential electoral supporters.

As far as the motivation of agency administrators is concerned, various ideas have been put forward in the economic literature. An early contribution by Von Mises (1944) made clear that the constraints and incentives provided by the governmental environment are fundamentally different from those provided by the market environment.

Subsequently, Tullock (1965) and Downs (1967) proposed specific assumptions about the objectives of public officials. In Tullock's view the public official is motivated by the objective of rising in the hierarchy. Downs recognizes objectives in the sphere of self-interest as well as in the sphere of altruism. To the former belong the desire for power, money income, prestige, convenience and security; to the latter belongs the desire to serve the public interest. The ideas of Von Mises, Downs and Tullock did not yet lead to a theory that could be used to derive precise and testable empirical hypotheses about outcomes (budgetary decisions). Such a theory was provided by Niskanen (1968, 1971).

Niskanen is particularly interested in the motivation of the administrator who holds factual authority over the economic behaviour of an agency. This official, denoted as 'the bureaucrat', is defined as 'the senior official of a bureau with a separate, identifiable budget'. According to Niskanen, the main objective of the bureaucrat is the maximization of the budget which is available for the bureau's activities. In his view this objective is instrumental for all the ultimate objectives that enter into the utility function of the bureaucrat, such as salary, perquisites of office, public reputation, power, patronage and output of the bureau. Furthermore, ease of making changes and ease of managing the bureau are enhanced by increases in the budget (not so much by its absolute size).

It has been noted that Niskanen's ideas about bureaucratic motivation can be elaborated in two ways. According to the first, budget maximization is the only bureaucratic objective; according to the second, budget maximization is one objective among others. In combination with a specific assumption about market structure, the first elaboration leads to a precise hypothesis about outcomes. In Niskanen's view the structure of the market in which the bureaucrat sells services is that of bilateral monopoly with a dominant supplier. This is the elaboration that Blais and Dion, in their review of the literature (1991) have called the 'formal model'. The second elaboration of the assumption of budget maximization only leads to a precise hypothesis about outcomes if the other objectives are specified in economic terms to the same extent as the objective of budget maximization. This is sometimes the case, for instance in the proposal of Migué and Bélanger (1974) to treat the maximization of 'managerial discretionary profit' (producer surplus) as a second bureaucratic objective, but sometimes it is not. The latter explains why Blais and Dion have denoted this elaboration as the 'informal model'.

There has been a substantial amount of empirical research on bureaucratic objectives. Results are not only dependent on the type of data being used, but also on methodological issues. A major distinction in this respect is whether assumptions about objectives are tested directly or indirectly. The direct approach attempts to establish the empirical validity of the assumption independently of a concrete model in which it may be applied. The indirect approach involves testing of complete models, including assumptions about the objectives of the actors, by data about outcomes (decisions). The choice between the direct and the indirect approach is not only a matter of expediency but also of methodological principle: the Friedman school rejects the direct approach to the testing of assumptions in general (Friedman, 1957). The general picture that emerges from the empirical literature is that budget maximization in the sense of the first elaboration (the formal model) finds little support in results that are based on the direct approach and some support in results that are based on the indirect approach. Budget mazimization in the sense of the second elaboration (the 'informal model') finds substantial support, especially in results that are based on the indirect approach.[2]

The choice of policy instruments will be examined in this chapter on the basis of the assumption that agency administrators are at least partially motivated by the size of the budget available to their agencies.

3.   NORMATIVE AND POSITIVE ASPECTS

Regulatory Tax versus Regulation

Regulatory ('Pigouvian') taxes are a well-known policy instrument in economic theory but in practice their application has been very limited in most Western countries. Until the development of environmental policy they have been in use mainly in the areas of tobacco and alcohol policy. In these areas their application is fairly widespread throughout the Western world. Usually the taxes on alcohol and tobacco take the form of excise duties, but in contrast to excise duties on other goods, the primary policy objective in these cases is the control of consumption rather than the generation of revenue. The excise on gasoline is a case of doubt. Originally the control of consumption was certainly not the primary objective of this excise in most Western countries, but since the development of environmental policy the need to recognize this objective has increasingly been emphasized.

The regulatory tax is often advocated by economists as the preferable alternative to regulation. The basic welfare-theoretic argument is that regulation fails to take into account the cost differences in emission reduction between private households. This implies that regulation does not produce the collective good of emission reduction in the most efficient way. A regulatory tax, on the other hand, equalizes the marginal cost of emission reduction between households and thus induces an allocationally optimal solution.

In practice we see very little regulatory taxation in the area of environmental policy. Politicians resist discriminatory tax increases for electoral reasons. Moreover, the complicated package deals that are necessary to compensate the affected minorities are not easy to implement. An additional reason is that producers in the private sector tend to prefer regulation to regulatory taxation, even if they are financially compensated for the increased tax burden. This is the case because regulation, especially if it comes in the form of private contracts with branch organizations, tends to protect existing producers against potential entrants.

From the point of view of agency administrators, the choice between regulation and regulatory tax is less straightforward. A determining factor in this respect is the role of the various ministries. Regulatory taxation is not an exclusive responsibility of the sectoral ministry. The ministry of finance has a strong role in policy making with respect to regulatory taxation and often also takes care of execution. For the sectoral ministry this means that a regulatory tax implies at least strong interference by the Ministry of Finance and often total surrender of the primary responsibility for the instrument and the associated administrative budgets (for policy development and execution). This is perceived as unattractive by the bureaucratic top of the sectoral ministry as well as by the agencies of that ministry that would be responsible for regulation. Obviously, bureaucratic interests in the ministry of finance may point in a different direction, but in the area of policy instrumentation the sectoral ministry is usually decisive.

The other side of the coin is that a regulatory tax raises revenue, which may partially accrue to the sectoral ministry. Moreover, the tax may be earmarked for expenditures of the sectoral ministry. If this is the case, the sectoral ministry avails itself of an independent source of income which is protected by law and does not require annual authorization. This is comparable to the protection of expenditures by entitlement legislation. The difficulty is to attain agreement on earmarking. Usually the ministry of finance will resist earmarking for the very reason that it weakens political control. From the welfare-theoretical point of view an argument in favour of earmarking is that the tax revenue is used to pay for a public facility which eliminates or reduces the negative external effect of the product that is being taxed. This argument implies that the tax is not a compensation for the external effect that ought to benefit the entire citizenry, but rather a price for the public facility that ought to accrue to the agency that exploits it.

It may be concluded that, in general, regulation will lead to larger agency budgets in the sectoral ministry than regulatory taxation, unless the tax is earmarked. In the latter case the reverse will usually obtain. The preference order of agency administrators in the sectoral ministry will vary accordingly.

Regulatory Tax versus Subsidy

There are many situations in which a regulatory tax and a subsidy can be considered as alternative instruments to attain the same policy objective. For example, production or consumption by a private household may have a negative external effect which can be eliminated by the production or consumption of a substitute product (which may differ from the original product only in the way it is produced). In those cases the government has the choice between taxing the negative external effect or subsidizing the substitute product. Examples are a tax on polluting emissions versus a subsidy on clean production technology, a tax on private transport versus a subsidy on public transport, a tax on energy use versus a subsidy on an energy-saving device.

In choice situations of this type, the tax is unambiguously the preferable alternative from the welfare-theoretical point of view. An optimal tax is a tax per unit of a harmful product that equals the sum of the marginal benefits from reduction of the negative external effect to the victims. An optimal subsidy is a subsidy per unit of a socially beneficial product that equals the sum of the marginal benefits from expansion of the positive external effect to the beneficiaries. Where a subsidy on a substitute product is used to reduce the negative external effect of a harmful product, an optimal subsidy can be defined as a subsidy per unit of the substitute product that equals the sum of the marginal benefits from reduction of the negative external effect of the harmful product to the victims. An optimal tax will in general lead to better results than an optimal subsidy because the effect of the tax will depend on the elasticity of the harmful product for its own price whereas the effect of the subsidy will depend on the cross-elasticity of the harmful product for the price of the substitute. Since this cross-elasticity will generally be lower than the elasticity of the harmful product for its own price, the tax will generally be less effective than the subsidy.

In reality we observe that politicians often prefer subsidies to taxes. In contrast to taxes, subsidies offer discriminatory benefits to certain private households and are attractive from an electoral point of view. Of course subsidies have to be funded, which may cause problems, and taxes raise revenue, which may solve problems, but these consequences are of little importance in comparison to the electoral effects. In particular, the funding of subsidies can be effected in various ways that politicians find less embarrassing than the imposition of a regulatory tax. One can think of a decrease of expenditures across the board, or of a small tax increase across the board. Other possibilities are an increase of the deficit, or accounting tricks, such as changes in the estimates of tax revenues or of expenditures for entitlement programmes. Each of these measures is less painful from an electoral point of view than the imposition of a regulatory tax on a specific group of citizens.

As far as agency administrators are concerned, the subsidy is also more attractive than the regulatory tax. As argued before, the ministry of finance has a strong say in policy development with respect to taxes and often that ministry is also responsible for execution. In contrast, the administration of subsidies is a task of the sectoral ministry. Subsidies increase the budget of the sectoral ministry because of both programme costs (the subsidies themselves) and administrative costs (costs of policy development and execution). Usually many jobs in the sectoral ministry are involved. In this case the earmarking of the tax is not a crucial factor. Given that the subsidy budget required to bring about a given reduction of a negative external effect will in general be larger than the total revenue from the tax to be imposed to induce the same effect, agency administrators will prefer the subsidy. Moreover, in view of the political resistance to discriminatory taxation, it is plausible that politicians will set lower targets for the tax instrument than for the subsidy instrument. This amounts to an additional reason to presume that the subsidy budget accruing to the sectoral ministry will exceed the revenue of an earmarked regulatory tax. The only advantage that an earmarked regulatory tax can have from a bureaucratic point of view is that it offers more legal protection. This is especially the case if the subsidy lacks the character of an entitlement, so that it can be amended or eliminated by executive action without change of substantive law.

Tax Expenditure versus Subsidy

Tax expenditures are exemptions from the general applicability of the tax rule in order to attain specific policy objectives. They are in use throughout the Western world in spite of criticism by fiscal experts. Examples are investment allowances, research allowances, and allowances for medical expenses.

From a welfare-theoretical point of view, subsidy and tax expenditure are equivalent policy instruments. The similarity between them consists in the fact that they lower the price of a product or production factor and thereby stimulate its use.

From the political point of view, tax expenditure is usually the preferable alternative. Both instruments provide discriminatory fiscal benefits and are therefore popular with the electorate and easy to implement. However, a tax expenditure offers more legal protection to the beneficiaries. This is especially the case if the subsidy does not take the form of an entitlement. But also if a subsidy is provided as an entitlement, it needs annual budgetary authorization. In contrast, tax expenditures usually do not need annual authorization and are thus completely withdrawn from the regular budget process.

Agency administrators often prefer subsidies. Subsidies increase sectoral budgets because of both programme costs (the subsidies themselves) and administrative costs. Since tax expenditures are exemptions from regular tax rules, both policy making and execution are in the hands of the ministry of finance. Whereas the administration of regulatory taxes is sometimes committed to special agencies, tax expenditures are necessarily administered by the general tax service.

Earmarked Tax versus Fee

In some situations citizens are paying for publicly provided services through earmarked taxes where fees on the basis of common law would also be possible. One can think of broadcast contributions, motorway levies, refuse collection duties, sewerage duties and social security contributions.

From a welfare-theoretical point of view, both ways of funding a public service can be considered equivalent if the one can be transformed into the other without any change in economic impact. However, such a transformation is not always possible. In particular, there are two cases in which it is not. First, earmarked taxes are sometimes income-dependent. This applies, for instance, to most social security contributions. In these cases one cannot make use of fees without abandoning the income distribution objective. One can debate in turn whether income-dependent contributions for public services are an efficient instrument of income policy from a welfare-theoretical point of view (they are not), but this is a different matter. Second, earmarked taxes are sometimes imposed on a basis that does not perfectly reflect the use of the service. This is largely a question of perception technology. Broadcast contributions are charged to the possessors of radio or television sets, not to people who watch or listen to broadcasts. Motorway levies are charged to possessors of cars, not to people who use roads. Refuse collection and sewerage duties are charged to possessors or renters of houses, not to people who produce refuse or use water. In these cases the tax is not an entirely efficient instrument, but it may still be the only viable instrument to put the cost of the service roughly on the consumer. It should be added, however, that although this argument sometimes explains the introduction of the tax, it may have grown obsolete in the course of time. Perception technology is developing and now it is sometimes possible to use fees, whereas it was not possible when the tax was introduced. This applies, for instance, to broadcast contributions, which can now be charged as fees through the technology of pay-to-view television, and to sewerage duties, which can now be charged as fees on the basis of water use. Political and bureaucratic interests become relevant when neither of these practial arguments stands any longer in the way of the fee option.

From the political point of view, the fee option is usually preferable. An earmarked tax is a discriminatory tax and will be unpopular with the affected citizens and hard to implement.

Agency administrators, too, tend to prefer fees. The proceeds of both fees and earmarked taxes accrue to agencies of the sectoral ministry and are roughly equally secure as sources of revenue, but the ministry of finance will play a larger role in policy making and sometimes in executive activities with respect to the tax. Therefore fees will usually lead to higher administrative budgets in the sectoral ministry.

4.   CONCLUSIONS

The preceding analysis has made it clear that in situations of choice concerning policy instrumentation, arguments of different orders are usually put forward. On the one hand there are arguments of a normative nature, often based on welfare theory. On the other hand there are arguments that have to do with the interests of politicians and bureaucrats. In this respect the effects of the policy instruments on discriminatory fiscal benefits and on the budgets of public agencies are relevant factors. Table 6.1 summarizes the various factors bearing on policy instrumentation in the cases of choice considered here.

Table 6.1   Normative, political and bureaucratic characteristics of policy instruments: rank order of instruments

Instruments	Allocative efficiency	Criterion Discriminatory fiscal benefits	Agency budgets
Regulatory tax	1	2	2*
Regulation	2	1	1*
Regulatory tax	1	2	2
Subsidy	2	1	1
Tax expenditure	1 (equal)	1	2
Subsidy	1 (equal)	2	1
Earmarked tax	2**	2	2
Fee	1**	1	1

*   Unless the tax is earmarked, in which case the order is reversed.
** If fee is technically feasible.

Table 6.1 shows that political and bureaucratic interests coincide in the cases of regulatory tax versus regulation, regulatory tax versus subsidy and earmarked tax versus fee, and that they are opposed in the case of tax expenditure versus subsidy.

As far as the relation between allocative efficiency and political interests is concerned, the following conclusions can be drawn. In the cases of regulatory tax versus regulation and regulatory tax versus subsidy, the political interest in the reduction of discriminatory fiscal sacrifices points in a different direction from that of allocative efficiency. In the case of tax expenditure versus subsidy, the political preference for tax expenditures is not inconsistent with the equal score of the instruments on the normative criterion. In this case, however, there are other normative criteria (expenditure control, budgetary authority of the legislator) on which the subsidy scores better and that ought to be taken into account as well. In the case of earmarked tax versus fee, finally, the political preference for fees is consistent with the normative criterion. The fact that in practice earmarked taxes are proliferating, even in cases where fees would be technically possible, can be seen as an indication that bureaucratic interests are sometimes more influential than political interests and efficiency considerations together.

A further conclusion regards the effects of the instruments on the total (macroeconomic) tax burden. These effects have to be distinguished from the discriminatory effects that cause the political resistance to certain fiscal instruments (regulatory tax and earmarked tax) and the political support for other fiscal instruments (tax expenditures and subsidies). It is not supposed in this chapter that effects on the total tax burden have normative implications (in the sense that a decrease of the burden is good and an increase is bad), but it is still important to be aware of these effects. Table 6.2 summarizes the effects of the alternatives on the total tax burden under the supposition that the rest of the budget is not affected (no expenditure cuts and no room for new expenditures). This implies that a regulatory tax will be compensated by tax decreases and that a tax expenditure and a subsidy will be funded by tax increases.

Table 6.2   Effects of policy instruments on total tax burden and burden from regulation

	Total tax burden	Burden from regulation
Regulatory tax	0	0
Regulation	0	+
Regulatory tax	0	0
Subsidy	+	0
Tax expenditure	0	0
Subsidy	+	0
Earmarked tax	+	0
Fee	0	+*

+ Increase of burden
0 No change
* If consumption is obligatory

Table 6.2 shows the consequences of both the introduction of a new instrument and the substitution of one instrument for another (by comparison of the signs of both instruments). Note, for instance, that the substitution of a subsidy by a regulatory tax leads to a decrease of the total tax burden! (Consider it as two changes: elimination of the subsidy allows a tax decrease without any effect on the rest of the budget and introduction of a regulatory tax can be compensated by reduction of other taxes without any effect on the rest of the budget.) The table can also be interpreted to show how the rest of the budget is affected if compensating tax decreases or increases are carried through in order to maintain the total tax burden (a plus means expenditure cuts).

Note that the effects of tax expenditure and subsidy on the total tax burden are different. Since the consequences of both instruments for the allocation of economic resources are identical, this difference is mainly optical. The effects of earmarked tax and fee are also different but this difference is not optical because the payment of a fee, in contrast to the payment of a tax, establishes an individual right of the citizen to receive a service in return.[3]

Table 6.2 also indicates what happens to the burden from regulation. This is an important aspect because a decrease of the total tax burden may not be attractive if it is fully compensated by an increase in the burden from regulation. This may be the case in the choice of regulatory tax versus regulation and in the choice of earmarked tax versus fee (namely if the consumption of the service is obligatory).

A final remark concerns the consequences of our findings for the role of welfare theory. The analysis has made it clear that sometimes there is a conflict between allocative efficiency and political interests and sometimes not. Provided that it neither make sense to offer advice to a politician in a direction that runs counter to basic political interest, nor in a direction that will be chosen anyhow, the question arises whether there remains any role for welfare theory in policy development at all. This question is particularly pressing for those who accept the basic claim of public choice theory that politicians and agency administrators decide on the basis of interests rather than norms. However, the answer is not necessarily negative. In the first place, our findings do not contradict in any way the premise that welfare theory provides an objective and precise yardstick for the measurement of allocative efficiency. Apart from any practical use, this is valuable on its own account. Moreover, there remain more practical roles for welfare theory as well. This has been emphasized in particular by Buchanan (1959). In the first place, welfare-theoretical analysis ought to stimulate economists to think about solutions that are Pareto-optimal, that is, efficient and beneficial to everybody simultaneously. In regard to the subject of this chapter this would imply the development of policy instruments that politicians like better than taxes but that are more efficient than regulations or subsidies. A policy instrument that offers good prospects in this respect is, for instance, the tradable permit. In the second place, welfare-theoretical analysis can be used for the development of institutional policy (Buchanan, 1987). Sometimes it is possible to reach agreement about institutional rules that make it harder to deviate from efficient solutions. One can think, for instance, of rules for the cases in which tax revenues can be earmarked. There is large scope for progress in both directions. Welfare theory remains indispensable in the toolkit of the economic analyst, but it is important to be critical about the purposes for which this tool can be applied.

NOTES

1. For a survey of the evidence see Wittman (1983).
2. For a survey of the record concerning the direct approach to the testing of budget maximization by bureaucrats see Young (1991). For surveys concerning the indirect approach see Niskanen (1975), Orzechowski (1977) and Kiewiet (1991).
3. In order to prevent the 'misuse' of fees for the purpose of increasing public revenue, the Dutch central government follows the rule that fees that cannot be avoided because consumption of a publicly supplied service is factually or legally obligatory have to be included in the computation of the total tax burden. The effect of this rule is that the political preference for fees is not only weakened if the economic effects of fee and earmarked tax are identical, but also if, in view of new perception technology, fees are the more efficient instrument. This is an unintended effect. It is good policy to monitor and control the burden from regulation on the economy, but the fact that some obligatory services are supplied by government is not a good reason to include the fees for these services in the total tax burden.

7. The political circumstances of instrument design: the case of privatization in Eastern Europe*

Lorene Allio, Mariusz Mark Dobek and David L. Weimer

1. INTRODUCTION

Policy scientists bring two very different perspectives to the study of policy instruments. One perspective seeks understanding of instruments as basic components for policy design. The origins of the design perspective can be found in two contrasted traditions: in efforts by economists to identify generic instruments for correcting market failures (Pigou, 1946; Kirschen et al., 1964; Weimer and Vining, 1989) and among students of implementation who sought a more disaggregated unit of study than the composite policy or programme (Bardach, 1980; Salamon, 1981; Elmore, 1987). From the design perspective, the political system is seen as part of a general context that affects the performance of, and restricts the choice among, instruments. The other perspective, which we call the policy process perspective, seeks to understand the relationship between the content of policy instruments and the political system (Lowi, 1972; Doern and Phidd, 1983; Linder and Peters, 1984, 1989a, 1989b and 1990). The policy process perspective sees a fundamental joint dependence between the content of instruments and the political system. In this chapter, we consider the efforts underway in the formerly communist countries of Eastern Europe to privatize large-scale industry from the two design perspectives.

Our central argument can be framed in terms of the distinction Peter May (1991) makes between policies without publics, which we see as consistent with the design perspective, and those with publics, which we see as requiring the policy process perspective. We argue that while the initial decisions concerning privatization in the countries of Eastern

* The authors wish to thank Daniel Diermeier, Joel Ericson, Tamas Fellegi, Tim Frye, Lyudmila Kareva, Brendan Kiernan, Steve Lewis, Nikolai Mikhailov, the late William Riker, and Randy Stone for advice and assistance.

Europe can reasonably be viewed as policy without publics, these initial decisions had distributional effects that created identifiable interests so that privatization of industry is now more appropriately viewed as a policy with publics. More generally, we argue that the relative simplicity and tractability of the design perspective, which facilitates practical application by analysts, is likely to be misleading in policy areas where instruments have large distributional effects. In other words, it may be necessary in such situations for analysts to embrace the more complicated and less tractable policy process perspective.

We begin our discussion by reviewing the economic theory of privatization, which roughly corresponds to the policy design perspective, and the political theory of privatization, which roughly corresponds to the policy process perspective. We then turn to the cases of large-scale industrial privatization in the Czech Republic and Slovakia, Hungary, Poland and Russia. In each case, we first consider the goals of privatization and the instruments initially selected to achieve them. We then consider the evolution of goals and instruments in response to the political interests that have emerged.

2. AN ECONOMIC THEORY OF PRIVATIZATION

Privatization is commonly used to describe two different processes. The first is the transfer of productive assets from state or collective ownership to private ownership. This might more descriptively be called 'desocialization', because it involves the state relinquishing ownership (Donahue, 1989, p. 215). The second process is the transfer of governmental functions from state to non-state organizations as, for example, when state bureaux contract for goods or services rather than produce them with their own employees (Savas, 1987). Such transfers of functions might more descriptively be called 'debureaucratization', and, though they may also involve the relinquishing of the ownership of productive assets by the state, they generally maintain some form of state funding of the functions. In the discussion that follows, we intend 'privatization' to refer to the former process. Indeed, we are concerned mainly with a specific form of privatization that is currently of great importance in formerly communist countries – the transfer of state-owned enterprises to private ownership.

Strictly speaking, there is no normative theory of either type of privatization. We can sketch such a theory, however, by considering what economic theory tells us about the relative efficiency of alternative ownership forms in various circumstances. A normative economic theory of ownership change calls for correction of deviations from optimal ownership forms. The normative theory of privatization refers to those corrections involving movements towards greater private ownership.

The simple distinction between private and non-private ownership provides an insufficient basis for discussion of efficient ownership forms. Ownership of things consists of a bundle of property rights involving various degrees of autonomy for the rights-holder with respect to the claim to income generated from them, their use, and the alienation of these rights. The strongest form of private ownership of productive assets is the idealized neoclassical firm in which the owner–manager has claim to the entire net income, has fully informed and effective control over the use of the firm's capital, and can freely dispose of these rights to another. In reality, however, the organization of modern industry typically involves a separation to some extent between the right to income from a firm (ownership) and the effective right to use the firm (management).

The consequences of the separation between ownership and management is a central focus of agency theory (Jensen and Meckling, 1976). Agents (managers) generally enjoy an informational advantage about their own effort levels and effectiveness relative to principals (owners). This opens the possibility that agents will be able to pursue their own interests, which may diverge from the interests of managers. Agency theory assumes that principals design contracts with agents so as to minimize agency cost, which is the sum of monitoring expenditures by the principal, the costs borne by agents to demonstrate their compliance with actions consistent with the principal's interests (bonding), and the residual loss to the principal from the exercise of the discretion remaining to agents after monitoring and bonding expenditures. Agency theory provides the basis for comparing private and state ownership of firms under different assumptions about the appropriate standard for social welfare and the market environment.

Undistorted Markets and Economic Efficiency

Consider initially the case of firms, which can be thought of as bundles of assets, operating in the absence of market failures; that is, the firms, or enterprises, use assets to produce pure private goods without externalities which they sell in competitive markets to fully informed consumers. If the goal of principals is to maximize the net present value of the income streams produced by the assets they own, then their minimization of agency costs will result in the economically efficient use of those assets. Further, if we take economic efficiency as the measure of social welfare, then several arguments can be made as to why private ownership is likely to be superior to state ownership.

The assumption that principals have the goal of maximizing the present value of assets is more reasonable for private owners than for public officials, because the latter generally cannot directly claim income from assets. For the public and private principals to share the goal of maximizing the present value of assets, we must posit it directly for public officials because, as we discuss in the political theory of privatization in Section 3, the private interests of public officials are not necessarily consistent with this goal. For example, in structuring and executing principal–agent relationships with the managers of state-owned enterprises (SOEs), public officials may be concerned with gaining political support by using the SOE for distributional purposes that may conflict with maximizing asset value. Depending on the particular political circumstances, such actions as supporting wage demands by unions in excess of market rates, requiring price subsidies for vocal consumer groups, and permitting questionable investment resources from public sources for SOE managers, may be seen by public officials as promoting their careers. Such political considerations may be especially consequential in situations in which the movement of assets to their most valued uses requires changes in existing structures that involve losses to identifiable interests.

Even in the absence of political motives, public officials are likely to have weaker incentives than private owners to engage in costly monitoring of agents because their exercise of ownership rights is generally non-transferable (De Alessi, 1980; Lott, 1987). Whereas a private owner can realize the gains in asset value that result from monitoring, public officials usually cannot. Public officials thus share in efficiency gains only indirectly as members of the polity while private owners share in direct proportion to their share of ownership. One apparent manifestation of the weaker incentives is the so-called 'soft budget constraint' that results in excessive borrowing from the state by SOEs (Kornai, 1986).

This line of argument raises the question of the incentive to monitor in situations of very diffuse private ownership, as in the case of joint-stock companies with no single holder of a large block of shares. The possibility of profitable management takeovers creates an incentive for specialization in monitoring (Manne, 1965). This incentive to specialize depends on the existence of efficient stock and capital markets, as those attempting management takeovers must be able to accumulate sufficient stock to gain control of the governing bodies of corporations. With respect to public ownership, public officials of smaller polities are likely to have a stronger incentive to monitor than those of larger polities because in the smaller polities a larger fraction of efficiency gains is likely to be realized by the officials. They may also see lower monitoring costs because they are closer to operation of the enterprise. The incentive to monitor is also stronger in smaller polities if public officials are more accountable to the local constituencies for the efficiency of enterprises or if they are subject to tighter fiscal constraints such as limits on borrowing (Zeckhauser and Horn, 1989). The latter may be especially relevant because of the problem of soft budget constraints at the national level. The national government can usually borrow or print money if SOEs fail to achieve targeted profit levels. National-level public officials may thus have difficulty making the budget constraints that they impose credible to the SOEs because the latter realize that the political costs of unemployment may be higher than those of borrowing to cover losses. The lack of credibility in the commitment to enforcing budget constraints is a measure of their softness (Kornai, 1992).

The possibility of takeover also creates an incentive for managers to reduce agency cost so as to make potential takeovers less profitable and thus less likely; it may also create an incentive to raise the costs of takeovers through actions that may contribute to increased agency cost. The greater the credibility of the threat of takeover, the stronger these incentives. So, for example, the privatization of some SOEs may increase the credibility of takeover perceived by the managers of other SOEs, thereby creating a strong incentive for efficiency (Vining and Weimer, 1990).

In summary, agency theory hypothesizes that in undistorted markets privately owned enterprises will be more efficient than SOEs. The empirical evidence strongly supports this hypothesis (Boardman and Vining, 1989; Vining and Boardman, 1992). Further, it appears that mixed enterprises, in which the state holds a share of ownership, perform more like SOEs than private enterprises (Vining and Boardman, 1992). Thus, economic theory argues for the transfer of SOEs selling products in undistorted markets to private ownership, though it does not address the process by which this privatization should occur.

Distorted Markets and Economic Efficiency

The comparison between private and state ownership becomes less conceptually clear when the markets in which enterprises sell are distorted by market failures. In such situations, the decisions of self-interested private individuals do not lead to economic efficiency. The most prominent example is that of natural monopoly. Profit maximization leads to allocatively inefficient restriction of supply to below the competitive level. In theory, the allocative inefficiency can be corrected by either regulation of the private firm or state ownership (Vickers and Yarrow, 1988). With respect to the minimization of agency costs, the relative advantage of private ownership is less clear than in the case of enterprises in competitive markets. One reason is that the regulation may impose constraints on management that interfere with the maximization of asset value. Another reason is that private owners face higher monitoring costs than they would for enterprises in competitive industries because direct comparisons of performance cannot be made with competitors (Vining and Weimer, 1990).

Other distortions in product markets, such as the presence of externalities or information asymmetries, raise the problem of allocative inefficiency under private ownership without regulation. Thus the appropriate comparison is between state ownership and regulated private ownership. The more efficient form depends on whether public officials are more effective as owners or regulators, an assessment that cannot reasonably be made without greater specification of government organization.

SOEs may be an appropriate ownership form in situations involving commitment problems. For example, if a government cannot make a credible commitment that it will not expropriate future profits from investments made by private owners, then there may be too little private investment and state ownership may be necessary to realize economic opportunities (Zeckhauser and Horn, 1989; Rodrik and Zeckhauser, 1988; Laffont and Tirole, 1993). State ownership may also be appropriate in situations in which private owners cannot make credible commitments. For example, governments rarely rely on private armies because their freelancers cannot make credible commitments that they will not turn on the government at critical times (Baumol, 1984).

State ownership may also offer advantages over private ownership when related markets are not well developed. For example, government may be able to bear risk at lower cost than the private sector when the latter does not have insurance or stock markets to facilitate diversification. It has even been argued that labour market imperfections, such as restrictions on the international movement of managerial expertise, could provide an economic justification for state ownership (Vernon, 1988).

The existence of distorted markets sufficiently complicates the comparison of private and state ownership that no strong general statements can be made. It does follow, however, that if the creation of an SOE was justified by a market distortion, then removal of the distortion suggests that privatization is appropriate: changing technology may eliminate natural monopolies; the performance of governmental institutions may enable the government to make credible commitments against expropriation; efficient insurance and stock markets may develop.

Broader Conceptions of Social Welfare

Our discussion so far has taken economic efficiency as the appropriate measure of social welfare. It can be argued that social welfare should also reflect distributional goals. If redistribution were costless, then first maximizing economic efficiency and then redistributing would be the socially efficient way to achieve any distributional goals. But redistribution is generally not costless because it tends to alter behaviour by distorting incentives to work and to invest. One might argue, therefore, that inefficiencies associated with state ownership can be justified in some circumstances by distributional goals. So, for example, an SOE might be justified as a way to direct subsidies to specific groups of consumers or workers. This argument, however, should take into account alternative policies to state ownership for achieving distributional goals.

Consider, for example, nationalization of a declining industry as a way to slow down losses of employment in a specific region. The nationalization is likely to involve large inefficiencies because it prevents the industry's assets from moving to more valued uses. At the same time, it may maintain jobs for a group of workers who might be slow to find new employment, perhaps because of their unwillingness to leave their region. The obvious question to ask is whether the workers could be assisted more efficiently through some other mechanism such as unemployment insurance, subsidized retraining, or the like.

By allowing social welfare to be defined as including goals other than economic efficiency, we open at least the possibility that private ownership is not superior to state ownership even in undistorted markets. In view of the theory and empirical evidence supporting the superior efficiency of private ownership, however, an explicit argument that distributional goals can be achieved more effectively through state ownership than through other policy instruments is needed to justify state ownership.

3. A POLITICAL THEORY OF PRIVATIZATION

Despite its importance, the politics of privatization has been given relatively little attention. The primary reason for this appears to be the commonly made assumption that privatizers are motivated by the pursuit of economic efficiency, and therefore that their political motives are of minor importance in the undertaking of public policies. Some recent work that emphasizes political motives, and offers a political approach to privatization, provides some valuable insights (Dobek, 1993a; Poznanski, 1992; Feigenbaum and Henig, 1994; Allio et al., 1997).

First, even if a particular programme is adopted initially to achieve certain economic goals, the government has to make it politically viable by generating sufficient political support for it. Policy options that optimally maximize economic outcomes may not be feasible politically. Second, it is also possible that the stimulus for privatization comes from the pursuit of the political goals of the ruling party, the major one being to retain office (Dobek, 1993a).

At the stage of policy planning, it may be difficult to determine whether a particular programme is more influenced by economic or political motivation. Deciding to leave privatized SOEs with monopoly power, for instance, trades off the goal of economic efficiency against the political goals of realizing government revenue, building a constituency among those who invest in the SOE, or reducing opposition from the SOE's workers. In the process of implementation, however, tension often develops between economic goals, which are assumed to benefit the general public, and political goals advantageous to the ruling political party. For example, in a particular case an open auction might be most consistent with economic efficiency, while a restricted sale to workers might be more politically advantageous.

Politicians, no matter how public-spirited, are likely to be concerned about their political futures when implementing privatization programmes. We can see privatization from this perspective as being driven more by the goal of building constituencies for the politicians themselves than necessarily promoting economic welfare for the general public. As a result, privatization policies may be designed to benefit selected groups in society whose political support the government is seeking to secure. This can be seen as the use of privatization as a political tactic (Feigenbaum and Henig, 1994).

Privatization has proved to be a very effective tactic for conservative political parties, that is, those advocating limited governmental intervention and restricted welfare responsibilities, to achieve their electoral goals. A clear example of this occurred in Great Britain under the

Conservative government of Margaret Thatcher (Dobek, 1993b). Politically, sales of public assets cannot only buy votes – often quite literally – but they can also further contribute to an electoral victory by, for example, reducing to a significant extent the need for new taxes in a situation of budgetary crisis. In the British case, privatization also served as a political weapon to weaken numerically the electoral base of the opposition – public sector employees, tenants of public housing and trade union members – while at the same time expanding groups from which the Conservative Party has traditionally drawn support (that is, the groups of shareholders, home-owners, employees of the private sector, and the self-employed). Finally, the Conservative Party used privatization to promote an ideology of private ownership and individualism, which can be thought of as a more strategic political function (Feigenbaum and Henig, 1994).

Privatization that involves massive redistribution of property rights may also be used as a strategy to legitimize a new political and economic system and to secure the irreversibility of changes that this system represents. This has been the case in post-communist countries since 1989. Privatization campaigns in countries such as the Czech Republic and Russia have been increasingly geared towards giving an immediate stake in the emerging market system and democracy to all adults through schemes involving free distribution of shares. Another political goal pronounced by governments in those countries is the creation of sound foundations of democracy and social stability, which in the political science literature are traditionally believed to be provided by a sizeable class of property owners (Almond, 1991; Rueschemeyer et al., 1992). While these lofty political goals may be important considerations in the designing of privatization plans in East Central Europe, the privatizers in those countries have occasionally exhibited a familiar pursuit of power in the process of implementing privatization.

In addition to domestic policy considerations, the impetus to privatize may also be provided by external factors. The World Bank and the International Monetary Fund (IMF), for example, have been actively promoting privatization in developing countries for over a decade (Mosley, 1988; Babai, 1988, pp. 269–75). This pro-privatization bias has not been attributed exclusively to their critical assessment of the performance of SOEs, but also to a private-business bias which has its roots in their founding articles established at Bretton Woods in 1944. The institutions created at Bretton Woods reflected the American liberal vision of what the world economy should look like. This was a vision that was, not surprisingly, conducive to advocacy of private property and advantageous to the American pre-eminence in the world economy at the time; it emphasized low tariffs, the *laissez-faire* state, and a stability that would encourage foreign investment (De Vries, 1986).

The IMF and the World Bank wield exaggerated influence among debtor states in that they perform a 'gatekeeper' function for the majority of international financial institutions (Assetto, 1988). Often a Letter of Intent with the IMF is required of borrowing states before foreign lenders will commit funds to them. It has been a common practice for the IMF and the World Bank to require borrowers to take stringent austerity measures, including reductions in their public sectors, as they access higher tranches of lending. East Central European countries have had experience (sometimes difficult, as in Poland) with the conditionality of these institutions in the raising and maintenance of their transitional financial arrangements (Sobell and Okolicsanyi, 1990; Sobell, 1989; Gatling, 1991). Though, in all fairness to the IMF and the World Bank, the programmes in East Central Europe have been of a highly heterodox nature (Taylor, 1988; Kolodko and Rutkowski, 1991), they have served to reinforce privatization drives as components of programmes designed to move economies towards fiscal stability and health.

4. DESIGN TRADE-OFFS IN PRIVATIZATION

The issues of programme design and their various dimensions have overlapping political and economic implications. Among the issues considered here, some are more clearly of a political nature while others are more of an economic nature. Yet none can be considered purely economic or political. We examine here some of the general questions of privatization in the post-communist context. In reviewing these considerations, set out in Table 7.1, the reader should bear in mind that the global experience with privatization does not necessarily provide policy guidance to decision makers in post-communist countries whose task is much more complicated because they must simultaneously build new economic and political institutions.

The Scope and Speed of Privatization

Among the most salient issues of privatization design are scope and speed. Considerations of scope include not only include how many enterprises should be privatized, whether the programme should be

Table 7.1   The design of privatization instruments

Design issue	Major dimensions	Considerations
Scope of privatization	Profitable/unprofitable SOEs	Short-/long-run fiscal concerns Employment effects Market demand for SOEs
	Broad/narrow	Administrative capacity
	Competitive/monopolistic SOEs	Regulatory capacity
Speed of privatization	Fast/slow	Administrative capacity Available domestic capital Commitment to reforms
Packaging of assets for privatization	SOE/local/central government	Entrenchment of managers Shedding of assets Stakeholder interests Information advantages
	Preservation/liquidation	Employment effects Economic efficiency Stakeholder interests
	Market valuation/audit	Market infrastructure Degree of stabilization Administrative capacity
Disposition of assets	Monetary/voucher	Concentration of ownership Popular political support Government revenue
	Contract/auction	Stakeholder participation Public perception of fairness
	Restricted/unrestricted ownership	Foreign participation Post-transfer regulation

broad or narrow, but also which enterprises to privatize. Though intended speed is related to the overall political and economic goals of privatization, it also depends on the effectiveness of various instruments and their sequencing. If speed is to be built into the programme, for example, a mass giveaway programme as opposed to a market sell-off programme may be required.

The intended scope of a privatization programme is a fundamental consideration. A broad programme that seeks to privatize all large enterprises may be ill advised in the context of a country's overall economic strategy. Privatizing enterprises in poor health may mean their speedy demise and a rapid rise in unemployment. Therefore, programme designers may decide to privatize healthier enterprises first, while forcing ailing enterprises to restructure. Restructuring of ailing enterprises, on the other hand, could lead to long-term fiscal drains on state budgets.

Another consideration is whether to privatize both monopolistic and competitive sectors of the economy. The centralized structure of Soviet-type economies encouraged the growth of monopolistic enterprises. Privatization of these enterprises without ensuring competitive conditions may result in inefficient markets. Whether these conditions develop depends on the extent to which other national policies permit foreign trade and facilitate the creation of new firms within the previously monopolized sectors.

Both considerations should take into account the capacity of the state to carry out the programme, first with regard to feasibility of broad privatization, and second, in relation to regulation and restructuring, which are relevant to decisions concerning the privatization of monopolies and the desirability of delaying privatization of troubled SOEs in favour of a turnaround period.

Speed is an issue with both political and economic implications. The more rapidly enterprises can be privatized, it is assumed, the more rapidly the economic environment in formerly socialist states will begin to resemble the robust capitalist economies of the West. It was often assumed that a rapid privatization would circumvent political opposition to restructuring, as the privatized industries would be presented to emergent interest groups as a *fait accompli*. Also, SOEs may represent a drain on the state treasury, making speed of privatization fiscally appealing.

Perhaps even more important than the speed and the scope of privatization is the fit of privatization instruments into the overall sequencing of economic and political reforms. Privatization, whether fast or slow, has both economic costs and benefits. A fortuitous sequence of measures can produce an increase in benefits, while a poorly designed sequence can exacerbate the myriad problems already presented by Soviet-type economies in transition. Although discussions of speed, scope and sequencing are numerous in the burgeoning literature on privatization, no convincing generalizations have been made.

The Packaging of Assets for Privatization

The fiscal costs and benefits of privatizing industry are relevant to programme design. SOEs are assets that may attract rent seeking by government officials, both local and central, and by enterprise managers. The possibility remains, however, that some enterprises will continue to be a drain on treasuries. The shedding of responsibility for these enterprises may be desirable for maintaining the budgetary health of government. Other considerations include administrative costs and the problem of the valuation of enterprises. These dimensions of programme design are likely to have great importance during implementation.

Different strategies for obtaining rents from privatization may be pursued by central governments, local governments and managerial élites. All these actors seek to gain something from the process of reallocating ownership. Whether that payoff consists of political pork-barrelling, as when local government officials obtain budget revenues from industry sales, or of personal rents, as when an enterprise manager 'parachutes' into an ownership position, all such redistributions are bound to involve political considerations for policy makers.

In view of expected rent seeking, programme designers may attempt to isolate day-to-day administration from politics by establishing an agency with some independence from the legislature. Doing so changes the relative costs and benefits of rent-seeking activity among the various actors. In any event, such an agency may develop technical expertise that permits implementation of the programme to be based on rules that restrain discretion.

The technical difficulties of the packaging of enterprises are legion and one of the most apparent is the difficulty of valuation in the post-communist context (Savas, 1992). Accounting procedures as they are known in the West were virtually non-existent under central planning. The valuation of enterprises has gone forward in many cases with assistance from foreign accounting establishments. There are many methods of valuation, each giving different asset values: replacement cost, liquidation value, book value, discounted cash flows, and price/earnings ratios. Each of these methods gives a somewhat distorted picture in post-Soviet-type economies (Young, 1991). Case-by-case valuation in the East European context has required accounting firms to rely on mixed methods developed specifically for the East European environment and subject to the enormous uncertainties of that environment.

Thus, valuation of individual enterprises presents a significant transaction cost for the post-communist governments. The obvious alternative would be to allow the market to determine the values of these SOEs, but in the initial period capital markets were virtually non-existent. Public stock offerings provide a means of valuation, yet such offerings may also be subject to high transaction costs. One of the appeals of mass privatization is that it offers a solution to the problem of valuation, generally involving a pool of assets from which the state does not expect to receive revenues and allowing a market to grow based upon these assets.

The Disposition of Assets

One of the most politically sensitive issues of privatization is the distribution of assets. Privatization involves moving property rights from a collective or public form to private hands. But to whose hands? Trade-offs arise between economic efficiency and social justice, and between ownership concentration and political support.

Among the alternatives for disposition is the auctioning of firms to the highest bidder. This strategy is appealing from a fiscal standpoint and may indeed create an owner with a strong incentive to maximize asset value. Yet to have a market for companies there must be buyers as well as sellers. The fact is that there are not enough domestic entre-preneurs with capital to privatize all SOEs in the short run at anywhere near their long-term market values. Even foreign capital may not be able to fill the gap. Another ownership option is the distribution of property rights to the public at large. As public assets under socialism were theoretically the property of all, it would seem a reasonable expec-tation that individuals would all receive some of the benefits of the privatization programme. General benefits of an improved economy, including improved individual economic opportunity, run the risk of being opaque and not being perceived as benefits accruing to the public as a direct result of the privatization of public property. It may therefore be more politically expedient to distribute nominally free shares in public enterprises or investment funds to create goodwill towards priva-tization and indeed to create political support for it.

Another dimension of the disposition of assets is whether there will be restrictions on ownership. Questions here include, for example, whether and the degree to which foreign participation will be allowed. Also, if the transfers of ownership are made, will the rights of new owners be attenuated by regulations?

The design of a privatization programme for a post-communist country is obviously a very complicated task. Economic and political considerations sometimes conflict. Further, as we argue in the next section, any privatization programme creates identifiable interests during its implementation that raise the relative importance of political considerations.

5. INTERPRETING POST-COMMUNIST PRIVATIZATION

In this section we focus on privatization of large companies, that is, those with 500 employees or more, in the post-communist countries. These enterprises constitute the bulk of state property slated for sale and their privatization has created the greatest difficulties. Privatization of medium and small enterprises, service and retail establishments, has progressed at a much faster pace despite involving some issues not addressed in this chapter (for example, restitution).

We present the major techniques used to privatize large companies, and specify the publics and their concerns that have influenced their choice and implementation in each country. By the term 'publics' we understand the 'identifiable groupings who have more than a passing interest in a given issue debate or are actively involved in an issue debate' (May, 1991). Following Peter May, we treat politics with and without publics as ideal analytical concepts – ends of a continuum of policy publics – and thus our cases differ by the degree of development of the relevant publics (interest groups) rather than by their existence or complete absence. Thus 'policies without publics' refers here to the relatively weak development of interest groups concerned with privatization except for a small number of political, technical and scientific élites involved in the formulation of government programmes. In contrast, the term 'policies with publics' denotes an ideal type in which conflict among different groups directly influences the decision making of the policy élites.

Hungary

Privatization of large enterprises was initiated in 1988 by the communist government with the adoption of legislation making it possible for state-owned companies to issue stock. This led in some cases to 'informal' privatization, whereby managers engaged in transferring ownership of the most profitable parts of their companies to newly created private enterprises. To the extent that managers exploited asset stripping for their personal gain, the process falls under the pejorative term, 'spontaneous privatization'. By mid-1990, when the communist government resigned, the general public was outraged by asset stripping of the communist élite. Therefore, it easily accepted the centralization of control over privatization in the hands of the State Property Agency (SPA), tightly controlled by the post-communist government of Prime Minister Jozsef Antall. This development gave the initiative on privatization back to the policy makers, thus approaching the situation of policy without publics.

The Antall government selected a general privatization strategy advocated by Hungarian technocrats and consistent with a desire to maintain the flow of foreign investment (Urbán, 1997). There was no comprehensive law on privatization to guide the process, however. Instead, a flexible approach was adopted. Privatization was carried out on the basis of *ad hoc* rules of the SPA, which responded to competing privatization plans from management and employees, and bids from outside investors. As a result, the dominant technique of privatization utilized by the SPA involved a mixture of direct sales to a majority holder, and management buyouts. The government was keen on finding foreign buyers to assume the role of the major shareholder, with the remaining shares or capital (usually up to 20 per cent) sold to the management and workers.

The major motivations for conducting privatization in such a manner were economic. Of primary importance was the search for new sources of revenue and foreign exchange (Hungary has the highest foreign debt per capita in the region and a large budget deficit). In addition, sales that would attract foreign investors were seen as the best way to improve the economic performance of privatized companies, because they were expected to provide an injection of capital, modern technology and connection to new markets. The liabilities of this strategy involved slow and expensive valuation of property, considerable insider control by former SOE managers, and marginalization of domestic entrepreneurs.

By the end of 1992, the issue of privatization moved towards the pole of policies with publics. As unemployment became a clear liability of privatization for common citizens, and the expected benefits of private ownership (for example, lower taxes and higher standards of living) failed to materialize, the public became increasingly concerned about immediate and tangible benefits of this policy. In addition to managers and employees, who wished to maintain their advantages as insiders in the privatization process, the public at large also became more interested in the redistribution of ownership. This was not lost on the opposition politicians, who started claiming that privatization had come to a standstill and broader participation of common citizens was necessary. Privatization became one of the issues generating sharp criticism of the government.

László Urbán (1997, pp. 249–53) details a number of politically motivated modifications to the privatization programme that the governing coalition adopted in an effort to respond to its emerging publics in the run-up to the 1994 election. First, as a concession to the Smallholder Party, a coalition partner that ran on the issue of reprivatization of land forcefully collectivized by the communists, the government introduced compensation notes that entitle those who lost land to assets such as annuities offered by the Social Security Fund or stocks offered by the SPA. The notes are transferrable, and they are publicly traded.

Second, in February 1992, in order to reassure the public of the government's commitment to maintaining the social security system, the parliament voted to transfer about US$3 billion of stocks to the Social Security Fund by 1994. When ex-communist union leaders were elected to the supervisory boards of the Fund, however, the government stopped the transfer, so that little was actually transferred before the election.

Third, the government attempted to politicize the SPA. Many members of the Democratic Forum parliamentary faction, whose constituents were beginning to draw them away from the increasingly unpopular government, were put on the boards of large SPA-owned corporations as a way of making staying in the coalition more attractive. When the board of directors and the technical staff of the SPA resisted government control, the government created the State Asset Management Company (SAMC) to guarantee greater control over the most valuable firms. The stock of the 160 most valuable companies was transferred from the SPA to the SAMC.

Fourth, a small trade union allied with the Democratic Forum convinced the government that majority employee ownership would be popular among skilled workers in profitable firms. In an effort to expand its electoral base, the government introduced special loans to facilitate employee buyouts. Initial buyouts occurred in firms of above average profitability, and the rate of buyouts increased dramatically in the six months before the election.

Fifth, shortly before the election, the government attempted to launch a small investor programme in an effort to expand its political support among groups who had been left out of the privatization programme. It was originally conceived of as a large-scale programme in which the general public would be given the opportunity to purchase stocks at preferential prices, but when it proved difficult to provide a sufficient portfolio of profitable firms for the programme, it was scaled back to an offering of stock in only five firms a month before the election.

In summary, the initial Hungarian privatization strategy seemed to be a largely technocratic decision responding to economic pressure to generate foreign exchange to service a large foreign debt. Between the first and second parliamentary elections, however, publics of electoral significance arose that prompted the government to modify the initial privatization strategy in search of greater electoral support.

Poland

Poland's path of privatization strongly reflected a movement from policy making without publics to policy making with publics. The first post-communist government of Tadeusz Mazowiecki (August 1989 to December 1990) was given an overwhelming mandate to move away from the Soviet-type economy. Society was united by its determination to bring down the communist system and policy-making was given primarily to a technocratic élite with group interests, including those of the workers' councils that had been organized under the last communist government within SOEs, left largely unarticulated. As decisions to marketize the economy were taken and redistributive effects became apparent, however, a complex array of interests has emerged.

In the immediate post-communist period, the Mazowiecki government adopted a *laissez-faire* privatization strategy similar to the one in Hungary. The pool of potential buyers for these firms proved to be far too shallow, while the sale of large enterprises, through a series of high-profile public stock issues, entailed significant transaction costs (for example, for the first five issues transaction costs were equal to some 13 per cent of the value of the privatized companies). It became apparent that there was not enough domestic capital (all private savings amounted to less than 10 per cent of the value of SOEs) to rely exclusively on the market-based strategy. Neither were foreign investors likely to fill the gap at this early stage, not only because Poland's needs were great (Poland is about four times the size of Hungary), but also because legalization of foreign ownership rights lagged and the political environment remained unpredictable.

Laissez-faire privatization also made the scope of privatization extremely broad. It attempted to privatize all enterprises and paid little attention to the need for restructuring where enterprises were ailing or monopolistic. Publics, especially workers in the public sector, felt the squeeze of a 'shock' austerity programme, without seeing any noticeable benefits from privatization. In fact, as in the early privatization period in Hungary, those who seemed to benefit the most were the former *nomenklatura* managers (Staniszkis, 1991). Mazowiecki's less than modest progress with 'large' privatization, his dismal showing in the 1990 presidential election, and the subsequent collapse of his government underscored the notion that ignoring political support for economic policies was dangerous for the government of a country with exploding unemployment and strong trade unions.

The succeeding government of Jan K. Bielecki (January–December 1991) tried to broaden both the spectrum of privatization techniques and their immediate beneficiaries. The major innovation was a programme of 'mass' privatization proposed in June 1991. Mass privatization, which was to apply to 400 large companies, was to address various economic and political goals and to overcome the valuation problem: (a) 60 per cent of shares of each enterprise were to be distributed among some 20 mutual funds, with a stake of 30 per cent going to one of them – the former to prevent creation of monopolies and the latter to address agency problems; (b) adult citizens residing in Poland were to exchange for an administrative fee their privatization vouchers for shares in mutual funds rather than in the enterprises themselves – to give the public a stake in the emerging market system without undue dispersion of ownership among investors new to capital markets; (c) 10 per cent of shares were to be distributed exclusively among the employees – to secure their support for the programme; and (d) 30 per cent of shares were to be retained by the treasury with the ultimate goal of selling them to private 'hard-core' owners when the domestic capital market developed – this was to create investors with large stakes and thus strong interest in companies' performance; at the same time, sales of 30 per cent of the shares rather than their free distribution were to generate revenue for the government. Shares of the mutual funds as well as shares of the companies themselves were to be traded a year from their distribution to the public (Dabrowski, 1991; Dobek, 1993a). The structure of this initial programme began what was to be a long journey through the legislature before its passage. The final programme would bear a strong resemblance to it.

The short existence of the Bielecki government prevented it from seeing adoption of the mass privatization plan. Political instability after the October 1991 parliamentary election delayed its introduction by either of the two short-lived governments that followed in the first six months of 1992. The pace of privatization in that period declined compared to previous years. A centrist government of Prime Minister Hanna Suchocka, created in July 1992, endorsed in principle the plan of mass privatization. In March parliament voted it down. It was resubmitted immediately in revised form, but its legislative enactment was to languish for years.

A gradualist capital sale continued after Suchocka's accession as the dominant technique, albeit with privatization attracting the attention of an increasing number of interest groups and with the government being increasingly responsive to their demands. After a wave of industrial strikes in the summer of 1992, the Suchocka government proposed broad negotiations to state workers represented by trade unions. The result was the 'Pact on State Enterprises and their Privatization', signed by seven trade union groups, the government and the national-level Employers' Association. The pact would make privatization more attractive to a number of interests, including employees of SOEs. It would give the workers more say as to the initial proposed method of privatization (the exception being companies selected for mass privatization, which would not have the option of choosing another method) and it would grant them 10 per cent of the shares free of charge (*Przeglad Rzadowy*, 1992), but it would also have granted a good deal of the decision-making powers to the Ministry of Ownership Transformation and, as a variety of interests became further articulated, the legislation of this 'pact' languished.

The victory of the Union of the Democratic Left (SLD) in parliamentary elections in 1993 signalled a shift in privatization interests and the strength of their articulation. To some degree, the vote was a referendum on the dismantling of the social safety net and the concurrent potential demise of large state enterprises that employed thousands. Indeed, privatization slowed under the SLD but continued to make significant progress, particularly towards the 'Law on the National Investment Funds' which provided the basis for mass privatization, and in the area of bank privatization. After the passage of this law the mass privatization programme became known as the National Investment Funds Programme. The funds were established in December 1994.

It is important to note the growing economic and political development that has occurred since the onset of the political and economic transformation in Poland. Not only has there been a shift to privatization with publics, but the nature of the publics has been changing very rapidly. Society at large is investing on a larger scale in new issues on the Polish stock market. And when *nomenklatura* benefits have been great, as in the undervalued first issue of the Bank of Silesia, the public uproar has been substantial. Additionally, a plethora of groups now represent business and investor interests, and these groups attempt to balance labour's influence with Poland's government. The explosion of foreign investment in Poland as mutual fund capital has poured into one of Europe's most promising 'emerging markets', and Poland's concern for conforming to the requirements of a future partnership with the European Union have meant an increasing responsiveness to international interests as well.

One of the most decisive indicators of the degree to which the issue of privatization has become one of privatization with publics is the conduct of the Privatization Referendum on 18 February 1996. The referendum put to popular vote the approval of the transfer of public property and an increase in the number of firms to be committed to the National Investment Funds Programme. It also contained questions regarding the disposition of privatization monies towards disability and pension payments, and other social expenditures. The measure was overwhelmingly approved (with the exception of a 'no' on expanding the number of enterprises in the National Investment Funds Programme) but in the end the referendum was not binding because turnout did not exceed 50 per cent.

Thus it would seem that in the Polish case there has been strong movement from 'policy without publics' towards 'policy with publics'. Indeed, as politicians became accountable for privatization policies and subject to scrutiny by a variety of interests that take notice of the minutiae of these policies, they felt compelled to put issues concerning the distribution of gains from privatization to a vote. The gradualism of Polish privatization has not been very successful in achieving privatization of large SOEs. Nevertheless, the rapid growth of the private sector resulting from the creation of new firms may ultimately prove to overshadow the consequences of the failure of privatization for economic growth and stability (Kaminiski, 1997).

The Czech and Slovak Republics

The Czecho-Slovak federal government initially took a cautious approach toward privatization of its large enterprises. Before a comprehensive plan was adopted in February 1992, few companies were privatized, mainly by sale to a majority foreign investor. In this early period, organized interests were relatively absent from the decision-making process. The government's plan called for free distribution of privatization vouchers. This method was to account for 40 to 80 per cent of the capital or stock of each large company (the remainder was to be sold directly to a major investor, management or employees). Citizens of the Czecho-Slovak federation could exchange their privatization vouchers for shares by subscribing to selected public issues at a set price or they could entrust mutual funds with this task (ultimately, about 75 per cent of them did the latter: *Polityka*, 2 May 1992, p. 12).

Opting for an extremely broad inclusion of beneficiaries did not prevent distributional conflicts from arising. A confrontation developed in the Czech Republic between the Ministry of Administration and Privatization of National Property, headed by Tomas Jezek, and the Federal Ministry of Finance, led then by Vaclav Klaus, one of the main authors of the voucher scheme. The February 1991 law on privatization of large enterprises left the Ministry of Privatization with wide discretion as to the extent to which particular techniques were to be utilized (for example, the voucher plan was to apply to anywhere from 40 to 80 per cent of the property of those companies). It became apparent that the ministry, under the pressure of management and employees, advocated limiting the voucher method in favour of employee and management buyouts and sales to foreign investors (the latter were sought by companies facing a shortage of capital). In turn, Klaus opted for the maximum use of the giveaway option, justifying it by the need to create a large group of property owners as well as to secure domestic ownership of the largest companies. Ultimately, the voucher privatization, scheduled to be conducted in two 'waves', turned out to be a compromise between the two positions. The government was determined to give priority to the voucher technique, thus pleasing the general public, but not without undue alienation of management and workers. Hence the first wave of voucher privatization, which took place from January to December 1992, included shares representing some 62 per cent of the property of the large companies privatized that year (*PlanEcon Report*, July 1993, p. 7).

In the meantime, deeply rooted ethnic animosities between Czechs and Slovaks and political differences between their leaders had resulted in growing divisions between the Czech and Slovak parts of the federation. The differences between the two republics as to the immediate effects of privatization, resulting in the widening gap in living standards and unemployment rates, had also contributed to the ultimate dissolution of the Czech and Slovak Federal Republic into two sovereign states on 1 January 1993. The Czech Republic had a great deal of light industry that made the transition to a market economy easier than in the Slovak Republic, which was burdened with heavy and armament industries.

The Czech Republic after Separation

The government of the Czech Republic, led by Klaus's Civic Democratic Party since its formation in June 1992, upheld its commitment to using vouchers as the dominant mode of distribution of privatized property. This policy favoured building a domestic constituency over attracting foreign capital and expertise. Shortly after the first wave of voucher privatization was completed, preparations for the second wave began. The second wave was launched in the Czech Republic in October 1993 and entailed shares in some 800 companies with a nominal book value of 130 billion Czech koruna, equivalent at that time to some $4.5 billion. This amount represented a smaller volume of shares as compared to the first wave of voucher privatization valued at some 199 billion koruna or $6.8 billion (*PlanEcon Report*, July 1993; p. 29).

By mid-1993 the process of privatization in the Czech Republic evolved to include a large spectrum of beneficiaries. A compromise was reached between the Ministry of Privatization, which supported the managers and workers in privatized companies, who were pushing for privileged treatment in the redistribution of property rights, and the Klaus group, which pressed for free distribution of shares to the entire society. Some 88 per cent of the book value of privatized companies was transformed into joint-stock companies. The remaining 12 per cent of the value of privatized property was disposed of in the following fashion: direct sales accounted for some 4 per cent (52 per cent of which were sold to domestic and 48 per cent to foreign investors); restitution claims amounted to some 3 per cent; employee shares totalled another 3 per cent; and the remaining 2 per cent were sold through intermediaries (*PlanEcon Report*, July 1993, p. 25).

As for the 88 per cent of the book value of privatized companies that were transformed into joint-stock companies, the majority of shares (some 62 per cent) were distributed through voucher privatization to the general public. The remaining shares were held temporarily by the Czech National Property Fund, transferred for free to municipalities, villages, and health and pension plans, given as restitution claims to prewar private owners, given to the employees, or sold to domestic and foreign investors. The 62 per cent of shares distributed to the public through vouchers constituted a compromise between the original positions of the Ministry of Privatization (arguing for 40 per cent) and the Klaus supporters (arguing for 80 per cent).

In 1995 and 1996 the third wave of privatization took place in the Czech Republic in the form of mergers and ownership consolidations. The impulse for this development was given by a pending new law making takeovers of Czech companies more difficult and expensive. The law, which was to be adopted in the spring of 1996, provided increased protection to minority shareholders who often found their holdings devalued as a result of mergers and takeovers. As the law was not to be retroactive, the second half of 1995 and early 1996 resulted in a buying frenzy on the Czech stock market as corporate managers attempted to build majority stakes in major companies (*PlanEcon Report*, November 1995a, pp. 1–9).

In conclusion, the government of the Czech Republic made a conscious and consistent effort to include voters and major political actors in the privatization programme. As indicated by the compromise over the fraction of stock to be transferred through vouchers, the government attempted to balance the interests of common voters with the interests of employees and managers of the privatized companies. This policy has been successful thus far from this perspective: it not only resulted in a relative absence of labour disputes and provided for popular support of privatization among the voters, but it also facilitated steady economic growth and generated confidence among foreign investors.

The Slovak Republic after Separation

Until the dissolution of the federation in January 1993, the voucher privatization campaign initiated by the federal government was also conducted in Slovakia. Thus, as in the Czech Republic, it was aimed at creating a large group of beneficiaries. Voucher privatization was until 1993 the main privatization method, accounting for over 88 per cent of the book value of privatized property; less than 12 per cent was privatized by other techniques (*PlanEcon Report*, April 1993, pp. 21–2).

This situation, however, changed during 1993 under the government of Prime Minister Vladimir Meciar. After the completion of the first privatization wave, Meciar announced that voucher privatization would be discontinued in his republic after the dissolution of the federation. Meciar explained this decision by saying that other forms of privatization, especially direct sales, were considered by his government to be more advantageous, mainly in terms of generating financial resources for the state.

The rationale expressed was that voucher privatization did not generate any income for the state and did not provide any capital for the enterprises, because the shares were distributed free of charge. Also, it excluded foreign investors from participation until the trading of distributed shares was to begin (*FBIS*–East Europe 29 December 1992; p. 28).

In order to justify his decision further, Meciar alluded to the fears of a sizeable part of the public, apprehensive of high unemployment rates and inflation commonly ascribed to the initially rapid pace of privatization. In reality, it was not the principle of voucher privatization but rather its fast pace that worried some Slovaks. Unlike Klaus in the Czech Republic, who constantly preached the virtues of a rapid privatization policy and the establishment of a market economy, Meciar kept promising his weary constituency a smooth transition, which he called a 'middle path between communism and capitalism'. He claimed that by slowing the pace of privatization it would be possible to save more jobs and to keep inflation in check.

The abandonment of the voucher programme led to a virtual halt in privatization in Slovakia in 1993 and the first months of 1994, despite Meciar's claims about his determination to continue the restructuring of property rights. While rejecting the Czech-designed privatization programme, Meciar did not have a coherent policy to replace it. An increasing number of his one-time supporters believed that his rhetoric about the 'middle path' was a disguise for the lack of a clear vision of revitalizing the Slovak economy. As popular support for Meciar's party was eroding (support for his party declined in public opinion polls from 60 per cent in mid-1992 to 14 per cent in December 1993), there was also mounting criticism and defection within the ranks of the party. At the end of 1993 increasing efforts were mounted within Meciar's own party to remove him from power. Also, the coalition partner in government, the Slovak National Party (SNP), was growing critical of Meciar. For example, the SNP leader, Ludovir Cernak, was publicly unhappy about the lack of progress in privatization and he described a series of public debates on privatization organized by Meciar in autumn 1993 as merely 'political theater' (*Economist Intelligence Unit Country Report: Slovakia*, 1st quarter 1994, p. 36).

It was in these circumstances that Meciar attempted a series of direct sales to individual investors. These sales led to a scandal and became one of the major factors triggering the downfall of his government in March 1994. In mid-February, the government sold thirteen companies to investors who were alleged to be Meciar's cronies. (Meciar was personally responsible for the sales because he retained for himself the portfolios of the privatization minister and the chairman of the Slovak National Property Fund.) On 9 March 1994, President Michal Kovac delivered a state-of-the-nation address severely criticizing Prime Minister Meciar for the 'ethics and the style of his politics'. In particular, Kovac claimed that Meciar personally told him that he wanted to design the privatization programme so as to ensure financial benefits for his

Movement for Democratic Slovakia (*Republika*, 10 March 1994). Kovac's speech additionally unified and motivated growing opposition to Meciar's government in the parliament and culminated in a no-confidence vote on 14 March 1994. It appeared at the time that, by discontinuing voucher privatization, Meciar lost a chance to generate support for his party from a broad constituency through the widespread distribution of material benefits.

The issue of voucher privatization was revived by the new government of Jozef Moravcik, which announced immediately after its formation in April 1994 that it would resume the voucher privatization abandoned by Meciar. The second wave, modelled after the Czech programme, was be launched shortly thereafter. An investigation was also initiated into the direct sales of companies conducted by the Meciar government in 1994.

Yet despite all the political controversies and scandals, Meciar and his party won parliamentary elections conducted in November 1994 and returned to power. The use of political patronage by Meciar and the fragmentation of the Slovak political scene appeared to allow a comeback. On the issue of privatization Meciar again changed his position as he committed his government to continuing voucher privatization. However, in reality nothing was done with this programme until July 1995, when the long-awaited second wave of voucher privatization was suddenly cancelled, even though 3.5 million Slovaks had already received their vouchers. Instead, a new programme was announced in which every eligible citizen would receive a bond guaranteed by the Slovak National Property Fund. The bonds could be used to purchase apartments in public housing, or to pay off instalment debts for a direct purchase of a public company. The bond programme seemed to be aimed at allowing insiders to buy bonds at discounts from ordinary Slovaks, most of whom could never afford to participate in the direct sale process (*PlanEcon Report*, November 1995b, p. 4).

In the meantime, the Meciar government continued privatization by direct sales of companies. The secrecy of this process and parallel developments on the political scene (harassment of opposition parties and free media, and the restoration of political patronage in the public sector by purges of people not loyal to the Meciar government) again brought accusations of 'large scale redistribution of state assets to political allies, transforming Slovak industry into a political patronage machine' (*PlanEcon Report*, November 1995b, p. 1).

In conclusion, the process of privatization in the Slovak Republic was distinctly different from that of the Czech Republic in its political and economic consequences. Privatization in the Czech Republic created a broad constituency of ordinary voters as well as employees and managers of privatized companies, all having a stake in the success of the process. This produced conditions favourable to a stable political and economic environment. In the Slovak case, a public for privatization also emerged, but it was an élite group of insiders and political allies of the ruling party (Movement for Democratic Slovakia). The result was an unstable and highly contentious political and economic system in which a 'divided majority' was repeatedly defeated by Meciar's political machine using patronage, intimidation and censorship of the media to remain in power.

Russia

Russia's political transition did not begin with as sharp a break with the previous system as in the countries previously discussed. Under Mikhail Gorbachev's leadership there had been raucous debate and ineffectual attempts to introduce private property, but the power of the communist managers endured. When President Boris Yeltsin consolidated his power after the failed August 1991 *coup*, there had not yet been much progress on large privatization, and opposition to it among management was still strong. This had a great impact on the radical character of Yeltsin's approach to privatization, as he was forced to turn for support for his reforms directly to the public at large. He attempted to overcome the resistance of the entrenched bureaucratic interests and to prevent the phenomenon of 'spontaneous' privatization from occurring on a large scale by moving towards the 'economic practices of populism' (*Pravda*, 25 July 1990 as quoted in Aslund, 1995). In addition, he had to look for ways to deal with the developing conflict between the local and the central government and the contradictory regulations on privatization that resulted from it. Equipped with special legislative powers, which entitled him to issue decrees, he was able to bypass the fragmented parliament in which managers organized around the Civic Union exercised significant influence.

On 29 December 1991 Yeltsin unveiled, in his presidential decree 'On the Acceleration of State and Municipal Privatization for 1992', an ambitious programme that called for some 25 per cent of state-owned property to be privatized by the end of 1992. According to this plan, 25 per cent of the nominal value of a company was to be distributed as non-voting shares to the workers, 10 per cent was to be sold to them, 5 per cent was to be sold to the top management, and the remaining shares would be sold to outside investors by auction (*Rossiiskaya Gazeta*, 10 and 15 January 1992).

But before implementation of this plan had actually started, a new, more ambitious and more radical programme was announced in June 1992. It envisioned privatization of one-third of the large industrial enterprises by the end of 1993, and the remaining two-thirds by the end of 1995. Excluded from privatization were certain categories such as the defence industry. Employees of every company could choose among three privatization options. According to the first option, 25 per cent of non-voting shares were to be distributed free of charge among the employees. They could also buy an additional 10 per cent of voting shares at a 30 per cent discount, and managers could buy 5 per cent of voting shares at full price. In the second option, employees were entitled to buy up to 51 per cent of voting shares at a price set by the *Goskomimushestvo* (The State Property Fund). According to the third option (limited to companies with up to 200 employees), a group of employees could buy 20 per cent of voting shares at a discount of 30 per cent and an additional 20 per cent of voting shares at full price. The remaining shares were to be sold as well as distributed free of charge in a voucher programme to be announced later. Prime Minister Yegor Gaidar, reformer and Yeltsin supporter, stressed that, in the light of the volatile political situation following the *coup* of August 1991, and the inconclusive parliamentary debate as to the direction of changes, a comprehensive privatization programme was aimed at making pro-market and democratic reforms irreversible and providing Russian citizens with tangible benefits from it (Frye, 1997, p. 92).

On 19 August 1992, the first anniversary of the failed *coup*, President Yeltsin disclosed a bold voucher privatization scheme. In its first tranche, it employed vouchers of a nominal value of 10 000 roubles (at the time equal to three months' wages) that could be used to bid for shares of privatized companies or shares of mutual funds. The vouchers also could also be sold immediately for cash (change of ownership did not have to be recorded). Vouchers were to be valid for a period of one year, and subsequent tranches could have different nominal values. All Russian citizens born before 1 September 1992 were eligible to participate. Distribution of vouchers started in October 1992, and exchange of stocks for vouchers of the first tranche began in early 1993. Each privatized company was to reserve 35 per cent of its equity to be exchanged for vouchers (Djelic, 1992).

Although not quite as desirable for managers as privatization plans that would have given insiders preferential access to all stock, the voucher programme did not challenge their primary objective – remaining free from external corporate control. Vouchers covered less than a majority of stock. Even if they had applied to a majority, their wide dispersion would have made it difficult for outsiders to gain a controlling interest. At the same time, managers may have shared with government a desire to make the privatization irreversible by creating a large constituency of people who had an economic stake in continued reform.

The programme moved forward with great speed but appears to have left SOE managers, the most powerful public at the beginning of privatization, largely in control of the newly privatized firms (Aslund, 1995, pp. 265–71). By mid-1994, 70 per cent of Russian firms had been transformed into joint-stock companies, but with outsiders holding only about 14 per cent of stock (Pistor, 1994; Frye, 1997).

Privatization in Russia has thus been amazingly fast and extensive, especially in comparison with privatization in Hungary and Poland, but it has not altered significantly the position of the managers, who remain largely unconstrained by external corporate control.

6. CONCLUSION

Although the circumstances of privatization in the post-communist countries are quite complex and varied, we think that they can be characterized as exhibiting movement from policies without publics to policies with publics. We do not mean to imply that the commitment to privatization by the new governments was apolitical – in Poland and Hungary, especially, it was used as one of several measures against the communists, and in Czecho-Solvakia, and more recently in Russia, it was seen as a way of creating a broad base of support for economic reform. Rather we mean that the initial privatization decisions, which seemed directed mainly at achieving economic goals, resulted primarily from bargaining among government actors with relatively little direct involvement from organized interests. As distributional consequences became clearer during implementation, however, affected interests gained voice through opposition parties, labour unions and other organizations, so that changes in the privatization instruments reflected greater concern for political goals.

An alternative explanation for the observed changes in privatization instruments is that the task was so complex, and our understanding of the interaction of simultaneous change in economic and political institutions so weak, that some false steps and miscalculations were inevitable. Indeed, in some of the countries designers seemed to be genuinely surprised by such implementation problems as the difficulty of valuing assets and the dearth of domestic investors. Yet many of the major changes in privatization instruments appear to be in favour of affected interests that have gained a voice through political parties or other organizations.

PART III

The Rhythms and Blues of Policy Instruments

8.   The dynamics of policy instruments
Roeland J. in 't Veld

1.   INTRODUCTION

A policy is shaped through a sequence of stages containing a number of loops before the outcomes become apparent. Once the life cycle of a policy system (as the paradigm to be relied upon) has been accepted, the question can be raised as to how policy instruments can be made to correspond to the phase in which the policy system finds itself (In 't Veld, 1991). In addition, the application of policy instruments is not once and for all. On the contrary, policy instruments are adjusted and replaced continuously as the needs of the societies and the effectiveness of the instruments change.

2.   POLICY INSTRUMENTS

The selection and application of policy instruments implies a number of embedded political choices. The first of these choices concerns the instruments themselves. Can instruments be designed effectively as if operating with a *tabula rasa*, or are instruments context-contingent? Similarly, what effect does the process by which instruments are applied exert on the policy outcomes and the utility of particular instruments?

The Design of Instruments

A closer look into the nature of policy systems reveals, however, that the choice of instruments is not 'free' (Ringeling, 1983). In other words, the policy system as a whole should be considered to a certain degree to constitute a 'Gestalt'. Given that, no policy maker is entitled to unscrew certain (policy) limbs and replace them with new ones. So the matter of policy instruments is more complicated, and less flexible, than may at first appear.

The Application of Instruments

The application of instruments is governed by at least two mechanisms. First, policy instruments become obsolete after some time, because stakeholders learn how to cope with and circumvent instruments. As a consequence, the effectiveness of instruments diminishes over time. Second, policy makers tend to respond in the same manner regardless of the effectiveness or ineffectiveness of instruments; that is, more of the same. The law of policy accumulation and the law of diminishing effectiveness are playing leapfrog. In the end, policy systems will collapse if no breakthrough is forced.

3.   POLICY DYNAMICS

As well as being seen as static entities, policy instruments must also be understood as part of a dynamic political process. This is true of the manner in which policies are made, and it is also true of the manner in which they are implemented. Again, typical assumptions concerning the capacity of government to implement policy successfully over time appear to be suspect when examined from a more sceptical perspective than is usually employed.

The Law of Diminishing Effectiveness

It is helpful to accept the hypothesis that in general the life-cycle effectiveness of any specific system of governance or any specific set of policies will be limited. The reasons for the limitation of the life of a system of instruments can be explained in the following terms: policy making aims for the realization of objectives which, by definition, will not be fulfilled automatically or by any spontaneous development. Policies are implemented by the authorities with the support of power in any form, for instance, visible sanctions or strategic threats. Such policy instruments bring with them both intended and unintended effects. Some of these effects are foreseen; others are unforeseen. Now, the general tendency will be that in the course of time the category of intentional foreseen effects will shrink, while the category of unintended unforeseen effects will increase in importance. We call this tendency *the law of the gradually diminishing effectiveness of public policies*.

The existence of this law of behaviour can be made acceptable by emphasizing the learning potential of individuals and organizations. People frequently experience the implementation of public policies as somewhat disagreeable, because of the divergence between their own preferred course of action on the one hand, and the course of action required by the policies on the other. The public use their abilities to avoid disagreeable effects by changing their visible behaviour in a strategic way. Avoidance, sabotage and resistance are very normal behaviours in respect of public policies. Because of their learning potential, the public will gradually succeed in using such strategies to reach their personal goals and to some extent undermine collective goals.

We may call this ability to learn, meaning here the ability to change behaviour in a strategic way, the *reflexivity* of social systems and individuals. This reflexive characteristic is decisive in all social structures, although some policies are more robust than others. Whatever the degree of sophistication of a certain set of public policies, the creativity of people will be the main cause of the temporary duration of success. Unless...? Unless, at the same time, the value patterns of the individuals concerned with the policy change in a direction which corresponds to the wishes and insights of the policy makers. We call this type of value change *internalization*. This is the only possible lasting exception to the law of gradually diminishing effectiveness of policy instruments.

The Law of Policy Accumulation

Historically we can see such processes of internalization at work in policy processes such as the abolition of slavery. If internalization is general and unanimous, public policies of abolition become superfluous. The desired effects of eliminating slavery will now emerge from spontaneous individual behaviour, for example, emancipating any slaves owned. So there remain two causes of death or change for systems of public policies:

1. The diminished effectiveness as a consequence of reflexivity.
2. The overwhelming success as a consequence of internalization.

Policy makers who do not understand the determinants of the restricted lifespan of public policies often react to diminishing effectiveness in the following characteristic way: if a measure becomes less successful or if policies lose their grip on the public, the stereotyped reactions by the policy makers are often to refine the nature of the norms and sanctions, to go into greater detail, to develop more stringent methods of enforcement, and so on. We call this stereotyped reaction pattern *the law of policy accumulation*. Ineffective policies lead to further policies. In the long run, this type of action will never be successful, again because of reflexivity. In the end, a policy crisis will emerge as a result of extremely detailed policies and the disappearance of effectiveness. The presumed existence of the Laffer curve in the world of taxes is a good example of such a crisis (higher marginal tax rates, designed to produce higher receipts, appear to cause a decrease of total tax revenues). The existence of such a crisis will enable the authorities to shift to a completely different paradigm of public policies and to a new system, so that a new life cycle may start.

The reflexivity on the part of people and organizations may be the general cause of learning, but the learning processes themselves take many different forms. Further, we should not forget that the highest level of the multi-layer system, the 'steering' organization, is itself capable of learning. The steering organization could, at least, postpone the appearance of the law of diminishing effectiveness or it could further processes of internalization by using intelligent 'lateral' policies to supplement failing ones. Thus, the steering organization and its 'targets' are engaged in a continuing process of mutual adjustment and attempts to outguess and outlearn each other.

4. THE ANALYSIS OF INSTRUMENTS

On the one hand, policy instruments to be utilized will have to interrelate with the relevant components of learning processes, if the dynamics of a policy system can be described adequately in terms of 'competing' learning processes (operating in different directions). The different categories of learning processes can be ordered as: first-order changes in performances, second-order changes in values, and so on, with higher-order processes being invoked when lower-order ones fail. These processes occur both on the side of the policy makers and on the side of the citizens and organizations being placed 'under control'.

On the other hand, however, any significant change of policy instruments results in serious transaction costs (defined in a broad manner). That is, shifting from one instrument to another requires changing administrative patterns as well as changing patterns of compliance by organizations and individual citizens. These changes upset routine patterns of administration and routine patterns of compliance (or avoidance), and hence impose costs on all parties concerned. Therefore, the relevant actors must discover guidelines for producing a wise compromise between the values of novelty and the values of stability in order to maximize their returns from the policy process.

Policy Learning

The learning processes of people and organizations which are subject to policies can be divided into two categories (Argyris and Schön, 1978):

1. First-order learning processes, as a consequence of which they change behaviour in a strategy to serve their own interests better.
2. Second-order learning processes, as a consequence of which they adapt other basic attitudes towards their position within the system: for instance, citizens try to overthrow the government, schools take strike action, universities no longer cooperate in a peer review system of evaluation, and so on.

The second-order processes are of a more 'constitutional' nature than first-order processes. Generally, second-order processes take place later and more gradually. Internalization is a good example of second-order learning processes. But the importance of second-order processes is inversely related to their speed. They are decisive for the general relationships between the layers in our policy system, and their impact may overshadow the issue at stake. As far as the 'survival' of an evaluation system is concerned, second-order learning processes may threaten the life of the system long before the law of diminishing effectiveness takes hold. In particular, the general confidence of one set of parties (citizens) may be destroyed by the use the other party (government) makes of the 'results' of the system. This is discussed in the following section.

5. THE USE OF PERFORMANCE INDICATORS

The laws and other regulations mentioned before may be generalized to include steering relations in a multi-layer system. One of the characteristics of a multi-layer system is the mutually interdependent relationship between different layers, so that one may speak about extrinsic steering as well as intrinsic steering. The components of a more or less integral system of governance – planning, allocation of resources, evaluation and control – are realized between different partners within and between organizations, and not infrequently in power structures which differ from component to component. Thus, governance must be conceived as a complex interaction among levels and components.

The policies will be subject to the law of diminishing effectiveness, and performance indicators may have an impact in any area of the steering system, and not simply in the area for which they were developed or even intended. The possibility of the use or, in the eyes of some parties involved, abuse of performance indicators, when they are employed for purposes other than the original ones, will influence the willingness of certain parties to cooperate in their preparation or implementation.

Once performance indicators exist, they are embedded in the integral power game among the parties involved. It will often be impossible to restrict the functions of performance indicators to those earlier agreed by the participants in the process. The careful strategic agent will therefore attempt to predict which unexpected functions others might wish the performance indicators to fulfil. The willingness of such an agent to cooperate with the development of indicators will depend not only on the results of these considerations, but also on his/her position in the debate on the precise definition of each of the components of a certain performance indicator. Those components may generally be expressed by the following formula: 'a certain output over a certain input'. The agent may wish to be involved in the definition of both the denominator and numerator of this ratio.

Performance indicators are always imperfect approximations of the 'real' situation, so there is always room for debate on the merits and deficiencies of any specific indicator. There can be only intersubjective truths about performance indicators, and intersubjective truth in a political environment is completely dependent on concepts such as consensus and conflict. Given that consensus is unlikely in a politically charged environment, indicators and their use will be a source of conflict.

The Life Cycle of Performance Indicators

The existing variety of insights regarding administrative performance in the public sector will determine the debate on the exact desirable properties of performance indicators in relation to their intended functions. The relative power positions of political actors may explain how the use of the performance indicator will expand to unintended functions.

The credibility gap arising from the expansion to unintended functions by the most powerful partner will heavily influence the future readiness of the other partners to cooperate in the near future. So the length of the life cycle of the performance indicator in a multi-layer system will be improved by:

- solid consensus between the parties involved on the functions of performance indicators in their mutual relationships during the first period of use;
- the acceptance of precise definitions of each of the components of the performance indicator to be developed (data element dictionary);
- accurate and well-balanced procedures to handle conflicts concerning either the development or the use of the performance indicator;
- the presence of so many performance indicators that each of the parties involved can sustain his/her own viewpoint with reference to 'his/her own' performance indicator;
- moderation on behalf of the more powerful partners as to the later expansion of the functions of well-established performance indicators;
- sufficient attention to the dangers of an over-mechanistic use of performance indicators (always accept a loose connection between performance indicators and the decisions to be based upon them, apart from exceptional cases).

It may be clear that performance indicators will flourish only in policy environments which are characterized primarily by dialogue and reasoning between the parties involved. If these are absent, the intersubjective truth sought will not emerge, and the performance indicators will soon disappear as a useless artefact.

Multifunctional Use of Performance Indicators

We have attempted to point out above that the multifunctional use of performance indicators is a potential source of conflict. Putting it more strongly, one might argue that the most important cause of hesitance about, and resistance to, the development of performance indicators in education (and other policy areas) is precisely the fear of abuse. And abuse might be defined simply as the use of the indicator in another functional relationship rather than the one agreed on beforehand. So if, for instance, the use agreed on beforehand was to develop performance indicators as tools to improve existing educational programmes on the basis of the results of evaluation, it might be seen as an abuse of power if decision makers in possession of these indicators utilized them as a basis for allocative decisions.

It is clear, however, that a series of performance indicators, once promulgated, could be used by anyone for any purpose. Therefore one might understand why many educators tend to refrain from any activity leading to the development of performance indicators or anything like them for their policy area. The usual method employed by educators to resist such development, often unsuccessfully, is an attempt to point out that it is unwise to try to capture such a precious thing as educational quality in terms of quantities, numbers or ranking orders. Apart from the fact that this reasoning is unsound, the outsider's impression is inevitably that this is a defensive posture. The stance appears to be chosen by educational administrators or teachers because they are hiding something – their ineffectiveness, their inefficiency, and so on – that could be revealed by using performance indicators.

The type of solution we want to offer here for the problem of multifunctional use of performance indicators is of a procedural nature. In most cases the professionals involved in educational evaluation and in the design of performance indicators will be involved in some kind of dialogue with the decision makers, who might pose a 'threat' by abusing the indicators. All kinds of future proposals are discussed, and in many cases there is a financial relationship. The restricted power of the educationalists has a negative character: they may resist or even sabotage the attempts to develop indicators or other measures by refusing to produce the necessary basic or background materials and data. The dialogue enables them, however, to utilize their integral strategic position to bargain over the future decision-making processes and the models and methods to be used, including the future use or non-use of indicators.

6.   CONCLUSION

Although the example of the application of performance indicators given here may seem extreme, it is our view that the conclusions reached above are, in principle, valid for all policy evaluations.

The interactive relationships between the 'constitutional' pattern (the rules of the political game, mutual trust, legitimacy) on the one hand, and the behaviour of the partners (keeping to earlier promises, being truthful) on the other, have been clarified. The evaluation system can be 'internalized' if the constructive constitutional pattern, existing at the start of the whole exercise, is reinforced by the behaviour of all partners concerned. It will then be consolidated and, in turn, gradually become a factor that influences its environment. Accreditation procedures in the USA, for instance, have to a certain degree determined the character of university management. In France, 'les concours' (competitive entry exams) are intertwined with the labour market, especially in the public sector. However, the system of evaluation is doomed to failure when the behaviour of one of the partners concerned weakens 'constitutional' relations, or if the law of diminishing effectiveness is fully in operation.

The first development is not always welcomed; nor is the second one always doomed. For the emergence of an internalized and predominant system of evaluation may be a major hindrance to the necessary flexibility of the labour market and thus to the educational system itself, and in turn hamper economic progress. On the other hand, the consciousness that systems and institutions have a limited lifespan will stimulate people and organizations to express innovative behaviour.

The awareness of the dynamic relationships developed above will aid the realization that efforts and investments into systems of evaluation, at any level, should be subject to depreciation. Costs and benefits have to be analysed in relation to the life cycle of the system concerned.

9. The acceptability and visibility of policy instruments

Kenneth B. Woodside

1. INTRODUCTION

Over the past decade or so a very rich and thought-provoking literature has grown up around the idea that politics and public policy can be studied from the perspective of the policy instruments employed by participants in the process. While the terminology used varies among such concepts as governing instruments, policy tools and policy instruments, they all share the fundamental insight that a range of different means (or instruments) is available to achieve a particular policy goal (Hood, 1986; Phidd and Doern, 1978; Woodside, 1986). This raises questions about why a particular policy instrument was used and how it was used. The study of the choice and design of policy instruments can play a useful part in the analysis of public policy.

The literature on policy instruments has commonly centred on the choice of one instrument over another. In this chapter we shall focus on the design or choice of characteristics of policy instruments. It will be argued that policy instruments can have at least two characteristics: acceptability and visibility. After discussing these two characteristics, we shall examine them in further detail through two case studies: the sale of beer in the Canadian province of Ontario and the application of rules of origin under the Canada–United States Free Trade Agreement (FTA). Whereas most attempts to use a policy instrument approach focus on domestic policy, this chapter will focus on international policy issues. International pressures on the domestic politics of all countries, but especially smaller countries, are becoming an increasingly common feature of policy studies. A subsidiary aim in the chapter is to extend the policy instrument approach to the study of international politics.

2. POLICY INSTRUMENTS

Policy instruments refer to the different means available to governments to attempt to achieve some goal. A wide range of instruments is available. These include exhortations to action by the public or some part of it. These and other symbolic measures usually involve very little action by the government beyond the initial announcement and possibly a public relations campaign to promote the ideas. Other policy instruments include tax expenditures and taxes more generally, expenditures, the many forms of public regulation, and public ownership and emergency measures of various types. In the section that follows, we shall examine some types of policy instruments used, first in the domain of national politics and then in international politics. We shall do so through a brief examination of the different perspectives that are brought to the study of these instruments.

Policy Instruments at the National Level

In national politics, the most commonly used instruments involve some form of taxation or tax relief, efforts to regulate various forms of behaviour and action, expenditure programmes to subsidize an activity that is considered desirable and, until recently, measures to establish public ownership in some sector of the economy. Sometimes governments may choose one instrument over another, deciding for instance to regulate an activity rather than invest public money in taking over ownership of a firm. In this way a limited market for policy instruments may develop, with policy makers choosing one instrument over another within such limitations as the instruments legally available to the departmental officials responsible for the policy or the prevailing budgetary conditions (Phidd and Doern, 1978; Woodside, 1986). Furthermore, debates over the choice of a policy instrument may pit one domestic constituency against another. Occasionally a foreign government may even develop an interest in the results of the debate, particularly if it will affect some of its firms or influence events within its borders.

One approach to the study of policy instruments and their use involves looking at this use in terms of the political relationship between the policy makers and the clients of the instrument, that is, those that will be influenced. Policy instruments may have ideological overtones or associations. Client groups that are strong advocates of policy solutions which emphasize the free market may strongly prefer such policy instruments as privatization or tax expenditures as much for their ideological congruence as for their record of success. The social standing of these groups may also make it important that the government listen to their concerns. Other groups may lack the social standing or status to expect and receive respect. Indeed it may even seen politically attractive to policy makers to force this clientele to live with a policy instrument that they do not find acceptable and that shows little respect for their status. Instruments may also differ in the extent to which they attempt to interfere or intervene in private individual decision making or the managerial prerogatives of private industry. Among the reasons that private businesses have preferred to receive public assistance through the use of tax expenditures instead of through the use of expenditure subsidies are the greater autonomy they thereby retain and the more limited accountability and interference this instrument involves between the user and the civil servants and treasury officials (Woodside, 1983). All these considerations look at policy instruments through the eyes of the clients of the instrument in use and their political relationship with the policy makers.

The use of policy instruments domestically can also be seen from the perspective of the policy makers acting as civil servants trying to implement a policy to achieve a particular goal. In this instance, the emphasis is likely to be on the relative merits of alternative instruments and their effectiveness and efficiency in achieving the desired result. In this situation the historical record of the use of a particular instrument will be important in determining which instrument will be used and how it will be used. It is assumed that this past experience will help policy practitioners to make choices among policy instruments and to design them to make it more likely that they will achieve the desired result. The supply of instruments legally available to a particular government department or institution becomes an important constraint on what policy makers may attempt and how they will try to implement their proposals. Policy makers with legal access to the most effective instrument may not be sympathetic to those with different goals. The educational background of the policy makers may also play a role. Practitioners such as economists, for instance, may be more comfortable with instruments that create incentives to guide the policy response of the clientele and less attracted to those that involve closer ties between government and the private sector.

Policy Instruments at the International Level

Most of the attention paid to the use of policy instruments in the international arena has traditionally focused on studying the use of these instruments in foreign policy, the provision of foreign aid, and the negotiation of international trade agreements like the GATT (General Agreement on Tariffs and Trade). This pattern has been changing over the last two decades as new types of international policy making have gained in importance. Several developments have led to an increased interest in international economic policy making and the use of policy instruments in the international arena. First, the continuing spread of trade liberalization and ongoing tariff reductions has led to increased access to domestic markets by foreign producers and their goods and services, with a resultant increase in trade tensions and conflicts because of greater competition. The proportion of the US economy, for instance, that is now open to foreign competition has increased sharply over the last decade or so, creating new fears about national competitiveness (US Joint Committee on Taxation, 1991). Second, and of more importance to our analysis, the lines that separate domestic from international policy have blurred significantly over the last two decades. This growth in what John Jackson has called the 'interface' problem between countries with differing policies to deal with similar problems involves competing countries reinterpreting the national policies of other countries as trade barriers (Jackson, 1991, pp. 218–19). For instance, there are growing pressures from countries such as the USA to force other countries such as Japan and Canada to proceed with measures such as privatization and deregulation in order to open up their markets to foreign investment and competition. These pressures are certain to continue to increase with the implementation of the GATT Uruguay Round agreements and the tremendous growth in economic interdependence. This will be particularly true of the various service agreements in the Uruguay Round that are still being negotiated. In February 1997 an agreement to liberalize telecommunications services by opening up many remaining monopoly services to international competition was completed. There is also the possibility of an agreement on financial services and a further OECD agreement on investment, the Multilateral Agreement on Investment, which extends the NAFTA (North American Free Trade Agreement) investments provisions to other OECD members.

The implementation of the agreements made in the Tokyo Round of the GATT during the late 1970s and 1980s led to a substantial reduction in the levels of tariff protection enjoyed by domestic industry in all developed countries. With the lowering of tariffs came a rapid increase in the volume of international trade (Woodside, 1992). Many public policies provide monetary advantages to domestic producers of goods and services and, as the volume of international trade has grown, foreign producers have increasingly questioned the aim and role of these policies. The fact that a policy or approach to a problem may have a long history, and not be a recent action designed to impede trade, may not be treated as very significant by foreign competitors. In this way any domestic policy can be seen to acquire a new and often disruptive international dimension.

Trade liberalization has not only meant increased mobility for goods across borders. It has also been accompanied by measures such as those under the North American Free Trade Agreement between Canada, the USA and Mexico and the ongoing deepening and widening of the European Union (EU) which seek to guarantee and expand the rights and opportunities of foreign investors under the domestic laws of the member states and establish new rules for trade in some services. This has brought new international actors into the domestic policy-making process. Increased international trade has put pressure on policy makers to defend existing protective measures through new instruments, as in the case of the very high tariffs being imposed under the programme of tariffication of agricultural subsidies. Further, some existing domestic policies have been targeted by foreign producers and their governments looking for explanations for their failure to penetrate those markets. All these developments have led to some domestic policies acquiring an alleged new international character as so-called non-tariff barriers and regulatory barriers. Efforts by countries such as the USA to force the removal of regulatory barriers in foreign markets generate pressures for policy harmonization that can be particularly difficult for smaller states. During the earlier period of GATT rounds which were concerned with the removal of so-called border measures such as tariffs and quotas, small countries could free-ride on the gains made in the system from negotiations between the larger states which would then be passed on to all GATT members. The emerging new trading system with its growing focus on the removal of regulatory barriers and other impediments to foreign trade and investment will probably be less beneficial for smaller states, which may find that they are forced to make policy concessions to the bigger states without receiving any concessions in return.

In this chapter we shall discuss two basic categories of policy instruments in the area of international economic policy making. The first involves border measures such as rules of origin and anti-dumping measures. Unlike in a customs union such as the European Union, where all member states harmonize their trade policies, in a free trade agreement such as the NAFTA there is no such requirement. This necessitates the establishment of rules of origin to determine which goods should receive the preferential treatment mandated by the agreement. These rules can have important implications for trade and investment and can be very complex (Johnson, 1993). Anti-dumping measures, for their part, are aimed at imported goods that are judged to have been sold in the domestic market of another country at a price that is lower than that at which they are being sold in their home market. In this case it is the manner in which countries postulate the existence of dumping that makes these measures complicated and subject to controversy (Boddez and Trebilcock, 1993; Jackson, 1991). One of the major attractions of the use of these policy instruments to restrict access by imports is that it is widely believed by politicians that only foreigners suffer as a result of the action. The impact on other domestic producers who use the imports as intermediate goods, and on consumers as a result of the higher prices these actions entail, often receives scant attention from the governmental agencies that police the system to monitor 'unfair' trade practices. This makes the use of these policy instruments seem relatively costless to politicians (Bovard, 1991). Later in the chapter we shall discuss a case study involving the application of rules of origin which we shall refer to as the Honda case.

The second category of policy instruments used in the international arena involves the capacity of a member of a liberalized trading area to retaliate against another member which has denied it some anticipated benefits of the trade agreement. These 'nullification or impairment' provisions are standard components of trade agreements such as the GATT and the NAFTA (Jackson, 1991, pp. 94–8). When retaliation occurs, it can be of at least equivalent value to the value of the trade believed to have been lost. The retaliating party can use any of the wide range of possible policy instruments to penalize the other party. Again, as with border measures, it is widely believed that only foreign producers are hurt by the use of these measures. Sometimes the retaliation may not be directly tied to a provision of the trade agreement but instead may reflect a perception on the part of one of the parties that some domestic policy of the other party offends against the spirit of the agreement. These types of disagreements have been common between the USA and Japan. They are also a potential basis for the harassment of smaller economies by larger economies where the government of the smaller state may feel constrained not to use the same policy instrument when they feel wronged. Later in this chapter we shall consider a case study of this type which will be referred to as the beer case.

3. THE CHARACTERISTICS OF POLICY INSTRUMENTS

As was stated in the introduction (Section 1), this chapter focuses on two characteristics of policy instruments: acceptability and visibility. It is argued that any policy instrument can vary in character in terms of each of these variables. Thus a policy instrument can be designed to be more or less acceptable to its clients, and it can also be designed to be more or less visible. Once the characteristics of a policy instrument that will be used in solving a particular problem for a particular constituent group are well established, they tend to be relatively stable. However, there is always at least some conflict over these characteristics as, for instance, when groups divide over the extent of use of corporate tax expenditures or over whether there should be a tightening of access to unemployment benefits.

The study of the use of policy instruments from the perspective of international economic policy raises two important areas of difference from their study in domestic policy. First, there is an ongoing need to take into account the behaviour of foreign governments and producers in understanding the choice and design of policy instruments. Where this behaviour has not been taken seriously, policy makers leave themselves and their fellow nationals open to retaliation through trade actions. The growing economic interdependence of the advanced economies has led to continuing pressure to harmonize, at least partially, policies that subsidize and protect domestic producers. It has also led to increased concern about how to design policy instruments so that they will help their intended beneficiaries without arousing retaliation from trading partners. Second, these policy instruments are used to penalize foreign producers. It may often seem that domestic policy makers, especially in the stronger economies, have little to lose by attacking foreign producers, since only the proponents of the actions can vote in domestic elections. This helps to increase the acceptability of these policy instruments among certain elements of the domestic business community. It also reflects the widespread presence of a mercantilist mindset among politicians – that exports are good and imports are bad.

The Acceptability of Policy Instruments

The idea of the acceptability of a policy instrument attempts to assess the political relationship between those in a position to choose which instrument they will use, the particular instrument that they do choose, and those that will be most directly affected by the instrument – its clientele. This idea is related to the idea of how coercive a policy instrument is in the sense of whether and to what extent it caters to the interests and preferences of its clientele. It is also related to the relative intrusiveness of the instrument in the sense of whether and to what extent it respects the autonomy of its clientele, letting them make their own managerial decisions, and the degree of supervision to which it subjects them.

A number of illustrations may help to explain this characteristic. In taxation policy, for instance, tax expenditures or incentives have traditionally been preferred to a more comprehensive tax base, with lower rates as a means of promoting business. This may now be changing, in the view of some. There is evidence that the number of these tax expenditures has been reduced during the 1980s in many of the developed countries but it will take some time to determine whether these changes are permanent and what impact this change has had on the acceptability of tax policy to encourage economic growth (Pechman, 1988). Similarly, professional groups have commonly preferred self-regulation over regulation by an independent agency. Again, change in the use of regulation has been occurring as more and more sectors of the world's economies are opened up through forms of deregulation. In both the above examples the same policy instrument is in use but its character has been modified as a response to changing pressures. One might examine these changes in terms of the extent to which they reflect a change in the acceptability of the use of the policy instrument to its traditional clientele.

The Visibility of Policy Instruments

The visibility of a policy instrument refers to the extent to which the use of a policy instrument can be readily documented and thus readily understood by the public. The less visible the use of a policy instrument, the more likely its consequences will be poorly understood, since there will be little information available to independent assessors. Less visible policy instruments are more likely to produce irrational policy consequences because their impact is subject to less careful and disinterested scrutiny. At the same time this lack of visibility may make the use of the policy instrument more attractive to its clientele. As a result, low visibility may be strongly related to high acceptability.

One of the primary goals of US trade negotiators during the Uruguay Round was to make the use of protective measures more transparent and visible. This would allow citizens everywhere to know, for instance, exactly how much protection the agricultural sector was receiving. Similarly, historically one of the attractions of tax expenditures for their beneficiaries was that their real cost in terms of revenue foregone by the government was largely unknown. Governments did not keep records on how much tax revenue they might have lost as a result of a particular tax break. In taxation policy some increased visibility has been achieved through the introduction by some governments of tax expenditure budgets, but these documents are still usually few and far between. At the same time, these budgets reflect the fact that visibility in the use of a policy instrument can and does change.

4.   ACCEPTABILITY AND VISIBILITY OF POLICY INSTRUMENTS – CASE STUDIES

Both the disputes examined in this section involve the governments of Canada and the USA. Each of these countries is the biggest trading partner of the other. The first dispute involves the sale of beer by American breweries in Ontario. This case raises issues involving different institutional and cultural approaches to organizing the sale of beer in Canada and the USA. Should the rationale of these differing policy approaches be accepted at face value or should each approach be treated as trade impediments that must be removed? This raises the issue of how to interpret a government initiative. Is it a necessary environmental safeguard or a disguised attempt to protect the domestic market from foreign competition? The acceptability of Ontario's beer policy to American brewers and trade policy makers became a new and important issue in the politics of beer regulation in Ontario. In addition, the visibility of Ontario's policy on minimum pricing was enhanced, with the government, for the first time, having to explain and justify why high beer prices were required. The resolution of the issue, at least for the time being, involved some effort to make Ontario's policy more acceptable to American brewers, who had now become part of the relevant clientele of Ontario's beer policy. The visibility of the minimum pricing regulatory policy was also enhanced somewhat, with more attention given to the existence of provincial policies that kept Ontario beer very expensive.

The second case involves rules of origin, an issue that has become increasingly important in the politics of international economic policy as free trade regions have proliferated. This case involves determining whether automobiles produced by Japanese car companies in North America and composed of auto parts from around the world and finally assembled in Ontario, qualified for duty-free access to the USA under the FTA or whether they should be treated as imports subject to the prevailing tariffs. Rules of origin deal with the question of when a good is produced to a sufficient extent within a jurisdiction or a defined trading area to be eligible for the favoured trading status available to such products. Rules of origin are fundamentally arbitrary and, unless a good wholly originates within a country, these rules may play havoc with its marketability in other countries. These rules also have to be implemented, and our second case raises some of the issues associated with the design of a policy instrument in the context of international trade policy. The design of rules of origin as a policy instrument can have a major economic impact. The resolution of this dispute, at least in the short term, involved a complete overhaul and restructuring of the rules of origin for automobiles under the NAFTA. These new rules have increased the acceptability of the rules for the two countries. They have also increased the visibility of the policy instrument by making it much clearer how local content will be determined.

The Case of Beer in Ontario

The sale of beer and wine in both Canada and the USA has long been an issue between the two countries. In the latter part of the 1980s trade actions were taken under the GATT by the European Community, the USA and by Canada to open up the beer and wine markets in the latter two countries. In the case of beer, GATT panels ruled against both Canada and the USA on the grounds that their governments were discriminating against the sale of foreign beer. In each country the discrimination occurred largely at the state or provincial level of government, but a resolution of the dispute would involve negotiations between the national governments. Although the GATT is a treaty between national governments, member governments commit themselves to 'take such reasonable measures as may be available to it to ensure observance of the provisions' of the agreement by regional and local governments within their boundaries (Stone, 1984, pp. 42–3; Jackson, 1991, p. 68). The case that we are examining involves that part of the dispute that involves Ontario and the USA.

Regulation of the sale of beer is a responsibility of provincial governments in Canada. Ontario's Liquor Control Act gives the Liquor Control Board of Ontario (LCBO) the authority to buy and sell beer, wine and liquor in Ontario and to authorize the beer companies in Ontario to establish, own and operate their own stores in the province (Bell and Pascoe, 1988, pp. 204–14). The beer industry has used this authority to establish a retail monopoly for the sale of beer called the Brewers Retail. This provincially regulated monopoly is owned by four breweries, of which the two largest – Molson's and Labatts – control the operation. Price competition is not permitted. Indeed, to enforce its opposition to price cutting the Ontario government has, for many years, established a minimum price at which beer could be sold. Ontario treated its minimum price policy as a social policy designed to discourage both price competition among brewers and beer consumption by Ontarians. When the brewers determined that they needed to raise their prices to cover their costs, they did so in concert.[1] The stores operated by the LCBO also sell beer but only in small quantities, up to a maximum of packs of six. They are also the only retail outlet for foreign beer. For a brief period in the mid-1980s there was talk of permitting the sale of wine and beer in convenience stores but the Liberal government of the day retreated from this position in the face of claims that the reform would encourage increased consumption and endanger the lives of those minding the stores at night. Thus the sale of beer remains highly regulated and controlled by the provincial government and, by delegation, the beer companies themselves.

The beer industry in Canada is highly concentrated. The two major breweries in the country control about 94 per cent of the market. At the same time, the Canadian breweries are relatively small by comparison with their American counterparts. The loss of economies of scale associated with the size of a brewery has been made more serious by the traditional requirement by Canada's provincial governments that beer sold within their boundaries must be produced locally as well. The result has been a highly concentrated industry characterized by a large number of small and inefficient plants that were highly vulnerable to the prospect of much lower cost competition from American brewers. While the federal government and the breweries themselves have persuaded some of the provinces to drop their inter-provincial barriers and permit the brewers to rationalize their production, the legacy of the small plants will take some time to be reversed. Two other factors require mention. The first is that the Canadian beer industry is much more dependent on the American market than US brewers are on the Canadian market. About 10 per cent of Canadian production is sold in the USA, while US sales in Canada are much lower. Canadian beer companies, therefore, have more to lose from a trade war than their American competitors. The second factor is that Canadian beer is sold in re-usable bottles, while most American beer is sold in non-returnable cans. Naturally, American brewers wished to be able to sell their beer in Ontario within a distribution structure that was similar to the one that they dealt with in the USA.

In 1991 a GATT panel ruled that the practice of imposing higher mark-ups and distribution costs on foreign beers by Canada's provincial governments was discriminatory.[2] Subsequently, in early 1992 another GATT panel ruled that US state regulation of the beer industry was also discriminatory; it meant, for instance, that domestic producers would receive tax expenditures and credits that were denied to foreign producers and domestic beer would be subject to lower excise taxes than its foreign competitors. The two panel decisions led to attempts to negotiate a settlement between the two countries and in April 1992 an agreement in principle was reached that would allow full access by the American beer industry to the Ontario market. The American government was apparently willing to accept minimum pricing by the Ontario government – despite the fact that it undermined the competitive advantage of American beer – as part of the agreement because the GATT panel had accepted this practice as an established social policy in Ontario.

However, the Ontario government subsequently introduced a 10-cent-per-can environmental levy for cans and non-returnable bottles in its budget of 30 April 1992. The integrity of this levy seemed particularly questionable as it applied only to cans of beer, not to cans of other beverages, and because it came at a time when the provincial government was not enforcing regulations that required 30 per cent of large containers of soda pop to be sold in refillable containers. While the Ontario provincial government was preoccupied with issues related to industrial policy, the new Social Democratic government was also giving considerable attention to environmental issues, especially those related to the approval of landfill sites and environmental assessment.[3] The introduction of the levy brought negotiations to a halt and led to re-opened hostilities between the two governments.[4] In July the US government introduced a countervailing duty of $3 per case on all beer entering the USA from Ontario. The Canadian government responded immediately with an equivalent duty of its own on some US beers, in particular the products of the US companies that were pushing the trade case.

This trade dispute has a number of dimensions. The American beer companies and their government regard the organization and regulation of the beer industry in Ontario as highly protectionist and designed to prevent US beer from competing effectively in the Ontario market. The concept of a minimum price was and is seen as an anti-competitive measure that eliminates most of the price advantage of the American breweries. The addition of the environmental levy was seen by these same brewers as being nothing more than a disguised trade barrier. The various charges levied by the Brewers Retail and the LCBO that penalize foreign beer, such as a warehouse charge, a handling charge and the LCBO's new brands listing fee, are obvious measures that discriminated against them. While these and some other measures had obvious industrial policy attributes – that is, they were intended to protect Ontario's beer industry against US competition – they also reflected Ontario's history in the regulation of alcoholic beverages. Actions by government to regulate the sale of alcoholic beverages such as minimum pricing have a long and sensitive history, and changes in the regulatory structure have been introduced only gradually and with great care. Subsequently, the Ontario government revamped its regulatory structure for beer. Since September 1993 US breweries have full access to the Brewers Retail distribution system and fees that discriminate between domestic and foreign beer have been eliminated. However, the American breweries also will have to live with a revamped regulatory structure that will continue to include minimum pricing. The American breweries now both export their beer to Ontario and continue to license the production of their beer by Ontario brewers. The licensing agreements have produced broader affiliations among the breweries in the two countries with Labatts affiliated with Anheuser Busch and Molsons with Coors and Miller Brewing. These high prices make the sale of US beer in Canada very profitable even if the prices restrict their market share. In essence, Ontario was able to defend its existing policy without making major concessions. However, the price advantage of US brewers is so great that this issue is unlikely to disappear. At the same time, the Ontario government was not particularly subtle in its approach to policy instrument design. While an environmental levy was quite acceptable in itself, the lack of consistency of the measure with the enforcement of other policies was noted and undermined its legitimacy. Ontario succeeded in maintaining its approach to the regulation of beer in the face of strong American oppostion, but its approach also raised the contentious issue of whether the measures were truly environmental in their intent or were, in fact, disguised instruments of industrial policy.

The problem in this case was that the US brewers were unhappy with Ontario's policies to control the sale of beer. Until recently, the acceptability of this policy to US brewers was not in question because they were not interested in having a direct presence in the Canadian market. In recent years, however, US brewers have become more interested in expanding their sales in Canada and have wanted to be able to take advantage of their sharply lower costs as compared to

Canadian brewers. The dispute led to Ontario making some small concessions in its approach to regulating the sale of beer and by giving US brewers access to the Brewers Retail outlets. The government marginally reduced the minimum price of beer and eliminated several charges that explicitly discriminated against foreign beer. However, the environmental levy on non-returnable cans was sustained. There was also a modest increase in the visibility of the government's regulatory policy. While many Ontarians continued to believe that the price of beer was excessively high, it wasn't until this case that the province was forced publicly to explain its policy and the concept of minimum pricing became better known. In conclusion, the acceptability to US brewers and the visibility of Ontario's regulatory policy were modestly improved.

The Case of Honda's Engines

The Honda case involves different interpretations of how to implement and apply a policy instrument. Rules of origin are a regulatory instrument and refer to the procedures used to determine the nationality of a particular good. Is a good American or North American in character? This issue is important because, in a liberalized trading zone such as the one that was created under the NAFTA, the trade benefits are supposed to be restricted to goods that satisfy the rules of origin described in the agreement. If a product is wholly manufactured within the trading zone, there is no problem. However, it is increasingly common for this not to be the case. This makes it necessary to decide what level of local content will be required and how it will be measured. This is a fundamentally arbitrary decision that will reflect some composite of the interests of the industries in the separate countries. Rules of origin, being protectionist in character, can have an industrial policy motivation in that the higher the percentage of local content required, the greater the supposed boost to the local economy. They also have to be enforced, and the higher the percentage of regional content required, the more important it becomes that officials in the member countries employ a common methodology to prevent goods from being too easily disqualified.

The Canada–US Free Trade Agreement (FTA) of 1989 enshrined a requirement of 50 per cent as the basic rule of origin for all goods in the new trading zone. This meant that 50 per cent of the combined value of the cost of the materials used to make the commodity plus the direct cost of assembling the good had to have originated in Canada or the USA in order for the good to qualify for duty-free status in moving between the two countries. Apart from the criterion of percentage of local output, another methodology is frequently used in applying rules of origin. This approach requires that a good must change tariff classification in order to be eligible for the special treatment provided in the trade agreement. Only when a change in tariff classification has occurred is it judged that a 'substantial transformation' of the good has taken place, and such a transformation is necessary for a good to qualify and comply with the rules of origin. Where the member countries apply the Harmonized Tariff System (HTS) established under the GATT, they will all be working with the same tariff classification system, with no opportunity to adjust the code to achieve some other goal (Morici, 1991). However, the HTS was not created to serve as an instrument to determine origin:

> In some cases substantial transformation coincides with a change in tariff headings... while in other cases substantial transformations may occur without products changing tariff headings. (Morici, 1991, p. 10)

In determining origin, both Canada and the USA use the general rule that requires that substantial transformation of a good take place. However, neither the FTA nor the NAFTA used the substantial transformation principle in determining origin for the automotive sector. Only regional value-added would be considered in determining whether an automobile qualified for the benefits of the FTA.

Under the FTA rules for automobiles, the two countries managed to develop different approaches to the calculation of content, despite the fact that these rules were derived from the same agreement. Ambiguities in the wording of the treaty were the source of the difficulty, allowing each side to make its own interpretation. The FTA rules defined 'direct cost of processing' and 'direct cost of assembly' in an identical fashion. However, the US Customs decided that if the wording was different, then their meanings must also differ. As a result, US Customs refused to interpret processing costs as regional costs in determining the direct cost of assembly unless those costs were associated with the actual act of assembly itself. In Canada the two terms were treated as equivalents. This meant that the Canadian Customs officials would see more North American content in a vehicle than their US counterparts. The impact of this difference in interpretation over which costs were included was exacerbated further by the application of so-called 'all or nothing' rules such as roll-up and roll-down. Roll-up occurs when a good or component, having been judged to have met the 50 per cent content rule, is then treated as if it were 100 per cent local in origin in the subsequent stage of content calculations where that part is being combined with other parts. In a roll-down, a good that fails to meet the content requirement, even if only by a small margin, will be treated as a completely foreign or non-originating good in any subsequent content calculations. Through roll-up a good with many subcomponents could actually have less regional content than another good that failed to qualify, depending on how and when the application of roll-down reduced the calculated amount of local content. The potential consequences of a difference in interpretation over which costs qualify for inclusion as regional content can be greatly exaggerated through the operation of these rules.

Before turning to the Honda case, a brief description of the organization of the automobile industry in Canada and the USA is necessary. Since 1965, the auto industry in Canada and the USA has been governed by the Autopact. This is a treaty between the two countries that allows the three major American automobile manufacturers to treat the market in the two countries as one market and thereby rationalize the North American marketplace. The Autopact and the associated Letters of Intent from the auto manufacturers and the Canadian government provided guarantees for the production in Canada of cars equal in number to those that were sold in the country (Eden and Appel Molot, 1993). At the time of the implementation of this agreement the Japanese auto makers were not a factor in the North American marketplace. However, this changed. Beginning in the early 1980s, when the Japanese manufacturers began to consider establishing plants in North America, the Canadian government sought to attract some of this investment to Canada by offering them duty remission agreements on exports to the USA and the possibility of entry into the Autopact by way of Canada. As it happens, the Canadian government had structured its legislation implementing the Autopact so that any country could join, whereas the American legislation was strictly an agreement between Canada and the USA. The success of the Canadian government in attracting more than Canada's proportionate share of Japanese investment created trade tensions between the two countries. When the FTA was negotiated in 1987, provision was made to prevent the Canadian government from using duty remission arrangements to encourage Japanese investment although existing plants could still enjoy duty-free passage across the Canada–US border, provided their output satisfied the rules of origin.

In March 1992, a preliminary ruling by the US Customs Service claimed that Honda Civic automobiles assembled at Alliston, Ontario did not meet the FTA's 50 per cent content requirement. In particular, Honda's engine blocks which were made in Ohio were declared to be 'non-originating' because they contained too many foreign parts. Automobiles contain about 10 000 parts, leaving substantial opportunity for the calculation of roll-up and roll-down to influence the measurement of the content of the final vehicle (Johnson, 1993). The Customs Service had treated the head and block of the engine as sub-assemblies of the engine. In calculating the regional content of the engine block, it was determined at less than the required 50 per cent. Certain costs of 'processing', such as occupational safety, medical care and compliance with environmental laws, were not treated as acceptable North American costs.[5] As a result, the North American content of the block was subject to roll-down to 0 per cent by the US Customs Service. This led to the entire engine being ruled to be 'foreign', and thus to the finished car assembled in Alliston, Ontario just missing the minimum 50 per cent content requirement. Officials at Revenue Canada came to a different conclusion about content because, unlike the US Customs Service, they calculated it differently. Their calculations were based on overall value alone, and the aforementioned processing costs were judged to be acceptable in the content calculations. This led to a favourable roll-up for Honda in Revenue Canada's calculation of North American content (Ritchie, 1997).

This trade dispute occurred during the negotiation of the NAFTA and resulted in important changes in the methodology for measuring regional content of automobiles as compared with that of the FTA. Roll-up and roll-down were eliminated from the calculation of regional content for automobiles. Instead, content would be determined by tracing the origins of all parts of an automobile and calculating the actual level of regional content. The parts that need to be traced are listed in the Uniform Regulations for the NAFTA. In addition, the levels of regional content required are to rise to over 60 per cent by the year 2002. These changes have increased the acceptability of the rules of origin for policy makers in both countries, eliminating some of the arbitrary features of the FTA rules and requiring that the content actually be 'North American' and not a product of the judicious use of roll-up and roll-down. These changes have also increased the visibility of the rules of origin, establishing common eligible costs and an unambiguous measure of regional content. At the same time, tracing will impose a severe administrative burden on the automotive industry and its suppliers, establishing the need for a very complex and lengthy paper trail for each automobile.

5. ACCEPTABILITY AND VISIBILITY OF POLICY INSTRUMENTS – REVIEW

In this chapter, we have argued that two characteristics of policy instruments are, first, the acceptability of the instrument to its clientele or those who will be affected by it and, second, its visibility. Every time that a policy instrument is used, choices are made as to the level of acceptability that it should meet and the extent of its visibility. Every policy instrument can be designed to be more or less visible and more or less acceptable to its clientele in its operation. This reality suggests an important feature that needs to be recognized in any discussion of instrument choice. Clearly any such discussion must focus on why one instrument or another is adopted. Policy makers can achieve their goals in a number of different ways and the choice of one instrument from among the population of available instruments is a reflection of that state of affairs. However, having selected one policy instrument over another, policy makers are then required to make further choices, involving the characteristics of the instrument that has been chosen. Thus, there are two stages at which choices have to be made.

This chapter has examined only two case studies. This is hardly the broad empirical foundation necessary safely to generalize the findings with respect to the characteristics of policy instruments. It is hoped, however, that this discussion may stimulate further attempts to apply the framework to other instances of instrument use. Examining the process of instrument choice from the perspective of both levels of choice – that is, the first level involving the choice of one instrument over another, and the second level involving the choice of the appropriate characteristics of the instrument that has been chosen – should introduce a sharper focus on the politics of instrument choice.

Policy instruments should be seen as a necessary part of any institutional explanation of the politics of a public policy. While the characteristics of a policy instrument are subject to change, there are likely to be situational factors that will limit those changes. This will give the characteristics of a policy instrument some degree of durability over the short and medium term. These characteristics are likely to have some impact on the politics of the policy. There is little question, for instance, that the relative lack of public knowledge about the extent and character of the use of the tax system to solve problems – that is, the relatively low visibility of the instrument – encouraged politicians to use the system and also made the use of this instrument attractive to its clientele.

This analysis suggests at least four profitable areas for study in the field of policy instrument choice. The first would be to explain why a particular policy instrument was chosen. Policy makers have alternatives and their choice of instrument needs to be explained and understood. Second, the policy instrument that was chosen has certain characteristics. What are these characteristics and why were they selected? Third, what has been the impact on conduct of the policy, the choice of policy instrument, and the choice of the characteristics of the policy instrument that was chosen? Fourth, if there is a change in either the characteristics of the policy instrument or even in the policy instrument itself, why did this change occur?

6. CONCLUSION

This chapter has argued that it is useful to think of the literature on the choice of policy instruments as having two levels of choice. The first involves the choice of one instrument over another. The second involves the choice of the particular characteristics of the policy instrument chosen. It is the second stage in the process that has been the focus of this chapter. It has been argued that two characteristics of policy instruments are its acceptability and its visibility. Two case studies were used to illustrate these characteristics. Further, it was argued that these characteristics can be generalized to the population of all policy instruments. Finally, various potential areas for research in the field of policy instrument choice were suggested.

NOTES

1. As a reflection of the sensitivity of the issue of the sale of alcoholic beverages in Ontario, until the 1960s Cabinet had to approve any increase in the price of beer by the industry. Thereafter, the system was changed to require the beer industry to put forward a joint request for a price increase. This approach changed in 1993 to allow the breweries to set their own prices independently.
2. The GATT decision ruled that Ontario had the right to continue its historic practice of setting minimum prices but criticized the means used by the province to establish these prices. The GATT panel preferred that Ontario use an approach that was based on the tax system – that is, a flat tax – rather than a mechanism tied to the price of domestic beer. Ontario agreed to switch over to this new system with effect from 1993.
3. The beer industry in Ontario appears not to have been involved directly in the decision to introduce the levy. The origins of the levy are said to have been with the Ministry of the Environment and the Treasury. The provincial premier at the time, Bob Rae, confirmed in a talk to one of my classes (in 1997) that the real intent was to serve as a trade barrier and protect against job loss.
4. One reason for the intense opposition to the environmental levy by the American

breweries may be the fear that other jurisdictions such as the state of California might adopt the system as well.

5. There are many confusions surrounding article 304 of the FTA, which provides the definitions relevant to the calculation of North American content.

PART IV

A Re-examination of the Study of Policy
Instruments

10. The sociogenesis of policy tools in the Netherlands

Nico A.A. Baakman

1. INTRODUCTION

For anyone nowadays involved in the study of Dutch public administration it is difficult to move without stumbling over policy tools. The concept of policy tools is everywhere: in many government sectors, new policy tools in the form of convenants are expected, badly chosen tools abound in a large number of policy analyses, and they sell like hot cakes in one theoretical discussion on policy after another.

Policy tools have not always been the focus of so much attention, and to ask how and why they have obtained that privileged position is to ask exactly what their sociogenesis actually is. Policy itself is a social phenomenon, but the ways in which it is analysed and regarded, as well as the developments in those approaches, are of course social phenomena too. One may therefore wonder how and in what circumstances these phenomena were generated, and that is exactly the question this chapter aims to answer. I shall sketch – and simultaneously criticize – a part of the historical development of thinking in terms of policy tools in the Netherlands. At the same time, I shall refer explicitly to the sociological origin of the impulses which underlie this approach and which explain the remarkable trend towards thinking and speaking in terms of policy tools.

The historical development I shall sketch does not, of course, begin with Adam and Eve; nor shall I deal with countries other than the Netherlands. I shall start with a personal recollection and finish with a plea – which I am not the first to make – for the clear separation of two different ways of studying public administration. The first way is guided by concern with the *improvement* of public administration and is therefore pursued for its practical use. The second way is in principle only concerned with *understanding* public adminstration and is pursued purely for its own sake. But we shall come to that in due time. Let me start with my personal recollection.

2. IN THE BEGINNING ...

I still vividly remember my first head-on collision with the term 'policy tools'. It was in February 1983 in Rotterdam during professor Ringeling's inaugural lecture, which he had entitled 'The tools of policy'. I was a little surprised that he had chosen that as his subject, because at the time I did not see how policy tools could possibly be the ingredients of a tasty little inaugural lecture. In that respect I was right. Despite the typical Dutch February weather outside, the speaker's concern was not to serve up something tasty to keep his audience warm. On the contrary, he made mincemeat of the whole policy tools school of thought.

Even so, his oration was very sympathetic and almost optimistic. Because of this ambiguity, and because of its mild tone, and in particular because at the end of the speech Ringeling unfolded the outlines of a programme for further research on policy tools, many of those present might have failed to notice the harsh blows he delivered here and there. After raising serious objections, Ringeling wound up his address with the statement that 'policy tools ... are connected with phenomena which are well worth studying'. Mind you, it was the *phenomena* which he said were worth studying, not the tools as such. He would have preferred to remove the term completely from the vocabulary of the study of public administration, because in his view it could too easily be misinterpreted as denoting a mechanistic concept. But the alternatives he mentioned, such as means, instruments or vehicles, unfortunately had the same shortcomings (Ringeling, 1983, p. 23).

That – and here of course starts the critique – is worth noting. One would be inclined to say that if other words lead to the same objections, the problem is not the *term* 'tools'. The obvious conclusion would be that there is something wrong with the theoretical context which necessitates the use of such a term. In other words, that there is a flaw in the underlying theory which defines what the concept of policy actually is. However, Ringeling did not formulate that conclusion as such.

Since he did not think that banning the term 'policy tools' from public administration would be feasible, he attached strict conditions to the scientific use of the concept (Ringeling, 1983, pp. 22–4). In my view, these ifs and buts are so far-reaching and involve such an extensive scientific research programme that it would be practically the same thing to say: let's just forget about the policy tools approach, at least for the next fifty years.

3. DE MORTUIS . . .

The mild tone of the inaugural lecture can be explained not only by the speaker's personality, but also by the special function which the lecture fulfilled: that of a scientific funeral oration on the occasion of the demise of the Committee for the Development of Policy Analysis, popularly referred to as COBA. This committee, which had originated within the Ministry of Finance and was obviously influenced by American technological optimism, assumed that government policy could be considerably rationalized, for instance by means of mathematically formalized decision-making techniques, a clear analysis of objectives, and the consequent 'logical' choice of the relevant policy tools (COBA, 1976, 1977). That the everyday reality of public administration in most cases now looks quite different, and looked different at that time as well, did not seem to matter; on the contrary, it was COBA's *raison d'être*. If reality was different, that was not rational, and so it would have to be changed.

The COBA, however, got itself desperately lost in the fog surrounding such factors as vague compromises and political rationality, internally contradictory or otherwise infeasible objectives, and office politics. In addition to this limited visibility, it was also faced with obstructive power, with the inertia of established routines, with bureaucratic and political rituals, conflicting interests, tribal disputes between departments, symbolic policies and strategic behaviour – matters, in short, which are daily elements in public administration and which are not really uncommon in other organizations either.

It may well be true that all these phenomena are everyday aspects of public administration, but it is highly debatable whether they are always recognized as such by the civil servants, politicians and administrators involved and, if so, whether they are always given their right names. The image of reality is usually (in politics practically always) retouched. This apparently has a function. If, under pressure from public opinion or parliament, for example, a department or agency is forced to rub off this make-up, and not telling the truth is once more called 'lying' and unwillingness to cooperate can no longer be called a 'coordinating problem', or a struggle for power in a policy field can no longer be concealed by referring to it as a 'matter of unclear cut competences', the effect on daily routine in the organizations is far-reaching and many people are unable to do their work properly for a long time.

This, however, is not deliberate deceit. It is one of the rules of the political–bureaucratic game that these phenomena should be hushed up as long as possible and, when that is no longer possible, provided with technical (and consequently euphemistic) labels. My impression is that many civil servants, politicians and even students of public adminis- tration often consider these rose-coloured labels as more realistic than the real, all-too-human phenomena which they obscure, and that many of them have started to believe sincerely that if the rules of the game do not allow certain matters to be mentioned, those matters can hardly exist in reality. To some extent, such a form of short-sightedness is indeed necessary for civil servants and politicians to allow them to function without becoming melancholy, apathetic or cynical, and conse- quently for students of public administration to allow them to remain on speaking terms with the administrators. In many cases, therefore, the retouching is probably highly functional. I shall return to that later on.

I would not wish to suggest that members of COBA also lived with such a retouched image of public administration, but nor can I exclude the possibility. Whatever the case may be, it is certain that, once political bodies have established their policy objectives, there is no room for the above-mentioned phenomena in COBA's normative monorational schemes.

But of course it was all there: the pushing and pulling, saying 'perhaps' while meaning 'over my dead body', the *reservatio mentalis*, the ritual behaviour and the bureau politics, the clash of interests and the hidden agenda. All those phenomena were present and simply did what they always do: turn goal-rational decision making and techni- cally neutral implementation into pious hopes. COBA, given its own opinion as to how policy should be rationally developed and implemented, could of course not handle them.

The effort to rationalize policy implies the wish to pursue a (meta) policy, and if the regular way of policy making is hardly goal rational, the result is a variation on the chicken-and-egg problem. One wants chickens because one wants eggs, but in order to have chickens, eggs must first be laid and hatched by chickens. By analogy, the same goes for democracy: democracy can only be implemented in a democratic way if there is already democracy, in which case it need not be implemented, and if it does not yet exist it cannot be effected in a democratic manner, and every other means of implementation seems incompatible with the principle.

Nevertheless, history – in the form of social and biological evolution – has produced both more or less democratic systems and egg-laying chickens. There are even government policies which are implemented effectively, efficiently and thus goal-rationally, for instance the monthly payment of salaries to state officials. On a national level there are

150 000 civil servants in the Netherlands, on a local level a total of 200 000, and in education, due to the large number of part-time employees, some 300 000 (Pont, 1991, p. 1). This is an extremely complicated, complex, massive and socially delicate affair, but – apart from the size of the amounts concerned – the transfer of payments usually works perfectly. On the other hand, the transfer of grants and loans to university students in the Netherlands, which is a comparable, even a somewhat less complicated task, looked for a long time more like a very convincing demonstration of Murphy's fundamental law. Just like 'democracy' and 'chickens which lay eggs', rational policy is in principle possible, but in order to understand the situations and circumstances in which it actually is or is not possible, a historicizing empirical approach is required. COBA, however, had a non-historical, purely normative–rational approach, which was bound to lead to the committee's undoing, notwithstanding all its good intentions, efforts and technical ingenuity.

'*De mortuis nil nisi bene*' (speak only good of the dead) must have been in Ringeling's mind when he gave COBA his scientific blessing after it had been suffocated politically and administratively. But in spite of all his sympathetic words, he could not of course conceal the fact that COBA's approach to government policy had never been viable and that the same had to be said to the instrumental elaboration of its ideas.

4.   THE HAZARDS OF PREDICTING

For the above reason I was never very serious about the 'programmatic' part of Ringeling's inaugural lecture, in which he broadly indicated a few lines of action for further research on policy tools. I considered it first as an obligation, part of the academic ritual connected with an inaugural lecture, and second as a token of reverence for the orphaned relatives of COBA – something like: it is undeniably dead, but it has not lived for nothing, because we can learn from its mistakes. In short, I simply did not believe that much attention would be devoted to the issue of policy tools in the future. Finished, over and done with, I thought. Nobody will ever seriously come back to this. But I turned out to be totally wrong.

Fifteen days after the inaugural lecture, Mr L.A. Geelhoed, a civil servant and as such chairman of the 'initial working group for the project plan for policy tools in a direct sense', presented his report *The interventionist state: proposal for a theory of policy tools* to the chairman of the Steering Committee for Departmental Reorganization, the then minister Mr Rietkerk.

The essence of the report was that the Dutch society consists of a budget democracy and a market democracy. Both are in disorder because they are too much intertwined. We must examine what tools the budget democracy has at its disposal and, on the basis of the possibilities offered by those tools, determine what its tasks should be. The budget democracy should be restricted to those tasks, and the remaining tasks should be left to the market democracy (Geelhoed, 1983).

The COBA concentrated primarily on analysing the objectives provided and thought that the selection of the corresponding tools would follow automatically, once the objectives had been split up into sufficiently concrete and simple sub-objectives (Bressers, 1983, p. 42). Geelhoed, however, shifted attention to the possibilities offered by the policy tools themselves. To overstate somewhat, the range of objectives to be set follows, in his view, from the possibilities offered by the available instruments, that is, the policy tools.

If we attempt to discover the scientific features of the report, such as a clear and unambiguous conceptual framework, valid argumentation, a strong theoretical basis, sufficient empirical elements, no confusion between the characteristics of theoretical models and of empirical reality, and a careful division between empirical and normative judgements, then we will have little work to do, because the report contains none of these. For that reason, Van Gunsteren (1984) disqualified the report in no uncertain terms as being a political programme. Geelhoed himself was put in the scientific pillory for being a political radical who had apparently not experienced the purifying and self-disciplining effect of writing a thesis.

Meanwhile, the political and administrative significance of the report – as well as that of its author, who rose via a professorship in law and a membership of the WRR (Scientific Council for Government Policy) to become the highest civil servant in the Prime Minister's Office – is something completely different. This significance can hardly be overestimated, although the programme drawn up by Geelhoed and his deregulation committee which made him famous has had as little effect as COBA's, for similar reasons.

The position of Geelhoed's report is clearly illustrated by the fact that it is referred to in the bibliography of many of the publications on policy tools which have since appeared, whereas I have not found a single article which elaborates theoretically or empirically on the conceptual framework or other aspects of the report. De Bruijn, for instance, refers to Geelhoed's categorization of policy tools but mentions a number of other classifications as well. He eventually rejects them all, for the simple reason that the categories are either too strict and too simple to do justice to the complexity of reality, or are not exclusive; they overlap, and consequently lack the power to make distinctions. The next step is his remark that a classification on the basis of the intrinsic characteristics of tools is not in fact possible, because the effects of a particular tool may be totally different, even opposite, in various policy contexts (De Bruijn, 1990, pp. 48–51). Although these statements are correct, they do not entice the author into banning the policy tools approach from the scene altogether. After some bowing and scraping, the tools leave by the back door (De Bruijn, 1990, pp. 55–7), only to come back later on in the role of prompter. Nor could De Bruijn bring himself to say that Geelhoed's conceptual work had thus been undermined completely.

My conclusion is that the large number of references to Geelhoed's report apparently had to do with a ritual rather than with the importance of its contents. The proliferation of these references implies that many publications on policy tools have appeared since then. That is indeed the case; the number is in fact very large. My conclusion, in 1983, could not have been wider of the mark.

5.   A SEMANTIC TEST AS CRITERION

The literature on policy tools has now become so vast that I have probably not seen everything. Nevertheless, I have a reasonable general impression of the literature, and on the basis of that I shall venture to divide the various publications into two groups. The first group includes the documents in which the word 'tool' is used as an ordinary term. Expressions such as 'the tool of subsidy X' or 'the tool of licence Y' are used, but it would have been the same (and shorter) to speak of 'subsidy scheme X' or 'licence system Y', because the specific instrumental aspects of the phenomenon studied are not discussed in a systematic way, that is, within the framework of an explicit theory of policy tools.

This does not necessarily affect the value of the analysis at hand. It is quite possible to make an interesting study of, for instance, the functioning of a subsidy scheme and call that scheme a 'tool' a hundred times in a row without analysing all kinds of other conceivable tools such as levies, licences, and so on, or going into the nature of policy tools as such. As long as we learn something about the subsidy scheme analysed, there is no real problem.

This characterizes the publications which I classify as belonging to the first group: if the word 'tool' is crossed out or replaced by, say, the empty word 'thingummyjig', this does not change anything in the analysis, the argumentation or the conclusions. Some linguistic patching up is all that will be required.

For all that, the totally superfluous, empty use of the word 'tool' has become widespread. For instance, I came across the following sentences in an otherwise rather good booklet on the council of ministers and its policy, written by a senior lawyer in the Department of General Affairs (Hoekstra, 1988):

> In 1983, the tool of the council of ministers and the office of the prime minister were incorporated into the constitution. (p. 11)

And a little further on:

> In this way, the unity of argumentation may be enhanced by means of the tool of the council of ministers. (p. 26)

You probably see what I mean. The word 'tool' does not add anything to what is already said, that is, that the council of ministers is now mentioned in the constitution and that the existence of the council may enhance the unity of argumentation. Numerous other examples of this kind could be given.

The empty language in this example is not very serious, but in other cases it may be more harmful. I shall give another example. In 1990, the National Audit Office (Algemene Rekenkamer) published a devastating report on the planning and construction of hospital facilities (Algemene Rekenkamer, 1990). I would like to emphasize that this is an excellent report in comparison with others of the same kind. The Hospital Facilities Act, the construction budget, the measures taken to reduce the number of beds and so on are consistently called 'tools' in this report. Naturally, one might think. But application of the semantic test reveals that the word 'tool' might as well be replaced by 'thingummyjig' or could simply have been left out. It would not have altered the data, nor the analysis, nor the devastating nature of the main conclusion. That conclusion (an undoubtedly justified one) is, in ordinary words, that planning and construction policy with regard to hospitals, nursing homes and mental hospitals has been far from successful. If the Audit Office had formulated its criticism in this way, the following questions would certainly have arisen: How is that possible? Whose responsibility is it? But since the Audit Office formulated it differently, the question as to the social origin of the problems was never even asked, though the answer was already implied. The Audit Office wrote:

> The National Government has not succeeded in initiating an effective and efficient policy process ... by means of the above-mentioned policy tools. (National Audit Office, 1990, p. 54)

This formulation suggests that the failure was due to the policy tools applied, and that other policy tools might have led to better results. The Audit Office even advised the Secretary to reconsider the set of policy tools, upon which the Secretary made known that he had already decided to do just that. This will surely be of no avail because there is nothing wrong with the relevant law or the other measures as such. In other fields of policy more or less comparable laws seem to work very well. The real trouble in this field is the permanent warfare between the many parties concerned (see Baakman, 1990, 1992, passim). But this true state of affairs was concealed by blaming the instruments. Besides, the Audit Office did not base its verdict about the instruments on an analysis of the data, but on the policy tools terminology which, in the report, is used without any discussion or justification. I do not know, of course, the meaning the researchers assigned to the word 'tool', but it really does not mean anything in the context of their analysis. If we leave out the word throughout the whole report, we are not faced with any semantic, logical or scientific puzzles, but at the most with a few easily solvable linguistic problems.

The above example is less trivial and raises the pressing question as to why the use of the word 'tool' is so popular. I shall come back to that later on. First, however, I must finish what I was doing, namely, classifying the literature on tools. In the first group of publications I distinguished, the word is used only in a nominal way, as a label, and not in an explicit theory of policy tools. The distinctive criterion is whether we can leave it out or replace it by a meaningless word. If this does not yield any problems or only linguistic ones, the publication belongs to the first group. It is a large and fairly incoherent group, of which I have only a global impression and certainly no clear overview.

The second, much smaller, group obviously does have a relevant theoretical framework. The connection between the publications is also much closer, which results from the fact that there is an actual research programme, with the quarterly journal *Beleidswetenschap* (Policy

Science) as an important forum. But this group also includes a number
of research reports, papers and even theses. Unfortunately, I cannot
deal with all of them. I shall follow the mainstream, and I apologize to
those whose work I shall have to ignore.

It all started with Bressers's thesis in (again) 1983, for which he
received the Van Poelje prize a year later. Although his thesis deals
with the effects of water quality policies and is consequently not directly
concerned with policy tools, Bressers discovered that levies had much
more effect than the other policy tools applied in this field (Bressers,
1983, p. 286). Bressers, who understandably enough was completely
unaware of Ringeling's oration when he carried out his research, distinguished various instruments within his area of study which he called
policy tools, but he did not yet develop an actual theory of policy tools.
In part, Bressers simply elaborated on the work of COBA, albeit far
from uncritically. His criticism, however, was not of a transcendent but
of an immanent nature. In other words, it was not concerned with
COBA's way of thinking about policy; it remained within the given
framework and tried to elaborate on that. A case of 'normal science',
to quote Thomas Kuhn.

In the meantime, Bressers's conclusion concerning the effectiveness
of the levy system compared to the other policy tools had become a
real eye-opener for the departmental policy makers in the field of
environmental protection. None of them had thought that the levy
system would be so effective, but it was certainly very convenient
since environmental policy was an important political issue and would
probably become even more so. Much work had to be done, and now
a prize-winning scientific study had revealed that certain policy tools
were apparently far better than others! It would be splendid if the
department knew more about them!

That is probably more or less what happened, I think, although I
was not there. In any case, contacts were established and a contract was
drawn up for conducting more research. One of the early fruits of these
activities was the research project *Comparative study of the effects of
tools in environmental policy* (quoted in Bressers and Klok, 1988, p. 6).
Soon afterwards the real work began. First came a *Preliminary theory
of policy tools for environmental policy* (Bressers and Klok, 1987a),
then for fellow scholars in public administration an article in *Beleidswetenschap* entitled 'Foundations for a theory of policy tools' (Bressers
and Klok, 1987b), for the civil service the report *Handbook of the
theory of policy tools* (Bressers and Klok, 1988), and quite a few more
articles in the journal *Beleidswetenschap*, eventually culminating in

Klok's thesis *A theory of policy tools for environmental policy* (Klok, 1991).

According to Klok, the theory of policy tools has ceased to be preliminary but is simply not yet complete, because the information content is not yet what it should be, the external circumstances have not been integrated systematically, informal tools have not been taken into account, and a number of other minor points (Klok, 1991, pp. 345–6). But, as I have said, Klok's work is still the culmination of the mainstream of the real theory of policy tools; a couple of important tributaries I would like to mention are the theses by De Bruijn (1990) and by Van der Doelen (1989).

6. AGAIN AD FONTES...

If we return to the beginning of my discourse, the speech by Ringeling, we are faced with an interesting problem. It does not have to do with the first group of publications, because that is, in fact, a variant on the theme of 'the emperor's new clothes'. The problem is related to the second group of publications, because that category is concerned with a real theory of policy tools, and that raises a few questions.

Has nobody read Ringeling? Have his comments been taken seriously, and have they been acted on after all? Has his extensive research programme, in which the theory of policy tools should have been embedded, been implemented? Or was he perhaps just wrong? And what if none of these is true? Presumably, Ringeling has indeed been read. Everybody has done his homework; the inaugural lecture figures in almost all lists of references. But, to begin with, he was apparently misunderstood.

For instance, in the programmatic article by Bressers and Klok, 'Foundations for a theory of policy tools' (Bressers and Klok, 1987b), the oration is included in the list of references, whereas the discrepancy with regard to content could hardly be greater. Bressers and Klok state, for instance, that

> There is a growing awareness that... a much greater variety of tools is possible. These tools constitute a sort of toolbox, from which a conscious choice can be made after careful consideration of the requirements of the intended effects and the circumstances (Bressers and Klok, 1987b, p. 78).

And what was Ringeling's view in that respect? He said, among other things, that 'a free choice of policy tools does not exist' (Ringeling, 1983, p. 10). And under the sub-heading 'A risky metaphor', he wrote:

> There is a . . . danger of thinking exclusively in terms of direct use and direct effects. One may easily be misled by the mechanical metaphor of the tool. It is . . . misleading because it suggests a representation of reality which has a rather poor empirical basis. (Ringeling, 1983, pp. 22–3)

Never the twain shall meet, one would be inclined to think, but the opposite is true. Ringeling and Bressers met in an evaluation committee and together published an article entitled 'Policy tools in three arenas: policy-making, implementation and effect' (Bressers and Ringeling, 1989).

The authors wanted to know if the two approaches could perhaps enrich one another, and the concept of the arena seemed to make that possible. Ringeling's point of view appears more clearly when the first arena (policy making) is discussed; Bressers's ideas are predominant in the other two arenas (the implementation and the effect of the policy in the field). In the real-life policy process, these arenas merge naturally into one another: what happens in one arena has certain effects on the other two. A theory of policy tools ought to do justice to that reality, the authors thought, and their joint conclusion was that this did not make it easier to formulate a theory (Bressers and Ringeling, 1989, p. 4). In my personal view, this is putting it very mildly.

The fact that Ringeling was right was not only recognized, but it also became even more evident because of the greatly increased number of empirical studies on the implementation of policy published since his inaugural lecture. The overall conclusion of all these studies is that the results of concrete policies are determined by a true profusion of highly specific factors, sometimes interacting, and at other times reinforcing or neutralizing one another. Or, if you like, that this profusion of factors determines the effects of the tools applied.

Klok summarized all this in a useful article (Klok, 1989) and made an effort to demonstrate that it was in fact all included in his theory of policy tools or, if not, could in principle be incorporated in it. The main problem in that respect is the continuous manoeuvring between the risk of an oversimplified theory on the one hand, and the risk of unmanageable complexity on the other. Klok writes:

> The complex character of the implementation process makes the use of relatively simple explanation models impossible. For the time being, however, it is inconceivable that models will be developed which do justice

to the complex character of the process by taking all relevant variables into consideration. (Klok, 1989, p. 274)

It is necessary to work out a compromise, and Klok expected that he would succeed in doing so.

When we realize that he was only thinking of policy implementation, and not of the other phases in the policy process which in practice cannot even be clearly distinguished from implementation, Klok's vision is shown to be far too optimistic. A more realistic conclusion to be drawn from the implementation literature might be that a middle course will probably suffer from a combination of both evils. It will be too simplistic to do justice to the reality, but at the same time too complex to be applied in the practice of policy.

But Klok did not draw that conclusion. And his thesis, in which his great ambitions would have to be achieved, does not correspond with his optimistic point of view. His theory, although restricted to the implementation of policy, the formal tools and a specific policy area, is not even complete, and I pity the policy maker who has to put this theory into practice. Few officials in policy making will have the courage to go through all those steps, quite apart from the fact that it is most uncertain whether anybody in public administration will ever get the opportunity to do so.

As I mentioned earlier, the objections raised by Ringeling and the extensive programme in which he wished to have the research on policy tools embedded, mean in my opinion the same as: let's just forget it for the next fifty years. Well, not even fifteen years have passed; Ringeling's criticism has not been refuted but rather confirmed by implementation studies; he has eventually been read by the instrumentalists and justice has even been done to him to some degree, although his major research programme has still not been carried out. Yet the words 'policy tool' are on everyone's lips and there is a theory of policy tools which, in fact, cannot exist. How is that possible? What is the social origin of this phenomenon?

7. FINALLY: THE SOCIOGENESIS. PROPOSAL FOR A SCHISM

The answer is simple: there is no theory of policy tools, at least not one that would in any way deserve the name. First of all, efforts to classify the empirically existing tools in an unambiguous way and to distinguish them from one another have been unsuccessful. However, an empirical theory designed to play a prescriptive role may be expected to provide operational terms that link up with the empirical reality – after all, the aim of the theory is to be applied. In every concrete policy context in public administration, terms like plan, law, information, licence, order, subsidy, by-law, and so on, have a well-defined meaning for the civil servants and administrators involved. These terms are used in and form part of their day-to-day practice; these concepts – whose connotation is implicit and goes without saying – are the basis of communication, and the policy context concerned is denoted by these and many similar terms. Any prescriptive theory of policy tools ought to be phrased in these terms, but that has always remained wishful thinking, because nobody has managed to categorize these actually existing tools in an unambiguous way. Out of desperation, the efforts were aimed instead at classifying abstractions of the real tools. According to De Bruijn, Van der Doelen has done very well in that respect.

Van der Doelen refers to policy tools as steering models. He differentiates between a legal model (regulations), an economic model (incentives), and a communicative model (information), each of which may either increase or restrict the number of possibilities (De Bruijn, 1990, p. 50). However, something as simple as a regulation that all foodstuffs must have a label indicating the ingredients is already too complicated for this conceptual framework: it has both legal, communicative and economic aspects. This would then be a 'mix of models', because all three models appear to be equally applicable.

Scientifically, that is of course untenable: a model is a simplified representation of the real world, and if a relevant piece of that reality fits into all three models, then the point is not that the real world is mixed, but that the models are unfit for an empirical description of that particular piece of the social reality. From an analytical point of view, Klok performs a little better by claiming that three different tools are applied respectively: a communicative, a legal and an economic tool (Klok, 1991, p. 172). However, for the civil servants, administrators and the business community involved – that is, empirically – there is only one tool, which is simply called a labelling regulation. That can be visualized, it exists, and that is what they must deal with.

I have attempted to think up a tool which is not mixed according to this train of thought, but I have failed. Is there any government activity which does not have a legal basis, or contain any economic component, or involve communication? Even if such activities do exist, they can never be very substantial or relevant. If our theory of policy tools for public administration does not, therefore, link up with the terms which define and must define the reality of public administration and consequently the tools involved, we are not going to get anywhere.

Second, we should realize that a theory of policy tools can only have significance within a relevant theoretical framework. After all, a tool is only a tool if it is instrumental in achieving a certain objective. With this in mind, we see something rather interesting. COBA concentrated on a proper analysis of objectives and assumed that once the main objective had been split up into simple sub-objectives, the choice of the appropriate tool would follow automatically. In their approach, the policy objectives are at the forefront. According to Geelhoed, the most sensible objectives to be chosen by the public administration follow from the possibilities offered by the available tools. Only what falls within the range of these possibilities is worth being made into a policy objective. Bressers and Klok, and others too, teach us that very little can be deduced from the intrinsic qualities of the tools, and that we should concentrate instead on the core circumstances in which the tools are applied. Indeed, those circumstances include objectives. Certainly, but these are not policy objectives, but rather the private objectives of those who implement the policy or are subjected to it. The policy objectives themselves have completely disappeared.

If anything is beautifully illustrated by this development in the policy tools approach, it is the fact that the interpretation of government policy in which objectives are chosen, the instruments (tools) pertaining to those objectives selected, those tools weighed on the basis of a cost–benefit analysis, and so on, is in most cases totally inadequate. It may look very rational, but it is also very normative, because it does not correspond with what we perceive. The empirical reality of policy making is very different. If the policy objectives fall, the policy tools fall too, because it is the policy objectives which make any government action instrumental, and if the policy tools fall, the related theory naturally falls with them.

Third, the existing theory does not say anything at all about the actual process of choosing policy tools. Klok distinguishes between a theory and a doctrine of policy tools. The theory deals with the effects, while, according to Klok, the doctrine is concerned with the choice of the tools. But alas, the content of the doctrine is nowhere to be found. Klok and the others only deal with the effects of the implemented tools. So what we have is merely an evaluation technique, and its authors have always acknowledged it rather shamelessly as such, but without being prepared to give up the term 'theory of policy tools'; witness a chapter by Bressers on the theory of policy tools in a book on policy evaluation (Bressers, 1991, *passim*).

The question we should now concentrate on and which will complete the sociogenesis of the policy tools approach, is: why is the term 'tools' used so frequently in an empty sense? Why does De Bruijn reject the theory of policy tools in his thesis (De Bruijn, 1990, p. 37 ff.) only to reintroduce it in an indirect way (tools as filter or technology of the organization), although he does not need that framework at all for his empirical analysis of the economic subsidies granted by the Department of Economic Affairs? Why did Bressers and Klok set out on their 'mission impossible' and why did they call the evaluation theory they developed a 'theory of policy tools'? Where on earth do that word and the thinking in those terms stem from?

Various social sources can be given. Firstly the spirit of the times. Weber distinguished 'wertrational' from 'zweckrational', Mannheim differentiated between instrumental and substantial reason, the Frankfurt school and Habermas waged war against the 'positivistisch halbierte Vernunft' which they saw arising everywhere, but it was to no avail. Nowadays, rational is always goal-rational, and goal-rational thinking means instrumental thinking. It is in the air and you can smell it everywhere.

But there are also more specific origins than the macrosocial context. Ringeling has worked out where the term 'policy tools' was used for the first time in the Netherlands. It was not in academia, but in public administration, in official reports and documents. From there it started its triumphant march through the country. COBA and Geelhoed, whose backgrounds were to be found not in science but in the civil service, are illustrative examples. I also have the impression that the extensive literature in which the word 'tool' occurs in an empty sense is predominantly written by reflective practitioners, by people whose daily activities are directly or indirectly concerned with public administration and who occasionally write about it.

Given the position public administration has assumed, due to the development of the welfare state, that is quite understandable. The public administration must act; there are evils to be fought; there are political and social pressures to be taken into account. Anyone who wants to achieve something within public administration is faced with problems, so it is better not to want too much; every civil servant, however, every administrator, every politician is supposed to do something. Activity, action – something must be done all the time, or at least the impression must be created that something is being done. Although that perspective of activity has always existed, it used to be much less dominant. Anyone who has to do anything will ask: 'How am I going to do it? What tools do I have at my disposal?' And in the case of a failure – which sometimes seems to happen – the same terminology offers a beautiful excuse: 'I didn't have the right tools.' That is of course nobody's fault.

As I mentioned earlier, a retouched image of reality is almost indispensable in order to function adequately in public administration. At least it is highly functional for the personal well-being of all persons involved. In public administration, a considerable proportion of the time is devoted to things which are not supposed to occur, or in any case should not be called by their real names and consequently do not really exist. Spending departments never make the slightest effort to fool the Ministry of Finance, office politics does not exist, civil servants do not steer policy decisions, departments do not have tribal disputes, there are certainly no symbolic policies, hidden agendas do not exist either, strategic information is never withheld, and so on. For that reason, the public administration can very well do without analyses of those kinds of phenomena – except when it happens to be convenient, for instance in a battle with another department – because such analyses are most confusing, damaging as they do the functional self-image. It is evident that these non-existent phenomena cause numerous problems, but such problems can be conveniently expressed in technical terms such as 'too complex objectives' or 'missing or inadequate tools'. Technical errors are also errors, of course, but they can more easily be forgiven and corrected than can the action of giving highest priority to the interest of the department, administrative obstruction or political activities by bodies which lack democratic legitimation by the electorate. In this way, criticism remains administratively and politically manageable, if things have got too obviously out of hand.

Professor Brasz wrote to me in a personal communication:

Eventually, all attempts to bind bureaucracies ... to a goal-rational approach result in increasing rigidity. These attempts ... have been extremely successful as regards the words used. The [public] administration has come to speak the language of policy analysis. But it does not help a great deal ...

That observation seems correct to me, because the difference between the professional language of many academic policy analysts on the one hand and civil servants, administrators and politicians with the proper education on the other hand is often hard to detect. They all talk about clear objectives, goal achievement, choosing the right tools, and the need for adequate coordination between them. But the important question here is, who has adopted whose professional language? Who, because of their structural social position, is obliged to think and speak about policy in terms of goals to achieve and tools to implement? In view of the observations we made earlier this is a rhetorical question, one is inclined to say. But whoever, in an attempt to be equally rhetorical, suggests that it is policy analysis itself which is responsible for choosing concepts which are so convenient for public administration, who furthermore suggests that policy analysis is not obliged to do so, because it is an intellectually independent activity, overlooks something. According to a particular interpretation of the field of study, that cannot be the case.

Public administration can only be improved directly by science by means of recommendations in terms of a goal-rational approach. After all, those who make strategic, tactical or political recommendations for the benefit of a certain government agency X, which is in dispute with department Y, are in favour of or serving X, and so are against Y, and are consequently no longer independent. In the long run, therefore, they lose – even in their own eyes – their scientific aura and the knowledge they produce will show partiality. However, civil servants are also very skilful in that respect – probably even more so, because many of them not only have a university degree but also know the field and the context in which the knowledge must be applied far better than any academic researcher.

In order to achieve direct improvements, recommendations must be made. Scientific recommendations, therefore, must be presented in the form of a goal-rational approach lest they be rejected as being partial. No self-respecting person can make recommendations in terms of a goal-rational approach if he/she does not sincerely believe that the most important component of the research object falls within that framework. I do not in any way doubt the integrity of such analyses. They can even be very critical and may be most unpleasant reading for the public administration.

However, it is immanent rather than transcendent criticism. It remains within the normative self-image which public administration must have. The fact that the starting-point of this type of analysis is of a purely normative nature can easily be concealed because the point at issue is not normativeness in the sense of a party-political view. The available models are, after all, purely rational, and their only normative aspect is the fact that the real world of policy making looks rather different. For that reason, we do have an ingenious method for scientifically designing goal-rational policies, but not for designing symbolic policies. For the same reason, there is a theory of policy tools for environmental policy, but not for the annual battle between the spending departments and the Ministry of Finance, although for each department this annually recurring confrontation consumes far more administrative energy than environmental policy.

Let there be no misunderstanding about it: I am not pleading for such subversive instrumental studies – I only want to point out why they do not exist. For public administration, there are officially no such problems. Those who look at policy in a rational way do not permit such phenomena other than in the form of regrettable blunders for which, of course, a rational remedy is recommended.

This constellation of the albeit functional, but nevertheless highly coloured self-image of public administration, the very respectable wish of scientists to improve the functioning of public administration, the normative but respectable (because totally rational) starting-point of a strong trend in the study of public administration – that complex of social factors has been responsible for the sociogenesis of the approach in terms of policy tools and has prompted studies such as that by Klok. His is a study which an otherwise sympathetic critic has called a classic misunderstanding between science and practice (Idema, 1991, p. 39).

My objections, however, do not only concern Klok; that would be extremely unfair. My objections are concerned with a manner of thinking and analysing which, because it aims at being useful for both the science and the practice of public administration, cannot fail to yield products which serve neither purpose. This is why I repeat once more the old plea for a distinction between scientific and practical knowledge. That distinction does exist and it makes sense, as every organizational consultant will confirm, and it should also become evident in the science of public administration. The first type of knowledge is not aimed at improving public administration, but at being subservient to society by analysing what happens within public administration. It attempts to be objective, uncovers and debunks myths, and does not care about the practical usefulness of its knowledge. Insight, understanding what happens – that is what it is interested in (for an example of such an analysis, see Baakman, 1990).

The other type of public administration knowledge is subservient to practice. It is clever, partial if necessary (in the way a lawyer may, within his professional code, be partial in respect of his client's interests), diplomatic, and concerned about the usefulness of its knowledge and recommendations (for an example, see Baakman, 1992). It is possible to play both roles, even for one single public administration expert, albeit not simultaneously. There are also legitimate arguments in favour of both viewpoints. But they should not be blended. That would be an intellectual disaster.

11. On instruments and instrumentality: a critical assessment

Frans K.M. van Nispen and Arthur B. Ringeling

1. INTRODUCTION

The policy sciences have been characterized by Lasswell by three objectives. They had to be problem-oriented and contextual in nature, multidisciplinary in approach, and explicitly normative in perspective. He called for 'a very considerable clarification of the value goals involved in policy' (Lasswell, 1951, p. 9). On the one hand, they were *descriptive*, looking for explanations. On the other hand, they have been *prescriptive* from the very beginning, looking for improvements. Not surprisingly, the diminished expectations about the capacity of government have made the question current again as to how to achieve the often conflicting policy objectives: the general welfare of the population has to be fostered, the government expenditure has to be put in order, inflation has to be stopped and the law has to be maintained. This has given birth to the study of policy instruments.

In this chapter we shall ask what the study of policy instruments has contributed to the body of knowledge of the policy sciences. A critical assessment will be made of the pros and cons of the instrumental view of policy making. In the traditional view a goal is set. The application of the means to attain that goal is seen as mechanic, as social engineering (Section 2). Much time and energy are spent on developing a distinct classification of instruments, but none turns out to be totally exclusive or exhaustive (Section 3). Besides, the selection of means is not only directed by goals, looking for the best tools to attain these goals. An instrument may be chosen for quite other reasons. It may be used because of a positive experience, because of its appeal, because of political reasons and because of the low visibility of that means (Section 4). The foundation of the study of instruments is provided by the rational central-rule approach. The view of the government as the central, dominant actor is heavily criticized, because it pays scant attention to policy implementation (Section 5). Besides, we have to be aware that we are using a metaphor when talking about instruments. A metaphor highlights specific characteristics, but may attribute to means qualities which they don't in reality possess. Not surprisingly, expectations about the potential of these instruments are not met (Section 6). Furthermore, goal attainment as the one and only yardstick to evaluate the application of instruments may be questioned (Section 7). It turns out that the means employed by the government are only one of the many variables that shape society, reflecting the revival of an old question in the policy sciences. In recent years we have seen a shift from instruments to the role of institutions as a resource as well as a constraint for the selection of means. A preference for a specific instrument, for example, may be seen as a constraint (Section 8). A summing-up completes our assessment of the pros and cons of the instrumental view of policy making and implementation.

2.   A QUESTION OF INSTRUMENTALISM?

In the past considerable attention has been paid to the relationship between goals and means. A policy was analysed in terms of its official goals and means, especially in government documents. The term 'policy instrument' became a popular one in Dutch official documents, more than among policy analysts. The systematic study of policy instruments was largely lacking. Even the arguments for the study of policy instruments were seldom heard, as a result of which many tools are overlooked in practice. This has produced a striking lack of prescriptive knowledge in public administration (Dror, 1971, p. 72).

The lack of attention to policy instruments in the American context may be explained by the habit of putting policies into programmes. Evaluation was also done on that level. It typically aimed at 'discovering whether programs work' (Langbein, 1980). The relative success of programmes was studied, but the insights from individual evaluations were often not related to the results of other programmes. The evaluations were restricted to specific means. The meta-question: what is the relative success of policy instruments and in which circumstances? was, with a few exceptions, not addressed. However, this is not to say that instruments and instrumentalism have no roots in public administration. Sometimes these phenomena were referred to as administrative techniques. They are seen as the 'nuts and bolts' of public administration (Henry, 1975, p. 22).

The study of policy instruments has also been stimulated by instrumentalism and social engineering. The importance of instrumentalism for the study of law is underlined by authors such as Holmes, Dewey and Pound, who have argued that the law may be used as a means to attain non-juridical goals. A rule is seen as the result of political aims and scholarly creativity. The realization of these goals demands a complicated implementation mechanism. So, a technology of law and social engineering is required or, to put it differently, a pragmatic view of government thinks in terms of instruments (Stillman, 1991, pp. 185–7).

3.   THE SEARCH FOR A CLASSIFICATION OF POLICY INSTRUMENTS

The question may be raised as to what constitutes a policy instrument and, more specifically, whether they are more than just means. Some authors refer to instruments as 'everything that is used to influence policy processes in order to reach a desirable situation' (COBA, 1976, p. 18), while other authors include the notion of a certain categorization or a set of means (Kuypers, 1980, p. 373). In that view means are seen as activities that have some characteristics in common, for example, a rule or a plan. A rule may be seen as a means. Still others state that instruments are only officially attributed, legitimate means. So Needham (1982) defines instruments as possibilities to govern that are 'legally available to public bodies' (p. 3). Sharing this definition are authors who stick to tools with a formal character. It is more or less acceptable nowadays to see instruments in terms of an object. Unfortunately, the conceptualization of instruments as objects runs the risk of reification. The government should even have a 'toolkit' (Hood, 1983; Bressers and Klok, 1987b, p. 78). However, a policy maker does not have a toolkit at his/her disposal from which he/she is free to choose one instrument to deal with a problem.

Much time and energy have been spent in developing a distinct classification of instruments (Van der Doelen, 1989). It is nowadays more or less accepted to make a distinction between three 'families' of instruments (Hoogerwerf, 1995, p. 230). The first family consists of *regulatory* instruments, such as orders and prohibitions (licences, permits, regulations). The second family embraces *financial* means. These instruments are more stimulative and less coercive than regulatory instruments. They may be positive (grants, subsidies) as well as negative (taxes and user charges) front a consumer's point of view. The third family includes *communicative* tools, which may be directed at the increase as well as the decrease of the degree of information of the other party. Hood has added a fourth category, that he called *organization*, referring to direct action as well as treatments (Hood, 1983).

The traditional instruments generated for a hierarchical relationship are no longer, if they ever were, appropriate in a network setting. A bottom–up approach will perform better, as many researchers state, than a top–down approach. The introduction of a second 'generation' of instruments (De Bruijn and Ten Heuvelhof, 1991a) has directed our attention to the importance of contingent variables, giving birth to bilateral or even multilateral means such as covenants. The new tools often have the same name, but the unilateral character has been replaced by a bilateral or even a multilateral character (Kooiman, 1993, p. 4). They take into account that you may lead a horse to the water, but you cannot make him drink. This reflects the changed view about the appropriate role of government, which is no longer seen as omnipotent. However, these tools still look for manipulative variables and, therefore, represent an instrumental view of government.

Unfortunately, we have to conclude that none of these classifications is exhaustive and mutual exclusive. However, this does not mean that the efforts to generate a classification of instruments have been totally useless. We were not trying to develop a classification on the basis of the characteristics of the effects of instruments in reality. A hammer may give the same result as a screwdriver in specific circumstances. Besides, it is sometimes difficult to single out the effects of a specific instrument, because means almost always turn out to be part of a mix. A tool frequently takes the form of a regulation. A public organization is, for instance, not allowed to allocate subsidies without a foundation in law because of the legality principle. This constitutes the difference between going by the book and arbitrariness, which may cause a problem for the development of a classification of instruments on the basis of their consequences. A distinction between very broad categories is what remains. However, that is not to say that it is useless: it may have a heuristic value in the analysis as well as the design of a policy.

Finally, the question may be raised as to why we should restrict ourselves to the formal means. Certainly an important part of the process of policy making is directed towards the production of instruments such as regulations, finance or money or, as Hood would say, planning procedures or organizational structures. A policy often consists of the combination and use of these means. A subsidy, for example, often appears as a rule configuration and is accompanied by an information campaign. Mostly, but not always. When we stick to the official tools, we miss all those informal instruments that are not mentioned in the process of policy making, but nevertheless are frequently used in practice. In practice, many other means are used to influence the developments in society: negotiations, mobilization of political support, persuasion, the appointment of people who have proved that they can be trusted, giving opponents the boot, threat, deceit and double-crossing. Moreover, formal instruments can be used in an informal way, for example, a regulation can be used in another way than was intended, a subsidy can be used to buy off a hazard. A public policy is often a combination of the formal instruments, put in writing, and the informal means of domination and persuasion, of pushing and pulling, of wheeling and dealing. The formal world is a paper world, a domain for armchair scholars. The informal world consists of political games with no other content than conquering and fortifying power positions. It is of little use to study just one of these worlds. A good policy analyst combines both.

4.   THE SELECTION OF INSTRUMENTS

A policy instrument may be chosen for a variety of reasons. The instrumentalist approach assumes that means are selected according to the goals. We can talk about the optimization of the relationship between goals and means. However, it is doubtful whether that presumption is correct. The selection of instruments often has nothing to do with optimization. The examples of the selection of instruments on other grounds than optimization are countless. They may be chosen because of cultural or institutional reasons. The organization may be more familiar with some instruments than with others. The application of rules, for example, is often associated with the Department of Justice, while subsidies are more characteristic of the Department of Economic Affairs. It is even possible that the goals change dramatically, but that the means stay untouched (Hufen, 1990).

A means may also be chosen because it is fashionable. Some tools are 'in', other means are 'out'. The question is not whether they are optimal or not, but whether they are popular or not. A policy maker who wants to show that he understands the current spirit of the times will choose instruments that are in vogue. A good example is privatization, which is rather fashionable nowadays. On the contrary, regulation is no longer fashionable. The call for deregulation is almost worldwide (Majone, 1990). One may question whether this is appropriate for all sectors of society in a variety of countries, because there is no evidence at all that regulation has gone too far everywhere. The regulations may have adverse effects in some post-industrialist countries and then in a specific policy area, but it is highly doubtful that the same is true for the regulations of the same policy area in, say, underdeveloped countries. Here fashion takes the lead over optimization again. The universal claim for deregulation seems to be more an expression of a fashion, a preference for the market or a prejudice against the government. Moreover, it underscores important functions that regulation can have (Breyer, 1982; Majone, 1989).

Finally, a policy instrument may be selected because it improves the position of some actors and/or weakens the position of others. A means with a great deal of discretion puts the implementing organization in a better position. When policy makers try to take a firm grip on the policy process they construct a tool that offers little leeway to the street-level organizations. Whether these efforts are successful is another question. Instruments are also chosen because the beneficiaries have a preference for them, more than the policy makers (Bagchus, 1996). A barely visible instrument, such as a tax expenditure, is often preferred by stakeholders than a more visible means, such as a subsidy. The selection of tools is, to put it differently, not made on more or less objective criteria such as effectiveness and/or efficiency, but upon subjective criteria such as availability, experience, preference or routine.

5. THE APPLICATION OF INSTRUMENTS

The instrumental approach to the government is built on the rational central-rule approach. The view of the government as the central, dominant actor is heavily criticized because of its mechanical and, therefore, unrealistic character (Van Gunsteren, 1976). It is built on the assumption that the actors who have to enforce the rule are puppets on a string. However, these actors have their own preferences. This approach may be appropriate for a relatively stable environment, but lacks the requisite variety to deal with dynamic systems. It smacks of 'social engineering', assuming that the fruits of scientific research may help to solve problems in society (Ringeling, 1983, p. 6).

Besides, it may give the false impression that the adjustment of market failures is the one and only rationale for the government intervention (Wolf, 1993). It might be true for the role of the government in America, but not in Europe. In the European context, the government exists in its own right and is not merely considered as a safety-net for the market (Rosenthal and Van Nispen, 1988; Ringeling, 1993a).

Moreover, it turns out that government is not the conductor – to use another metaphor – of an orchestra, but one of the musicians. Indeed, society can be considered as an orchestra without a conductor. The actors in society not only have their own values and goals; they also have their own preferences with respect to the instruments. They may prefer the sermon to the whip, the carrot to the stick. But regulation can also be a source of rights, and subsidies can bring competitors in a better position. An important part of the political struggle over a public policy results not only from different political preferences, but also from interest groups fighting among each other about the means that government should use.

Finally, interest groups have contra-instruments at their disposal. It is an illusion to think that regulations are, and economic means are not, influenced by political pressure as Majone has stated (Majone, 1989, pp. 143–4). First, because economic tools have also been shaped as regulations. Second, because interest groups will fight as hard on incentives as they do on regulation. In the Netherlands the proposal for an energy tax was contested so hard by the big energy consumers, heavy industry, that they were exempted. The experience with policy instruments provides a totally different view of the role of government from that offered by the rational central-rule approach. The expectations about the potential accomplishments of government have to be reduced.

6. POLICY INSTRUMENTS AS A METAPHOR

One of the criticisms of the instrumentalists is that they ignore the dynamic character of the relationship between goals and means. The goals are considered as given once and for all, whereas a continuous process of goal-succession is taking place (Hogwood and Peters, 1983). It makes no sense to use a goal that is no longer up to date as a criterion to evaluate the effectiveness of a policy. On the one hand, it may give the false impression that a policy was a success. On the other hand, it may conceal that a policy was a failure (Hoogerwerf, 1977, p. 304; Herweijer, 1981, pp. 357–62).[1] Besides, means are not related to one single goal, but to a number often conflicting goals referring to a variety of interests or stakes. It is sometimes easier to agree upon the means than on the goals, leaving the goals silent (Lindbolm, 1959).

The opposite may also be true. The goals are sometimes seen as very general, often symbolic statements without any reference to the means.

The instrumentalists do not take into account that goals and means are relative concepts, that is, a goal might be a means and a means might be a goal or, to put it differently, 'instruments cannot be neatly separated from goals' (Majone, 1989, p. 117). This is not the first time, and certainly not the last time, that political rhetoric has slipped into the analysis. It is difficult to study the machinery of government without getting grease on our hands. There are some risks. Misleading metaphors easily slip into our analyses when we use political language. We become part of the political scene and lose the distance needed for good analysis.

The concept of policy instruments – whether used in academia or in practice – is a metaphor. One can speak of figurative language. The utilization of metaphors is quite common in our daily conversation, in scientific research and, more specifically, in the study of policy instruments (Hogwood and Peters, 1985). It highlights specific characteristics of a phenomenon. In his well-known study Landau has suggested that a metaphor can be a great help in giving direction to research activities, in developing interpretative systems and criteria to determine what is important and what is not (Landau, 1979). In brief, metaphors are an important means for the generation of knowledge.

The comparison of a policy instrument with a hammer, a pair of pincers or a screwdriver is appealing, but may also be misleading (Ringeling, 1983, pp. 22–3). A metaphor may influence the way in which political and social problems are perceived and the direction in which solutions of these problems are sought. The implementation of the solutions found in that way may lead to unintended and unforeseen problems that overshadow the original problems (Schuyt, 1982, pp. 15–17). A metaphor attributes qualities to means that they do not have in reality and, therefore, may raise expectations that cannot be met. A rule, for instance, is based on a mechanistic view. It reflects a causal or deterministic method of inquiry, directed at the creation of the conditions to make a rule as effective as possible. A rule is, as such, typically the expression of 'social engineering' (Ringeling, 1983, p. 8).

The danger of misconception is present every time we use a metaphor, at least when Schuyt's argument holds. So, inevitably the question arises as to what extent the metaphor fits and where it leads us astray. We run the risk of instrumentalistic thinking, of a mechanistic approach to policy processes: the planning and implementation fit neatly, the goals and means are linked to each other, the means are ready for utilization and the effects are clear. The picture thus created of policy processes is one in which there is no uncertainty. The policy maker is a craftsman who has mastered his toolkit.

The instrumentalistic metaphor may lead to three wrong tracks. The first is that we consider instruments as neutral means and deprive them of their political character. However, tools are not neutral at all. The second is that effectiveness becomes the only relevant yardstick for the evaluation of the utilization of tools. However, the government has to take other values into consideration. The third track is that we assume that the policy maker controls the instruments, but in practice policy makers often turn out to be the victims of their instruments. They don't have a free choice from the toolkit. Their knowledge of the effects of means is limited and their possibility of manipulating the tools is restricted.

Finally, we would like to add that not only official policy makers use instruments. A policy is shaped in a process with a number of actors, with instruments of their own. Sometimes means are shared, but more often tools are confronted with each other. We shall elaborate on this later.

7.   EFFECTIVENESS AS THE ONE AND ONLY YARDSTICK

The instrumentalists have goal attainment in their sights, but they have not been very successful in relating instruments to changes in society. This is partly due to methodological problems. A control group – as required by the experimental model – is often not at their disposal or is rejected from a moral point of view. Besides, we often miss empirical data about the situation before the intervention. Furthermore, effectiveness doesn't necessarily mean goal attainment and visa versa, as the Dutch retrenchment policy in the 1980s shows. At first sight, the efforts to reduce the deficit were very successful – the targets were met – but a closer look revealed that the achievements were mainly due to a boost in the economy.[2] However, the effectiveness of the retrenchment policy of that time wasn't very high. In addition, it is very hard to isolate the impact of the application of instruments because of the interdependence of instruments and the interrelation of all kinds of processes in society.

Furthermore, a distinction has to be made between instruments on paper and instruments in practice. It may be argued that the *application* of instruments is more important than the instruments laid down in policy. The application of instruments is governed by at least two mechanisms (In 't Veld, 1993). First, policy means become obsolete after some time, because stakeholders learn how to cope with instruments and resist them. As a result, the effectiveness of tools diminishes over time. Second, policy makers tend to respond in the same way to the effectiveness or ineffectiveness of instruments. They ask for more of the same. The law of policy accumulation and the law of diminishing effectiveness play leapfrog. In the end, policy systems will collapse if no breakthrough is forced.

Effectiveness may be a shaky standard by which to measure the success of a policy instrument, especially when it is chosen on grounds that have little to do with the optimization of the relationship between goals and means. It is not enough to take considerations other than this optimization into account. It is even questionable whether it is desirable to use effectiveness as the unique standard. The choice for effectiveness is by no means neutral (Simonis and Lehning, 1987, p. 19; Lehning, 1991, p. 9; Ringeling, 1993a, pp. 74–6). The question was not relevant for the logic positivist paradigm or for pragmatism, because a distinction is made between value premises and factual premises (Simon, 1945).[3] The value premises were given; the factual premises had to be found. They could be the product of good analysis. It was another way of saying that means were neutral. The means, as Machiavelli has stated, are sanctified by the goals.

A policy instrument is not neutral and represents values of its own. We have to make a distinction between acceptable and unacceptable means. In most circumstances negotiations are preferred to the utilization of force, and prevention is considered better than the solution of societal problems. A public inquiry is often directed to the acceptability of a specific instrument by public authorities rather than to the legitimacy of the goals. Perhaps it is characteristic of the value-loaded public sector that the means are not neutral. When we use the instrumentalist metaphor we easily neglect the political or ideological character of means. The instrumental metaphor may lead us astray, because political parties have a preference for a specific instrument. The liberals of the nineteenth century, for example, stressed the importance of regulation as a defence against the arbitrariness of rulers. The Christian democrats emphasized the importance of voluntary organizations as a prevention of an omnipotent public sector. The social democrats have put planning on the throne as a weapon against the waste of the market. The political debate has often concentrated on the means and these discussions had nothing to do with optimization, but a deeply rooted difference of opinion about the appropriate role of government (Ringeling, 1988). Furthermore, some degree of ineffectiveness has to be accepted due to the interrelationships of instruments. The discretion of governments to use a means in a flexible, even optimal way will be restricted considerably when a subsidy or an organization is structured by a regulation. A subsidy is not granted when there is a change in behaviour, but when the applicant meets the criteria. A treatment is not used when it is apt, but when there is a legal basis.

We have to conclude that effectiveness is a highly dubious standard with respect to instruments. The means of government will always have a certain degree of ineffectiveness as a consequence of the interrelationship of tools and, therefore, we have to accept some degree of suboptimization. Furthermore, by using effectiveness as an unique, dominating value, we easily lose the value-loaded character of the public sector from sight.

8.   WHAT MATTERS: INSTRUMENTS OR INSTITUTIONS?

The relationship between instruments and organizations is a double one. On the one hand, organizations apply means. On the other hand, organizations are seen as tools. However, it has to be stressed that an organizational unit is hidden behind an instrument. A subsidy, for instance, may be allocated by an organizational unit of a department, but that organizational unit is not like clay in the hands of the head of that department. On the contrary, it has a mind and preferences of its own. It raises the question of alternative rule configurations such as rule-guided versus discretionary behaviour (Kiser and Ostrom, 1982).

In addition, an organizational unit will structure the problem at hand along familiar lines. For example, an organizational unit granting licences will perceive a problem as one that can be solved by licences. However, the provision of better information might have been a more effective or a less expensive means. Besides, regulations are often more profitable for beneficiaries than taxation, although taxation may be more attractive from a theoretical point of view (Buchanan and Tullock, 1975). The formulation of strict standards for vehicles, for instance, makes it more and more difficult for new car manufacturers to enter the market. However, stakeholders don't always have a preference for regulations above taxation, as the case of international freight transport shows. It is clear that freight transport by road causes much more damage to the environment than that by rail or by water. However, regulation of freight transport has failed due to the opposition of the truckers. Instead, they have accepted a higher taxation on petrol (Theeuwes, 1993); Rietveld and Van Wissen, 1993, p. 102).

Recent developments in the policy sciences have directed our attention once again to the role of institutions[4] as a resource as well as a constraint for policy making.[5] A variety of approaches, concepts, methods and theories is put forward. The principal–agent model, amongst others, seeks attention for incentives as a tool. The role of incentives is at least twofold. First of all, a policy maker may use incentives to stimulate subordinates to meet his/her demands. Second, incentives may be used to direct the behaviour of the stakeholders. However, the utilization of incentives is not new. The same point was made earlier in the area of public choice (Olson, 1965; Niskanen, 1971; Breton and Wintrobe, 1982). Moreover, one may question what else a subsidy is than a positive incentive.

9. SUMMING-UP: WHERE DO WE STAND?

The instrumental view of government seems to fit more into the American than into the European tradition. In the European view, the government is not merely a safety-net for the market. A number of services is traditionally provided by or on behalf of the government. Surprisingly, instrumentalism has received much more attention in the European context, though that may be due to a difference in terminology. The whole bulk of literature on policy analysis, seen as utilization-focused research, for instance, points in the same direction. A positive exception is Majone, who has made a strong stand for a more argumentative approach in policy analysis (Majone, 1989, pp. 116–45).

The instrumental view of the government has left its mark. The direct impact on the policy sciences may be small, especially in the USA, but the indirect impact on public policy is hard to neglect. It has forced policy makers to think in terms of goals and means, in terms of effectiveness, which they did not do before. It has improved the communication between policy makers as well as between these policy makers and policy analysts.

Much attention is paid to specific instruments and their classification. It is nowadays common to make a distinction between three 'families' and two 'generations' of instruments. Unfortunately, none of these classifications is exhaustive and mutually exclusive. Furthermore, they pay scant attention to the informal means. It is time to admit that the efforts to produce a classification of instruments on the basis of their characteristics and the characteristics of their effects is a dead-end street.

In the last few years we have experienced a shift to the selection of instruments. The instrumentalists assume that means are chosen because of the optimization of the relationship between goals and means.

However, the selection of tools has often nothing to do with optimization, for example, they are often chosen because they are fashionable
or unobtrusive. It may be argued that the application is even more
important than the selection of instruments. The instrumentalists assume
that the actors who have to enforce the rules are puppets on a string.
However, these actors have their own preferences. Besides, it turns out
that government is one of the players in the policy arena.

The instrumentalists have goal attainment and, therefore, effectiveness in their sights. However, it is often difficult to single out the effects
of a specific instrument, because instruments are often revealed as a
part of a mix of instruments and, therefore, we have to accept some
degree of sub-optimization. Besides, effectiveness is not the one and
only value that the government has to allocate. Furthermore, we have
to be continuously aware that we use a metaphor when we talk about
instruments. The comparison of a means with a hammer, a pair of
pincers or a screwdriver is appealing, but may also be misleading to
some extent. A metaphor attributes to instruments qualities which they
do not have in reality and, therefore, may raise expectations that cannot
be met. We easily neglect, for example, the political or ideological
character of instruments.

A number of adjustments has been made in the last few years, of
which establishment of a link with the institutional and the contextual
variables is the most important. However, they still represent an instrumental view of the government and are – as such – fine-tunings of an
old song rather than a new song about the role of government in society.
The recent debate on the appropriate role of government has shifted
the study of policy instruments away from the characteristics of specific
policy instruments to the interaction of policy instruments as applied
by multiple actors. On the one hand, it has enriched the study of policy
instruments by introducing new policy instruments. On the other hand,
it has extended the scope of the study of policy instruments to policy
processes (Ringeling, 1993b, p. 201) in which policy instruments are
'only' one of the many variables that shape the outcome of these policy
processes. It reflects a more enlightened view of instruments in which
means are no longer associated with instrumentalism.

NOTES

1. A different question is whether the official goal is the right criterion to evaluate a
    policy. There is a number of alternative yardsticks, such as adequacy, efficiency, equity
    or equality and legitimacy (Brewer and DeLeon, 1983; Wolf, 1993). Besides, the

criterion of intersubjective agreement is used to evaluate a policy in the hermeneutic or interpretative approach.

2. The Dutch government, therefore, has decided no longer to relate the spending cap to a yardstick such as GDP.

3. Behind that distinction traces can be found of the old dichotomy between politics and administration (Wilson, 1887).

4. We would like to stress that an institution isn't the same as an organization. The latter can be seen as an institution, but an institution also includes, for instance, a rule configuration.

5. The growing interest in the meaning of institutions was recently articulated in a conference of the Netherlands Inter-university Institute of Government on *The Role of Institutions in the Public Sector: Constraints or Resources for Policy Making?*, Oosterbeek, The Netherlands, 9–10 November 1995. The meeting was part of a broader research project on the importance of institutions in public administration.

Epilogue

B. Guy Peters and Frans K.M. van Nispen

1. THE ROLE OF GOVERNMENT

Government is under attack. In most industrialized countries a debate is going on about the appropriate role of government. The government is forced to step back in favour of the market. The people in the street don't like politicians; bureaucrat bashing is a popular pastime. Not surprisingly, the study of policy instruments is facing the consequences of this attitude to government.

The first development that may affect the study of policy instruments has to do with the debate about the appropriate role of government. In his last *State of the Union* address President Clinton announced that the era of big government is over, though nobody seems to have a replacement in mind (Eisenach in Solomon, 1996, p. 866). He called for:

> a leaner, but not a meaner government that cuts yesterday's programs and bureaucracy to make room for tomorrow's solutions, rooted in responsibility, empowerment of our citizens, the strength of our communities. (Clinton, 1996)

The American government has never been that big, but the market is more regulated than in most European countries. Not surprisingly, deregulation is more of an issue than on the other side of the Atlantic. The opposite is true for privatization which, especially in England, has taken off. However, the consequence is the same, that is, a *smaller* government.

Second, the Clinton administration has established a large-scale effort to re-invent government, referring to David Osborne and Ted Gaebler's bestseller (Osborne and Gaebler, 1992). The vice-president has launched a plan for a more *entrepreneurial* government, that 'works better and cost less' (Gore, 1993). The majority of the ideas are not new, but they are for the first time combined together in a conceptual framework. The last development is the introduction of performance-oriented organizations, which in Europe is matched by the creation of agencies or semi-autonomous bodies to improve efficiency in the public sector.[1]

A third development that will have an impact on the study of policy instruments is related to the efforts to reduce the budget deficit. One of the requirements for entry into the European Monetary Union (EMU) is a budget deficit of not more than 3 per cent of GDP. The retrenchment policy of the American government is even targeted at a balanced budget. The budget deficit has to be zeroed out over a period of six years. The consequences are clear: the welfare state is under attack. All kind of provisions will be cut back and we shall have to wait and see whether the market will take over.

2. THE STUDY OF POLICY INSTRUMENTS: WHAT'S UP?

The study of policy instruments has a long history that goes back to the very beginning of the policy sciences. The present attention to policy instruments in academia is preceded by the efforts of the government to determine the consequences of its actions (Baakman, Chapter 10, p. 200). The interest in the impact of its tools has stimulated policy makers to think in terms of (the link between) goals and means, which may be seen as one of the most important improvements in government since the war (Klaassen and Van Nispen, 1995).

The study of policy instruments has for a long time been dominated by efforts to categorize policy instruments according to their character- istics. None of them turns out to be mutually exclusive and/or totally exhaustive. It is nowadays common to make a distinction between three *families* of policy instruments (Van der Doelen, 1989). The recent introduction of a second *generation* of policy instruments may be seen as fine-tuning to a new situation. The new policy instruments often go under the same label as the old policy instruments, but the emphasis is no longer on the unilateral aspect of governance. The focus is more on the bilateral or even the multilateral aspect (Kooiman, 1993, p. 4). This is the admission that the government is only one of the players in the game and the other players also have instruments, call them contra-instruments, at their disposal. It reflects another view of the role of government. Government is no longer seen as a conductor, but more as one of the musicians (Van Nispen and Ringeling, Chapter 11, p. 210).

The agenda is more or less set by De Bruijn and Hufen (Chapter 1) who claim that the study of policy instruments moves away from the *classical* approach in favour of a more *contextual* approach to policy instruments.[2] This opens the door to all kinds of other variables, because instruments are only one of the many variables that explain what happens in society. Besides, it has raised the study of policy instruments from the micro to the meso-level, that is, to the level of a network.

The shift away from the traditional approach to policy instruments has important consequences for the focus of study. The process of implementation has become more important than the outcome of that process and, therefore, goal attainment is less of an issue. The reduced significance of the stated goal is especially true for the hermeneutic approach to policy instruments in which effectiveness is of less importance than mutual understanding (Linder and Peters, Chapter 2, pp. 40–42).

The relationship between the characteristics of the policy instruments on the one hand and the characteristics of the environment on the other is the subject of Bressers's chapter (5) about the choice of policy instruments in a network. He argues that it is more likely that a policy instrument will be chosen when it does not challenge the existing network. A regulation, for instance, has a better chance when the objectives of the actors are in line (cohesion) and the interaction between the actors (interconnection) is weak than when the opposite is true.

The study of (the choice of) policy instruments may be seen through a political filter. A politician may favour policy instruments that lead to discriminatory fiscal benefits, while a bureaucrat may prefer policy instruments that may increase his/her discretionary budget (Kraan, Chapter 6, p. 108). Besides, the lack of *visibility* of policy instruments may be in the interests of an interest group. A low visibility may be strongly related to a high acceptability. It may make an instrument more attractive to its clientele (Woodside, Chapter 9, pp. 169–70). However, it also decreases the likelihood that an instrument is selected on implementability and effectiveness (Bressers, Chapter 5, pp. 100–101). The interest group may even capture the policy maker (Mitnick, 1980, p. 14). The support for such a capture theory is rather weak, but it is clear that the efforts to deregulate were in the interests of the private sector.

The role of time is introduced by In 't Veld (Chapter 8), who has made an analysis of the utilization of policy instruments from a more *dynamic* perspective. On the one hand, policy instruments need some time to become effective. On the other hand, they become outmoded over time, that is, instruments may no longer be up to date. As a result, stakeholders learn to deal with the negative consequences of the application of instruments with diminishing effectiveness. In 't Veld uses social indicators as an example, but the same is true for other instruments. The application of policy instruments is subject to what Ashby has called the 'law of requisite variety' (Ashby, 1969). They are not chosen once and for all, but have to be adjusted and refined continuously in order to catch up with developments in society.

3. LOOKING INTO THE CRYSTAL BALL

The era of big government may be over, but that does not mean that no role is left for government. On the contrary, government still has a role to play, as President Clinton said in his speech at Penn State University recently:

> we still need a government that is strong enough to give people the tools they need to make the most of their own lives, to enable them to seize opportunities when they are responsible. (Clinton, 1996)

The same is true for most European countries, though the state exists there in its own right and is not merely seen as a safety-net for the market (Rosenthal and Van Nispen, 1988). Furthermore, people in Europe are not ready to give up the welfare state and are, therefore, willing to accept a modest budget deficit.

The view of the appropriate role of the government goes up and down. The government may not be that popular nowadays, but we can already see signs of a revaluation. The government is not doing so badly after all. In some ways, it is doing a better job than the market. In the end, it is a choice between imperfect alternatives (Wolf, 1993).

NOTES

1. The agencies may look alike at first sight, but a closer inspection reveals that there is at least one important difference. Contrary to an American agency, a European agency is not led by a political appointee, but by a career civil servant.
2. We use the contextual approach here as a container for all kind of studies that take the contextual variables into account. It consists of the proceduralist as well as the contingentists' view of instruments (Linder and Peters). Furthermore, it contains the refined as well as the institutional view of instruments (Bagchus).

Bibliography

Algemene Rekenkamer (1989–90), *Planning en bouw van Ziekenhuisvoorzieningen*, Tweede Kamer, White Paper 21 674, nos. 1–2.

Allio, L., M.M. Dobek, N. Mikhailov and D.L. Weimer (1997), 'Post-Communist Privatization as a Test of Theories of Institutional Change', in Weimer (1997), pp. 319–48.

Almond, G.A. (1991), 'Capitalism and Democracy', *Political Science and Politics*, **24** (3), 461–6.

Anderson, C. (1987), 'Political Philosophy, Practical Reason and Policy Analysis', in F. Fischer and J. Forester (eds), *Confronting Values in Policy Analysis*, Beverly Hills: Sage, pp. 22–44.

Anderson, F. et al. (1977), *Environmental Improvement Through Economic Incentives*, Baltimore, MD: Johns Hopkins University Press.

Arentsen, M.J. (1991), *Beleidsorganisatie en beleidsuitvoering*, Enschede: Universiteit Twente.

Arentsen, M.J. and J.Th.A. Bressers (1992), 'Het belang van de factor macht bij de uitvoering van beleid', *Beleidswetenschap*, **6** (2), 103–25.

Argyris, C. and D.A. Schön (1978), *Organizational Learning: A Theory for Action Perspective*, Reading, MA: Addison-Wesley.

Ashby, W.R. (1969), 'Selective Regulation and Requisite Variety', in F.E. Emery (ed.), *Systems Thinking: Selected Readings*, Harmondsworth: Penguin Books, pp. 105–24.

Aslund, A. (1995), *How Russia Became a Market Economy*, Washington, DC: The Brookings Institution.

Assetto, V.J. (1988), *The Soviet Bloc in the IMF and the IBRD*, Boulder, CO: Westview Press.

Baakman, N.A.A. (1990), *Kritiek van het openbare bestuur. Besluitvorming over de bouw van ziekenhuizen in Nederland tussen 1960 en 1985*, Amsterdam: Thesis Publishers.

Baakman, N.A.A. (1992), 'Het managen van de besluitvorming over de bouw van ziekenhuizen', in De Jong et al., pp. 28–34.

Babai, D. (1988), 'The World Bank and the IMF: Rolling Back the State or Backing its Role', in R. Vernon (ed.), *The Promise of Privatization: A Challenge For U.S. Policy*, New York: Council of Foreign Relations, pp. 254–85.

Bagchus, R. (1996), *Waardevolle instrumenten*, Delft: Eburon.

Baggot, R. (1986), 'By Voluntary Agreement: The Politics of Instrument Selection', *Public Administration*, **64** (1), 51–67.

Bardach, E. (1980), 'Implementation Studies and the Study of Implements', paper delivered at the Annual Meeting of the American Political Science Association, Washington, DC, 28–31 August.

Baumol, W.J. (1984), 'Toward a Theory of Public Enterprise', *Atlantic Economic Journal*, **12** (1), 13–20.

Bekke, A.J.G.M. (1990), *De betrouwbare bureaucratie*, Alphen aan den Rijn: Samson.

Bekke, H., J. de Vries and G. Neelen (1994), *De salto mortale*, Alphen aan den Rijn: Samsom.

Bell, G.G. and A.D. Pascoe (1988), *The Ontario Government: Structure and Functions*, Toronto: Wall and Thompson.

Bezemer, H., W.T. de Groot and G. Huppes (eds) (1988), *Instrumenten voor milieubeleid*, Alphen aan den Rijn: Samsom.

Blais, A. and S. Dion (eds) (1991), *The Budget Maximizing Bureaucrat. Appraisals and Evidence*, Pittsburgh: University of Pittsburgh Press.

Boardman, A.E. and A.R. Vining (1989), 'Ownership and Performance in Competitive Environments: A Comparison of the Performance of Private, Mixed, and State-Owned Enterprises', *Journal of Law and Economics*, **32** (1), 1–33.

Bobrow, D.B. and J.S. Dryzek (1987), *Policy Analysis by Design*, Pittsburgh: University of Pittsburgh Press.

Boddez, T.M. and M.J. Trebilcock (1993), *Unfinished Business: Reforming Trade Remedy Laws in North America*, Toronto: C.D. Howe Institute.

Borman, C. (1993), *Aanwijzingen voor de regelgeving, en andere voor de regelgeving relevante aanwijzingen*, Zwolle: Tjeenk Willink.

Bovard, J. (1991), *The Fair Trade Fraud*, New York: St Martin's Press.

Bovens, M.A.P. and W.J. Witteveen (eds) (1985), *Het schip van staat, beschouwingen over recht, staat en sturing*, Zwolle: Tjeenk Willink.

Braybrooke, D. and C.E. Lindblom (1963), *Strategy of Decision*, New York: Free Press.

Bressers, J.Th.A. (1983), *Beleidseffektiviteit en waterkwaliteitsbeleid. Een bestuurskundig onderzoek*, (s.n.), Enschede.

Bressers, J.Th.A. (1985), *Milieu op de markt: een controverse tussen twee marktbenaderingen. Een aanzet tot een instrumentenleer voor milieubeleid*, Amsterdam: Kobra.

Bressers, J.Th.A. (1987), 'Geld voor milieubeleid of milieubeleid met geld?', *Tijdschrift voor Milieu en Recht*, **14** (4), 114–22.

Bressers, J.Th.A. (1989), 'Beleidsevaluatie en beleidseffectiviteit', in Hoogerwerf (1989), pp. 165–83.

Bressers, J.Th.A. (1991), 'Hoe valt de effectiviteit van beleid te verklaren? Instrumenten theorie', in Bressers and Hoogerwerf (1991), pp. 136–54.

Bressers, J.Th.A. (1993), 'Beleidsnetwerken en instrumentenkeuze', *Beleidswetenschap*, **7** (4), 309–30.

Bressers, J.Th.A., P. de Jong, P.J. Klok and A.F.A. Korsten (eds) (1993), *Beleidsinstrumenten bestuurskundig beschouwd*, Assen: Van Gorcum.

Bressers, J.Th.A. and A. Hoogerwerf (eds) (1991), *Beleidsevaluatie*, Alphen aan den Rijn: Samsom.

Bressers, J.Th.A. and T.P. Huzen (1984), 'Een politicologische benadering van bestuursinstrumenten', in J.Th.A. Bressers et al. (eds), *Bestuursinstrumenten*, Enschede: Universiteit Twente, pp. 47–96.

Bressers, J.Th.A. and P.J. Klok (1987a), *Een voorlopige instrumententheorie van het milieubeleid*, Enschede: Universiteit Twente.

Bressers, J.Th.A. and P.J. Klok (1987b), 'Grondslagen voor een instrumententheorie', *Beleidswetenschap*, **1** (1), 77–97.

Bressers, J.Th.A. and P.J. Klok (1988), *Handleiding instrumententheorie*, 's-Gravenhage: Publicatiereeks Milieubeheer (no. 3).

Bressers, J.Th.A., L.J. O'Toole and J. Richardson (1994), 'Networks as Models of Analysis: Water Policy in Comparative Perspective', *Environmental Politics*, 3 (4) (special issue), 1–24.

Bressers, J.Th.A., H. Pullen and J. Schuddeboom (1990), *Toetsing van beleidsinstrumenten*, Enschede: Universiteit Twente

Bressers, J.Th.A. and A.B. Ringeling (1989), 'Beleidsinstrumenten in drie arena's: beleidsvorming, uitvoering en doorwerking, *Beleidswetenschap*, 3 (1), 3–24.

Breton, A. and R. Wintrobe (1982), *The Logic of Bureaucratic Conduct: An Economic Analysis of Competition, Exchange and Efficiency in Private and Public Organizations*, Cambridge, MA: Cambridge University Press.

Brewer, G.D. and P. de Leon (1983), *The Foundations of Policy Analysis*, Homewood, IL: The Dorsey Press.

Breyer, S. (1982), *Regulation and Its Reform*, Cambridge, MA: Harvard University Press.

Browne, A. and A. Wildavsky (eds) (1983), 'Implementation as Mutual Adaptation', in J. Pressman and A. Wildavsky, *Implementation*, Berkeley: University of California Press, (3rd edition), pp. 206–31. ·

Brunsson, N. and J.P. Olsen (1993), 'Organizational Forms: Can We Choose Them?' in N. Brunsson and J.P. Olsen (eds), *Reforming Organization*, Chatham, NJ: Chatham Publishers, pp. 1–5.

Buchanan, J.M. (1959), 'Positive Economics, Welfare Economics and Political Economy', *Journal of Law and Economics*, 2 (1), 124–38.

Buchanan, J.M. (1967), *Public Finance in Democratic Process*, Chapel Hill: The University of North Carolina Press.

Buchanan, J.M. (1987), 'Constitutional Economics', in J.M. Buchanan, *Explorations into Constitutional Economics*, College Station: Texas A&M University Press, pp. 57–67.

Buchanan, J.M. and G. Tullock (1975), 'Polluters' Profits and Political Response: Direct Control versus Taxes', *American Economic Review*, 65 (1), 139–47.

Cadsby, C.B. and K. Woodside (1993), 'The Effects of the North American Free Trade Agreement on the Canada–United States Trade Relationship', *Canadian Public Policy*, 19 (4), 450–62.

Caudle, S.L. (1987), 'Regulatory Management: Government as a Regulated Industry', *International Journal of Public Administration*, 10 (1), 155–69.

Centrum voor Energiebesparing (Energy Conservation Centre) (1991) *Milieu en economie: sterke hand of onzichtbare hand*, Delft.

Chenery, H. (1964), 'Choice of Policy Instruments', in G. Meier (ed.), *Leading Issues in Development Economics*, Oxford/New York: Oxford University Press, pp. 503–10.

Clinton, W.J. (1995), *Radio Address by the President to the Nation*, 14 January.

Clinton, W.J. (1996), *State of the Union*, 23 January.

Clinton, W.J. (1996), *Remarks by the President, Pennsylvania State University Graduate School Commencement*, State College, PA, 10 May.

COBA (1976a), 'Handleiding voor de departementale doelstellingenanalyse', *Beleidsanalyse*, 5 (2), 2–32.

COBA (1976b), 'Het instrument subsidie: een leidraad voor het subsidie-onderzoek', *Beleidsanalyse*, 5 (1), 11–72.

COBA (1977), *Het formuleren van de probleemstelling*, 's-Gravenhage: Ministerie van Financiën.

Coleman, W.D. and G. Skogstad (eds) (1990), *Policy Communities and Public Policy in Canada: A Structural Approach*, Mississauga, Ontario: Copp Clark Pitman.

Comfort, L.K. (1985), 'A Model for Organizational Learning', *Journal of Policy Analysis and Management*, **10** (1), 100–118.

Croskery, P. (1995), 'Conventions and Norms in Institutional Design', in Weimer (1995), pp. 95–112.

Dabrowski, M. (1991), 'Privatization in Poland', *Communist Economies and Economic Transformation*, **3** (3), 317–25.

Dahl, R.A. and C.E. Lindblom (1953), *Politics, Economics and Welfare*, New York: Harper and Row.

Dahme, J. and D. Grünow (1983), 'Implementation persuasiver Programme', in Mayntz (1983), pp. 117–41.

Damen, L.J.A. (1987), *Ongeregeld en ondoorzichtig bestuur: staats-bestuurlijke beschouwingen naar aanleiding van de steunverlening aan individuele ondernemingen*, Deventer: Kluwer.

Davis, O.A., M.J. Hinich and P.C. Ordeshook (1970), 'An Expository Development of a Mathematical Model of the Electoral Process', *American Political Science Review*, **64** (2), 426–48.

De Alessi, L. (1980), 'The Economics of Property Rights', *Research in Law and Economics*, **2** (1), 1–47.

De Bruijn, J.A. (1990), *Economische Zaken en economische subsidies: een instrumentele en organisatorische analyse van de toepassing van economische subsidies*, 's-Gravenhage: Vuga.

De Bruijn, J.A. (1993), 'Sturen met geld. Operationele, strategische en institutionele aspecten van het gebruik van bedrijfssubsidies', in Bressers et al. (1993), pp. 55–67.

De Bruijn, J.A. and E.F. ten Heuvelhof (1991a), *Sturingsinstrumenten voor de overheid: over complex netwerken en een tweede generatie sturingsinstrumenten*, Leiden: Stenfert Kroese.

De Bruijn and E.F. ten Heuvelhof (1991b), 'Recht en netwerken: een bestuurskundige beschouwing', *Bestuurswetenschappen*, **45** (2), 105–16.

De Bruijn and E.F. ten Heuvelhof (1993), 'Management of Environmental Policy Networks', in Dutch Committee for the Long Term Environmental Policy, *The Environment: Towards a Sustainable Future*, Dordrecht: Kluwer, pp. 85–109.

De Bruijn, J.A. and E.F. ten Heuvelhof (1995a), *Netwerkmanagement: strategieën, instrumenten en normen*, Utrecht: Lemma.

De Bruijn, J.A. and E.F. ten Heuvelhof (1995b), 'Policy Networks and Governance', in Weimer (1995), pp. 161–79.

De Bruijn, J.A. and J.A.M. Hufen (1992), 'Instrumenten van overheidsbeleid,' *Beleidswetenschap*, **6** (1), 69–93.

De Haan, P., Th.G. Drupsteen and R. Fernhout (1986), *Bestuursrecht in de sociale rechtsstaat*, Deventer: Kluwer.

De Jong, P. and A.F.A. Korsten (1993), 'Beleidsinstrumenten bestuurskundig beschouwd: Inleiding', in Bressers, De Jong, Klok and Korsten (1993), pp. 1–15.

De Jong, P., A.F.A. Korsten and J.H. van der Made (eds) (1992), *Ziekenhuizen, besluitvorming en management*, Assen: Van Gorcum.

Dercksen, W.J. (1986), *Industrialisatiepolitiek rondom de jaren vijftig*, Assen: Van Gorcum.

De Vries, M.G. (1986), *The IMF in A Changing World: 1945–1985*, Washington, DC: IMF.

DiMaggio, P.J. and W.W. Powell (1983), 'The Iron Cage Revisited: Institutional Isomorphism and Collective Rationality in Organizational Fields', *American Sociological Review*, **48**, (2), 147–60.

Djelic, B. (1992), 'Mass Privatization in Russia: The Role of Vouchers', *RFE/RL Research Report*, **1** (41), 40–44.

Dobek, M.M. (1993a), *The Political Logic of Privatization*, Westport, CT: Praeger Publishers.

Dorek, M.M. (1993b), 'Privatization as a Political Priority: The British Experience', *Political Studies*, **41** (1), 20–36.

Doern, G.B. and R.W. Phidd (1983), *Canadian Public Policy: Ideas, Structure, Process*, New York: Methuen.

Donahue, J.D. (1989), *The Privatization Decision*, New York: Basic Books.

Donaldson, G. and J.W. Lorsch (1983), *Decision Making at the Top: the Shaping of Strategic Direction*, New York: Basic Books.

Donaldson, L. (1982), 'Comments on "Contingency and Choice in Organization Theory"', *Organization Studies*, **3** (1), 65–72.

Dowding, K. (1995), *The Civil Service*, London: Routledge.

Downs, A. (1957), *An Economic Theory of Bureaucracy*, New York: Harper and Row.

Downs, A. (1967), *Inside Bureaucracy*, Boston: Little Brown.

Dror, Y. (1970), 'Law as a Tool of Directed Social Change', *The American Behavioral Scientist*, **13** (4), 553–9.

Dror, Y. (1971), *Design for Policy Sciences*, New York/London/Amsterdam: Elsevier.

Dryzek, J.S. (1990), *Discursive Democracy: Politics, Policy and Political Science*, Cambridge: Cambridge University Press.

Dunn, W.N. (1988), 'Methods of the Second Type: Coping With the Wilderness of Conventional Policy Analysis', *Policy Studies Review*, **7** (4), 720–37.

Economist Intelligence Unit (1994), *Country Report: Slovakia*.

Eden, L. and M. Appel Molot (1993), *The NAFTA's Automotive Provisions: The Next Stage of Managed Trade*, Toronto: C.D. Howe Institute.

Eijsbouts, W.T. (1989), *Recht en toeval, premissen van 'het beleid' in het licht van de feiten* (n.p., anon.)

Ekkers, P.D.J. (1984), *Toewijzers en woningzoekenden: een case-studie naar de aard en de dimensies van het proces van woonruimteverdeling in Nijmegen*, Nijmegen: Katholieke Universiteit Nijmegen.

Elmore, R.F. (1980), 'Backward Mapping: Implementation Research and Policy Decisions', *Political Science Quarterly*, **94** (4), 601–16.

Elmore, R.F. (1987), 'Instruments and Strategy in Public Policy', *Policy Studies Review*, **7** (1), 174–86.

Feigenbaum, H.B. and J.R. Henig (1994), 'The Political Underpinnings of Privatization: A Typology', *World Politics*, **46** (2), 185–208.

Festinger, L. (1957), *A Theory of Cognitive Dissonance*, Stanford: Stanford University Press.

Fischer, F. (1990), *Technocracy and the Politics of Expertise*, Newbury Park: Sage.

Forester, J. (1985), *Critical Theory and Public Life*, Cambridge, MA: MIT Press.

Franssen, J.C. and A.B. Ringeling (1977), 'De COBA en de overheidssubsidie', *Bestuurswetenschappen*, **31** (5), 340–50.

Friedman, M. (1957), 'The Methodology of Positive Economics', in M. Friedman, *Essays in Positive Economics*, Chicago: The University of Chicago Press, pp. 3–43.

Frye, T. (1997), 'Russian Privatization and the Limits of Credible Commitment', in Weimer (1997), pp. 84–108.

Gatling, R. (1991), 'Focus on Finance', *Business Eastern Europe: A weekly report to managers of East European operations*, 30 September.

Geelhoed, L.A. (1983), *De interveniërende staat: aanzet voor een instrumenten-leer*, 's-Gravenhage: Staatzuitgeverij.

Gerrichhauzen, L.G. (1990), *Het woningcorporatiestelsel in beweging*, Delft: Delftse Universitaire Pers.

Glasbergen, P. (1989), *Beleidsnetwerken rond milieuproblemen*, 's-Gravenhage: Vuga.

Godfroij, A.J.A. (1981), *Netwerken van organisaties: strategiën, spelen, structuren*, 's-Gravenhage: Vuga,

Gore, A. (1993), *From Red Tape to Results*, Washington, DC: US Government Printing Office.

Gore, A. (1994), 'The New Role of the Federal Executive', *Public Administration Review*, **54** (4), 317–21.

Granovetter, M. (1985), 'Economic Action and Social Structure: The Problem of Embeddedness', *American Journal of Sociology*, **91** (3), 481–510.

Grimberg, B.F.J., J.Th.A. Bressers, P.J. Klok and A.E. Steenge (1988), *Schadever-goeding als stimuleringsinstrument: een toepassing van de instrumententheorie op de schadevergoedingsregeling voor bedrijven in het kader van de wet inzake de luchtverontreiniging*, Enschede: Universiteit Twente.

Hahm, S.D. et al. (1992), 'The Influence of the Gramm–Rudman–Hollings Act on Federal Budgetary Outcomes', *Journal of Policy Analysis and Management*, **11** (2), 207–234.

Hall, P.A. (1993), 'Policy Paradigms, Social Learning, and the State', *Comparative Politics* **26**, 275–96.

Heclo, H. and A. Wildavsky (1974), *The Private Government of Public Money*, London: Macmillan.

Henry, N. (1975), *Public Administration and Public Affairs*, Englewood Cliffs, NJ: Prentice Hall.

Herweijer, M. (1981), 'De dynamiek van het doelstellend gedrag', *Bestuurswetenschappen*, **35** (5), 348–66.

Hjern, B. and C. Hull (1982), 'Implementation as Empirical Constitutionalism', *European Journal of Political Research*, **10** (2), 105–15.

Hoekstra, R.J. (1988), *Ministerraad en vorming van regeringsbeleid*, Zwolle: Tjeenk Willink.

Hogwood, B.W. and B.G. Peters (1983), *Policy Dynamics*, Brighton: Wheatsheaf Books.

Hogwood, B.W. and B.G. Peters (1985), *Pathology of Public Policy*, Oxford: Clarendon Press.

Honigh, M. (1985), *Doeltreffend beleid*, Assen: Van Gorcum.

Hood, C. (1983), *The Tools of Government*, London: Macmillan.
Hood, C. (1986), *The Tools of Government*, Chatham, NJ: Chatham Publishers.
Hoogerwerf, A. (1977), 'Effecten van overheidsbeleid', *Beleid & Maatschappij*, **4** (11), 302–15.
Hoogerwerf, A. (1983a), 'Aanzet voor een instrumentenleer, kantekeningen bij "De interveniërende staat"', *Tijdschrift voor Openbaar Bestuur*, **9** (14), 359–62.
Hoogerwerf, A. (ed.) (1983b), *Succes en falen van overheidsbeleid*, Alphen aan den Rijn: Samsom.
Hoogerwerf, A. (ed.) (1989), *Overheidsbeleid*, Alphen aan den Rijn: Samson, (4th edition).
Hoogerwerf, A. (ed.) (1992), *Het ontwerpen van beleid: Een handleiding voor de praktijk en resultaten van onderzoek*, Alphen aan den Rijn: Samsom.
Hoogerwerf, A. (1992), 'Het ontwerpen van beleid als onderdeel van een politiek proces', in ibid., pp. 34–49.
Hoogerwerf, A. (1995), *Politiek als evenwichtskunst: dilemma's rond overheid en markt*, Alphen aan den Rijn: Samson H.D. Tjeenk Willink.
Hufen, J.A.M. (1990), *Instrumenten in het technologiebeeld: een onderzoek naar instrumenten die gericht zijn op de technologische vernieuwing van de industrie* (s.n.) Groningen.
Hufen, J.A.M. and A.B. Ringeling (eds) (1990), *Beleidsnetwerken: Overheids-, semi-overheids- en particuliere organisaties in wisselwerking*, 's-Gravenhage: Vuga.
Hufen, J.A.M. and A.B. Ringeling (1990), 'Beleidsnetwerken in het openbaar bestuur', in ibid., pp. 1–19.
Hufen, J.A.M. and J. Schuilenburg (1990), 'De politieke economie van het MKB-beleid', *Maandschrift Economie*, **54** (1), 39–48.
Hult, K.M. (1987), *Agency Merger and Bureaucratic Redesign*, Pittsburgh: University of Pittsburgh Press.
Hupe, P.L. (1990), 'Intenties en interacties', in Hufen and Ringeling (1990), pp. 223–34.
Idema, R.A. (1991), 'Ex post, ex ante', *Openbaar bestuur*, **1** (9), 39.
Ingram, H. and A. Schneider (1990), 'Improving Implementation Through Framing Smarter Statutes', *Journal of Public Policy*, **10** (1), 67–88.
Ingram, H. and A. Schneider (1993), 'Social construction of target populations: implications for politics and policy', *American Political Science Review*, **87** (2), 334–47.
In 't Veld, R.J. (1984), *De vlucht naar Esfahan*, 's-Gravenhage: Vuga.
In 't Veld, R.J. (1991), 'Autopoiesis, Configuration and Steering: Impossibility Theorem or Dynamic Steering Theory', in R.J. in 't Veld et al. (eds), *Autopoiesis Configuration Theory: New Approaches to Societal Steering*, Dordrecht: Kluwer, pp. 3–17.
In 't Veld, R.J. (1993), 'The Dynamics of Educational Performance Indicators', in J.L. Mikesell (ed.), *International Perspectives of Regional Development and Regional Organization*, Bloomington: Indiana University.
Jackson, J. (1991), *The World Trading System: Law and Policy of International Economic Relations*, Cambridge, MA: MIT Press.
Jenkins, I. (1980), *Social Order and the Limits of Law: A Theoretical Essay*, Princeton, NJ: Priceton University Press.
Jensen, M.C. and W.H. Meckling (1976), 'Theory of the Firm: Managerial

Behavior, Agency Costs and Ownership Structure', *Journal of Financial Economics*, **3** (4), 305–360.

Johnson, J.R. (1993), 'NAFTA and the Trade in Automotive Goods', in S. Globerman and M. Walker (eds), *Assessing NAFTA: A Trinational Analysis*, Vancouver: The Fraser Institute, pp. 87–129.

Jordan, G. (1990), 'Sub-governments, Policy Community and Networks', *Journal of Theoretical Politics*, **2**, 319–338.

Kaminiski, B. (1997), 'Comment on Institutional Structures, Labor Interests and Evolving Privatization Bargains in Poland', in Weimer (1997), pp. 232–8.

Kaufmann, F.X., G. Majone and V. Ostrom (eds) (1986), *Guidance, Control, and Evaluation in the Public Sector*, Berlin: Walter de Gruijter.

Kaufmann, F.X. and B. Rosewitz (1983), 'Typisierung und Klassifikation politischer Massnahmen', in Mayntz (1983), pp. 25–49.

Kiewiet, D.R. (1991), 'Bureaucrats and Budgetary Outcomes: Quantitative Analyses', in Blais and Dion (1991), pp. 143–73.

Kirschen E.S. et al. (1964), *Economic Policy in Our Time: General Theory* (volume 1), Chicago: Rand McNally.

Kiser, L. and V. Ostrom (1985), 'Three Worlds of Action. A Metatheoretical Synthesis of Institutional Approaches', in E. Ostrom (ed.), *Strategies of Political Inquiry*, Beverly Hills: Sage, pp. 179–222.

Klaassen, H.L. and F.K.M. van Nispen (1995), 'Policy Analysis in the Netherlands', paper presented at the 17th Research Conference of the Association for Public Policy and Management, Washington, 2–4 November.

Klijn, E.H. (1990), 'De vissen en het aas', in Hufen and Ringeling (1990), pp. 157–74.

Klok, P.J. (1987), 'Gebruiksmogelijkheden van een instrumententheorie: afvalverwijdering als voorbeeld', *Beleidswetenschap*, **1** (4), 356–83.

Klok, P.J. (1989a), *Convenanten als instrument van milieubeleid*, Enschede: Universiteit Twente.

Klok, P.J. (1989b), 'Beleidsuitvoering en instrumententheorie', *Beleidswetenschap*, **3** (3), 264–81.

Klok, P.J. (1991), *Een instrumententheorie voor het milieubeleid; de toepassing en effecten van beleidsinstrumenten*, Enschede: Universiteit Twente.

Klok, P.J. (1992), 'Beleidsinstrumenten als stromen hulpbronnen', paper presented at the Dutch Political Science Annual Conference Day.

Kocken, E.H.A. (1966), *Het vergunningenstelsel in de Hinderwet en Woningwet*, Alphen aan den Rijn: Samsom.

Kolodko, G.W. and M. Rutkowski (1991), 'The Problem of Transition from a Socialist to a Free Market Economy: The Case of Poland', *The Journal of Social, Political, and Economic Studies*, **16** (2), 159–79.

Koningsveld, H. (1984), *Het verschijnsel wetenschap*, Meppel: Boom.

Kooiman, J. (1993), 'Social–Political Governance: Introduction', in Jan Kooiman (ed.), *Modern Governance: New Government–Society Interaction*, London: Sage Publications, pp. 1–6.

Koolhaas, E. (1990), 'Rotterdamse handhavingspraktijken', in Hufen and Ringeling (1990), pp. 175–88.

Koppenjan, J.F.M., A.B. Ringeling and R.H.A. te Velde (eds) (1987), *Beleidsvorming in Nederland: Een vergelijkende studie naar de totstandkoming van wetten*, 's-Gravenhage: Vuga.

Kornai, J. (1986), 'The Soft Budget Constraint', *Kyklos*, **39** (1), 3–30.

Kornai, J. (1992), *The Socialist System: The Political Economy of Communism*, Princeton, NJ: Princeton University Press.

Korsten, A.F.A. et al. (eds) (1991), *Overheidsmanagement en de menselijke factor*, 's-Gravenhage: Vuga.

Kotler, P. and A.R. Andreason (1987), *Strategic Marketing for Nonprofit Organizations*, Englewood Cliffs: Prentice Hall.

Kraan, D.J. and R.J. in 't Veld (eds) (1993), *Environmental Protection: Public or Private Choice*, Dordrecht: Kluwer.

Kraan-Jetten, A. and J.B.D. Simonis (1987), 'Theorievorming binnen de beleidswetenschappen; het kritisch-rationalistisch perspectief', in P.B. Lehning and J.B.D. Simonis (eds), *Handboek beleidswetenschap*, pp. 319–36.

Krasner, S.D. (1988), 'Sovereignty', *Comparative Political Studies*, **21** (1), 66–94.

Kuks, S.M.M. (1987), 'Instrumententheorie voor effectiever milieubeleid', *Bestuur*, **6** (8), 238–41.

Kuypers, G. (1980), *Beginselen van beleidsontwikkeling*, Muiderberg: Coutinho.

Laffont, J.J. and J. Tirole (1993), *A Theory of Incentives in Procurement and Regulation*, Cambridge, MA: MIT Press.

Landau, M. (1979), 'On the Use of Metaphor in Political Analysis', in M. Landau, *Political Theory and Political Science: Studies in the Methodology of Political Inquiry*, New York: Macmillan, pp. 78–102.

Langbein, L.I. (1980), *Discovering Whether Programs Work: A Guide to Statistical Methods for Program Evaluation*, Santa Monica: The Rand Corporation.

Lasswell, H.D. (1951), 'The Policy Orientation', in D. Lerner and H.D. Lasswell (eds), *The Policy Sciences: Recent Developments in Scope and Method*, Stanford: Stanford University Press, pp. 3–15.

Leeuw, F.L., R.C. Rist and R.C. Sonnichsen (eds) (1994), *Can Governments Learn? Comparative Perspectives on Evaluation and Organizational Learning*, New Brunswick; Transaction Publishers.

Lehning, Percy B. (1991), *Beleid op niveau. Over de architectuur van overheidsinterventie*, Meppel: Boom.

Lindblom, Ch.E. (1959), 'The Science of the Muddling Through', *Public Administration Review*, **19** (2), 78–88.

Linder, S.H. and B.G. Peters (1980), 'From Social Theory to Policy Design', *Journal of Public Policy*, **4** (3), 237–359.

Linder, S.H. and B.G. Peters (1986), 'A Design Perspective on Policy Implementation: The Fallacy of Misplaced Precision', *Policy Studies Review*, **6** (3), 459–75.

Linder, S.H. and B.G. Peters (1989a), 'Implementation as a Guide to Policy Formulation: A Question of "When" Rather than, "Whether"', *International Review of Administrative Sciences*, **55** (4), 632–52.

Linder, S.H. and B.G. Peters (1989b), 'Instruments of Government: Perceptions and Contexts', *Journal of Public Policy*, **9** (1), 35–58.

Linder, S.H. and B.G. Peters (1990), 'An Institutional Approach to the Theory of Policy Making: The Role of Guidance Mechanisms in Policy Formulation', *Journal of Theoretical Politics*, **2** (1), 59–83.

Lott Jr, J.R. (1987), 'The Effects of Nontransferable Property Rights on the Efficiency of Political Markets', *Journal of Public Economics*, **32** (2), 231–46.

Lowi, T.J. (1964), 'American Business, Public Policy, Case Studies, and Political Theory', *World Politics*, **16** (16), 677–715.

Lowi, T.J. (1972), 'Four Systems of Politics, Policy and Choice', *Public Administration Review*, **32** (4), 298–310.

Luhmann, N. (1984), *Soziale systeme*, Frankfurt am Main: Suhrkamp.

Mahar, M. (1992), 'Wolf at the Door: A Failing Economy Threatens Survival of the New Russia', *Barron's*, 19 October, pp. 8–26.

Majone, G. (1976), 'Choice among Policy Instruments for Pollution Control', *Policy Analysis*, **2** 589–613.

Majone, G. (1989), *Evidence, Argument and Persuation in the Policy Process*, New Haven, CT: Yale University Press.

Majone, G. (ed.) (1990), *Deregulation or Re-regulation: Regulatory Reform in Europe and the United States*, London/New York: St Martin's Press.

Manne, H. (1965), 'Mergers and the Market for Corporate Control', *Journal of Political Economy*, **73** (2), 110–20.

March, J.G. and J.P. Olsen (1984), 'The New Institutionalism, Organizational Factors in Political Life', *American Political Science Review*, **78**, 734–49.

March, J.G. and J.P. Olsen (1989), *Rediscovering Institutions*, New York: The Free Press.

March, J.G. and J.P. Olsen (1995), *Democratic Governance*, New York: The Free Press.

Marin, B. and R. Mayntz (eds) (1991), *Policy Networks: Empirical Evidence and Theoretical Considerations*, Boulder, CO: Westview Press.

May, P. (1991) 'Reconsidering Policy Design: Policies with Publics', *Journal of Public Policy*, **11** (2), 187–206.

Mayntz, R. (ed.) (1983), *Implementation politischer Programme II: Ansätze zur Theoriebildung*, Opladen: Westdeutscher Verlag.

Mayntz, R. (1983), 'Implementation von regulativer Politik', in ibid., pp. 50–74.

McGuire, A. and P. Stuart (1987), 'The Role of the Test Discount Rates in the NHS', *Public Policy and Administration*, **2** (3), 11–22.

McLean, R. and B. Fountain (1989), 'The Strategic Implications for Canada's Negotiating Strategies of Recent Findings on U.S. Subsidies', paper presented at the Conference on Subsidies in the United States, Ernst & Young, Toronto, 1 November.

Meltsner A.J. and C. Bellevita (1983), *The Policy Organization*, Beverly Hills: Sage.

Migué, G.J. and G. Bélanger (1974a), 'Toward a General Theory of Managerial Discretion', *Public Choice*, **17** (1), 27–43.

Migué, G.J. and G. Bélanger (1974b), 'Reply on Niskanen', *Public Choice*, **17** (1), 45–7.

Miller, T. (1984), 'Conclusion: A Design Science Perspective', in T. Miller (ed.), *Public Sector Performance*, Baltimore, MD: Johns Hopkins University Press, pp. 251–68.

Minister van Binnenlandse Zaken (1985–86), *Notitie van de minister van Binnenlandse Zaken over de vermindering en verbetering van circulaires*, Tweede Kamer, White Paper 18 315, no. 5, p. 2.

Mintzberg, H. (1979), *The Structuring of Organizations: A Synthesis of the Research*, Englewood Cliffs, NJ: Prentice Hall.

Mitnick, B.M. (1980), *The Political Economy of Regulation: Creating, Designing and Removing Regulatory Forms*, New York: Columbia University Press.

Montjoy, R.S. and L.J. O'Toole (1990), 'Policy Instruments and Politics: Multiple Regression and Intergovernmental Aid', paper presented at the annual meeting of the American Political Science Association, San Francisco, August 30–September 2.

Morici, P. (1991), 'Rules of Origin in a North American Trade Accord', paper presented at the conference on How is Free Trade Progressing? Toronto, 18–19 November.

Mosley, P. (1988), 'Privatisation, Policy-Based Lending and World Bank Behavior', in P. Cook and C. Kirkpatrick (eds), *Privatisation in Less Developed Countries*, New York: St Martin's Press, pp. 125–40.

Needham, D. Barrie (1982), *Choosing the Right Policy Instruments, an Investigation of Two Types of Instruments, Physical and Financial, and a Study of Their Application to Local Problems of Unemployment*, Aldershot: Gower.

Niskanen, W.A. (1968), 'The Peculiar Economics of Bureaucracy', *American Economic Review*, **58** (2), 293–305.

Niskanen, W.A. (1971), *Bureaucracy and Representative Government*, Chicago: Aldine Atherton.

Niskanen, W.A. (1974), 'Comment on Migué & Bélanger', *Public Choice*, **17** (1), 43–45.

Niskanen, W.A. (1975), 'Bureaucrats and Politicians', *Journal of Law and Economics*, **18** (3), 617–43.

Niskanen, W.A. (1991), 'A Reflection on Bureaucracy and Representative Government', in Blais and Dion (1991), pp. 13–31.

Noorderhaven, N.G. (1990), *Private Competence and Public Responsibility: Anatomy of a Government–Firm Relationship* (s.n.), Groningen.

Olson, M. (1965), *The Logic of Collective Action, Public Goods and the Theory of Groups*, Cambridge, MA: Harvard University Press.

Onderzoekers Kombinatie Utrecht (1989), *Voorlichting over Energiebesparing*, Utrecht.

Orzechowski, W. (1977), 'Economic Models of Bureaucracy: Survey, Extensions and Evidence', in Th.E. Borcherding (ed.), *Budgets and Bureaucrats*, Durham, NC: Duke University Press, pp. 229–59.

Osborne, D.E. and T. Gaebler (1992), *Reinventing Government: How the Entrepreneurial Spirit is Transforming the Public Sector*, Reading, MA: Addison-Wesley.

Ostrom, E. (1986), 'A Method of Institutional Analysis', in: Kaufman, Majone and Ostrom (1986), pp. 459–75.

O'Toole, L.J. (1990), 'Contingentie van beleid en organisatorische arrangementen', in Hufen and Ringeling (1990), pp. 121–35.

O'Toole, L.J. and K. Hanf (1990), 'Na de top-down versus bottum-up controverse: De interorganisatorische context van beleidsprocessen', in Hufen and Ringeling (1990), pp. 21–37.

Pechman, J. (1988), *World Tax Reform: A Progress Report*, Washington, DC: The Brookings Institution.

Peters, B.G. (1996a), 'Deinstitutionalization and Reinstitutionalization: The Institutions of Regulatory Policy in the United States', paper presented at a conference on Regulatory Policy and Institutions, University of Exeter, 7–8 April.

Peters, B.G. (1996b), 'Political Institutions, Old and New', in R.E. Goodin and H.D. Klingemann (eds), *New Handbook of Political Science*, Oxford: Oxford University Press, pp. 205–20.

Phidd, R. and G.B. Doern (1978), *The Politics and Management of the Canadian Economy Policy*, Toronto: Macmillan.

Piers Consultancy (1991), *Literatuurinventarisatie energiebesparing en gedragsverandering*, 's-Gravenhage.

Pigou, C.A. (1946), *The Economics of Welfare*, London: Macmillan, (4th edition).

Pistor, K. (1994), 'Corporate Governance in Russia: An Empirical Study', in: M. McFaul and T. Perlmutter (eds), *Privatization, Conversion, and Enterprise Reform in Russia*, Stanford, CA: CSIA, pp. 69–84.

Podgorecki, A. (1970), 'Law as a Tool of Directed Social Change', *The American Behavioral Scientist*, **14** (3), 553–9.

Poister, H. and G. Streib (1989), 'Management Tools in Municipal Governments: Trends over the Past Decade', *Public Administration Review*, **49** (5), 240–48.

Pont, H.A.P.M. (1991), 'Het Nederlandse model van arbeidsverhoudingen', in Korsten et al. (1991), pp. 29–36.

Poznanski, K.Z. (1992), 'Privatisation of the Polish Economy: Problems of Transition', *Soviet Studies*, **44** (4), 641–64.

Pressman, J.L. and A. Wildavsky (1973, 1979), *Implementation*, Berkeley: University of California Press.

Pröpper, I.M.A.M. and M. Herweijer (1992), *Effecten van plannen en convenanten*, Deventer: Kluwer.

Richardson, J.J. (1983), *Policy Styles in Western Europe*, London: George Allen and Unwin.

Richardson, J.J. and A.G. Jordan (1979), *Governing under Pressure: The Policy Process in a Post-Parliamentary Democracy*, Oxford: Martin Robertson.

Rietveld, P. and L.J.G. van Wissen (1993), 'Transport Policies and the Environment: Regulation and Taxation', in Kraan and In 't Veld (1993), pp. 91–110.

Ringeling, A.B. (1983), *De instrumenten van het beleid*, Alphen aan den Rijn: Samsom.

Ringeling, A.B. (1990), 'De overheid naast andere actoren? Dwaalsporen en mispercepties', in Hufen and Ringeling (1990), pp. 55–70.

Ringeling, A.B. (1988), 'De wet en andere beleidsinstrumenten', in R. Depre et al. (eds), *Handboek beleidsvoering voor de overheid*, Alphen aan den Rijn: Samsom, pp. 1–23.

Ringeling, A.B. (1993a), *Het imago van de overheid*, 's-Gravenhage: Vuga.

Ringeling, A.B. (1993b), 'De ontwikkeling van het denken over beleidsinstrumenten. Enige kanttekeningen', in Bressers et al. (1993), pp. 191–201.

Ritchie, Gordon (1997), *Wrestling with the Elephant: The Inside Story of the Canada–U.S. Trade Wars*, Toronto: Macfarlane, Walter & Ross.

Rodrik, D. and R.J. Zeckhauser (1988), 'The Dilemma of Government Responsiveness', *Journal of Public Policy and Management*, **7** (4), 601–20.

Rood, M.G. (1985), 'Van loonpolitiek tot budgetpolitiek. Enkele gedachten over loonvorming en overheidssturing', in Bovens and Witteveen (1985), pp. 161–78.

Rosenthal, U. (1988), 'Van Sturing tot toeval', in W.C.M. van Lieshout et al. (eds), *Bestuur en meesterschap: opstellen over samenleving, staat en sturing*, 's-Gravenhage: Staatsuitgeverij, pp. 19–27.

Rosenthal, U., M.P.C.M. van Schendelen and A.B. Ringeling (1984), *Openbaar bestuur: Organisatie, beleid en politieke omgeving*, Alphen aan den Rijn: Samsom.

234 Public policy instruments

Rosenthal, U. and F.K.M. van Nispen (1988), 'Privatization. Reflections from Another Culture', in Ch.F. Bonser (ed.), 'Privatization', *SPEA Review*, **10** (2), 68–73.

Rueschemeyer, D., E. Huber Stephens and J.D. Stephens (1992), *Capitalist Development and Democracy*, Chicago: University of Chicago Press.

Sabatier, P.A. (1988), 'An Advocacy Coalition Framework of Policy Change and the Role of Policy-oriented Learning Therein', *Policy Sciences*, **21** (2–3), 129–68.

Sabatier, P.A. and H.C. Jenkins-Smith (1993), *Policy Change and Learning: an Advocacy Coalition Approach*, Boulder, CO: Westview Press.

Salamon, L. (1981), 'Rethinking Public Management: Third Party Government and the Forms of Changing Government', *Public Policy*, **29** (3), 255–75.

Salamon, L. and M. Lund (1989), *Beyond Privatization*, Washington, DC: Urban Institute Press.

Savas, E.S. (1987), *Privatization: The Key to Better Government*, Chatham, NJ: Chatham House Publishers.

Savas, E.S. (1992), 'Privatization in Post-Socialist Countries', *Public Administration Review*, **52** (6), 573–81.

Schon, D. (1971), *Beyond the Stable State*, New York: Random House.

Schrama, G.J.I. (1991), *Keuzevrijheid in organisatievormen*, Enschede: Universiteit Twente.

Schreyögg, G. (1980), 'Contingency and Choice in Organization Theory', *Organization Studies*, **1** (4), 305–26.

Schreyögg, G. (1982), 'Some Comments about Comments: a Reply to Donaldson', *Organization Studies*, **3** (1), 73–83.

Schuyt, C.J.M. (1977), 'Problemen van wetgeving', *Beleid & Maatschappij*, **4** (7–8), 186–97.

Schuyt, C.J.M. (1982), *Ongeregeld heden: naar een theorie van wetgeving in de verzorgingsstaat*, Alphen aan den Rijn: Samsom.

Schuyt, C.J.M. (1985), 'Sturing en het recht', in Bovens and Witteveen (1985), pp. 113–24.

Self, P. (1995), *Government by the Market?*, Boulder, CO: Westview.

Siemons, J.C.M.M. (1992), *Occupational Safety and Health Policy Implementation: A Comparison between Japan and the Netherlands*, Enschede: Universiteit Twente.

Simon, H.A. (1945), *Administrative Behavior. A Study of Decision-Making Processes in Administrative Organizations*, New York: The Free Press.

Simonis, J.B.D. and Percy B. Lehning (1987), 'Een pluriforme beleidswetenschap', in Percy B. Lehning and J.B.D. Simonis (eds), *Handboek beleidswetenschap*, Meppel: Boom, pp. 9–20.

Slay, B. (1993), 'The East European Economies', *RFE/RL Research Report*, **2** (1), 113–18.

Sobell, V. (1989), 'The IMF's Pivotal Role in Transforming Poland's Economy', *Radio Free Europe Research*, 10 October.

Sobell, V. and K. Okolicsanyi (1990), 'The IMF's Negotiations in Hungary and Poland, *Report on Eastern Europe*, **1** (4), 43–6.

Solomon, B. (1996), 'Something Big?', *National Journal*, 20 April, pp. 864–8.

Staniszkis, J. (1991), 'Political Capitalism in Poland', *East European Politics and Societies*, **5** (1), 127–41.

Steinberger, P. (1980), 'Typologies of Public Policy: Meaning Construction and the Policy Process', *Social Science Quarterly*, **61** (2), 185–97.

Stillman II, R.J. (1991), *Preface to Public Administration*, New York: St Martin's Press.

Stone, C.D. (1975), *Where the Law Ends: The Social Control of Corporate Behavior*, New York: Harper and Row.

Stone, F. (1984), *Canada, the GATT and the International Trade System*, Montreal: The Institute for Research on Public Policy.

Summers, R.S. (1980), *Het pragmatisch instrumentalisme: een kritische studie van de belangrijkste Amerikaanse rechtsfilosofie*, Zwolle: Tjeenk Willink.

Tak, Th. van der (1988), *Vergunning verleend. Een bestuurskundige studie naar vergunningen op grond van de wet inzake de luchtverontreiniging en de wet algemene bepalingen milieuhygiëne*, Delft: Eburon.

Tassey, G. (1985), 'The Technology Policy Experiment as a Policy Research Tool', *Research Policy*, **14** (1), 39–52.

Taylor, L. (1988), *Varieties of Stabilization Experience: Towards Sensible Macroeconomics in the Third World*, Oxford: Clarendon Press.

Termeer, C.J.A.M. (1993), *Dynamiek en inertie rondom mestbeleid: een studie naar veranderingsprocessen in het varkenshouderijnetwerk*, 's-Gravenhage: Vuga.

Thain, C. (1985), 'The Education of the Treasury: The Medium-Term Financial Strategy', *Public Administration*, **63** (3), 261–85.

Theeuwes, J.J.M. (1993), 'Regulation or Taxation', in Kraan and In't Veld (1993), pp. 51–69.

Thelen, K. and S. Steinmo (1992), 'Historical Institutionalism in Comparative Politics', in S. Steinmo, K. Thelen and F. Longstreth (eds), *Structuring Politics, Historical Institutionalism in Comparative Analysis*, Cambridge: Cambridge University Press.

Tinbergen, J. (1956), *Economic Policy: Principles and Design*, Amsterdam: North Holland.

Toonen, Th.A.J. (1979), 'Publieke organisatie en complexiteit', *Bestuurswetenschappen*, **33** (5), 274–92.

Toonen, Th.A.J. (1993), 'Bestuur en Beleid', in J.W. van Deth (ed.), *Handboek Politicologie*, Assen: Van Gorcum, pp. 250–81.

Tullock, G. (1965), *The Politics of Bureaucracy*, Washington, DC: Public Affairs Press.

Tullock, G. (1967), *Towards a Mathematics of Politics*, Ann Arbor: University of Michigan Press.

US Joint Committee on Taxation (1991), *Factors Affecting the International Competitiveness of the United States*, Study prepared for the Committee on Ways and Means, Washington, DC: US Government Printing Office.

Urbán L. (1997), 'Privatization and Institutional Change in Hungary', in Weimer (1997), pp. 239–55.

Van de Graaf, H. and R. Hoppe (1990), *Beleid en politiek: Inleiding tot de beleidswetenschap en beleidskunde*, Muiderberg: Coutinho.

Van der Doelen, F.C.J. (1989), *Beleidsinstrumenten en energiebesparing*, Enschede: Universiteit Twente.

Van der Vlies, I.C. (1986), 'Dweilen met de kraan open', *Regelmaat*, **1** (1), 20–21.

Van Dijk, J.W.A. (1986), *Innovatie en overheidsbeleid: duwen en trekken in de industriepolitiek*, Amsterdam: VU Uitgeverij.

Van Gunsteren, H.R. (1976), *The Quest for Control, A Critique of the Rational Central-Rule Approach in Public Affairs*, New York: Wiley.

Van Gunsteren, H.R. (1984), 'Wie in zijn graf ligt maakt geen fouten meer; een interventiete ontwikkelen door ambtenaren, *Beleid & Maatschappij*, **1** (6), 159–63.

Van Gunsteren, H.R. (1985), 'Het leervermogen van de overheid', in Bovens and Witteveen (1985), pp. 53–74.

Van Nispen, F.K.M. (1983), 'De bezuinigingsinstrumenten van de overheid: iets minder mag dat?', *Bestuurswetenschappen*, **37** (6), 367–79.

Van Nispen, F.K.M. and J.F.W. Rijntalder (1990), 'Bezuinigen op zijn Amerikaans', *Openbare Uitgaven*, no. 1, pp. 18–25.

Van Ommeren, F.J. and H.J. de Ru (1993), *Convenanten tussen overheid en maatschappelijke organisaties*, 's-Gravenhage: Sdu.

Van Riel, C.B.M. (1986), *Overheidsvoorlichting en intermediaire kaders: een studie naar de intermediaire rol van organisaties in het voorlichtingsproces van de centrale overheid*, Delft: Eburon.

Van Twist, M.J.W. and L. Schaap (1991), 'Een theorie over autopoietische systemen', *Beleidswetenschap*, **5** (4), 299–322.

Van Woerkom, C.J.M. (1988), 'Wetgeving en communicatie als beleidsinstrument: een integrerende benadering', *Bestuurswetenschappen*, **42** (5) 322–33.

Vereniging van Nederlandse Gemeenten (1985), *Bestuur per circulaire*, 's-Gravenhage.

Vermeend, W.A.F.G. (1983), *Fiscale investeringsfaciliteiten*, Arnhem: Gouda Quint.

Vermeulen, W.J.V. (1988), 'De effectiviteit van een subsidie bij multi-instrumentele beleidsuitvoering: regionaal zware metalenbeleid als voorbeeld, *Beleidswetenschap*, **2** (4), 245–359.

Vermeulen, W.J.V. (1993), 'Niet alleen waar gesubsidieerd wordt, vallen spaanders,' in Bressers et al. (1993), pp. 69–73.

Vermeulen, W.J.V. and R.A.J. Goes (1989), *Tussen financiële prikkel en overreding*, Utrecht: Rijksuniversiteit Utrecht.

Vernon, R. (ed.) (1988), *The Promise of Privatization: A Challenge For U.S. Policy*, New York: Council of Foreign Relations.

Vickers, J. and G. Yarrow (1988), *Privatization: An Economic Analysis*, Cambridge, MA: MIT Press.

Vining, A.R. and A.E. Boardman (1992), 'Ownership versus Competition: Efficiency in Public Enterprise', *Public Choice*, **73** (2) 205–39.

Vining, A.R. and D.L. Weimer (1990), 'Government Supply and Government Production Failure: A Framework Based on Contestability', *Journal of Public Policy*, **10** (1), 1–22.

Vogel, D. (1986), *National Styles of Regulation: Environmental Policy in Great Britain and the United States*, Ithaca, NY: Cornell University Press.

Von Mises, L. (1944), *Bureaucracy*, New Haven, CT: Yale University Press.

Wamsley, G.L. and H.B. Milward (1985), 'Policy Subsystems, Networks and the Tools of Public Management', in K.I. Hanf and Th.A.J. Toonen (eds), *Policy implementation in Federal and Unitary Systems: Questions of Analysis and Design*, Dordrecht: Nijhoff, pp. 71–96.

Weimer, D.L. (ed.) (1995), *Institutional Design*, Dordrecht: Kluwer.

Weimer, D.L. (ed.) (1997), *The Political Economy of Property Rights*, New York: Cambridge University Press.

Weimer, D.L. and A.R. Vining (1989), *Policy Analysis: Concepts and Practice*, Englewood Cliffs, NJ: Prentice Hall.

Wildavsky, A. (1979), 'Policy Analysis is what Information Systems are Not', in A. Wildavsky, *The Art and Craft of Policy Analysis: Speaking Truth to Power*, Boston, MA: Little, Brown, pp. 26–40.

Wilson, G.K. (1985), *The Politics of Health and Safety*, Oxford: Clarendon Press.

Wilson, W. (1887), 'The Study of Public Administration', *Political Science Quarterly*, **2**, 197–222.

Wittman, D.A. (1973), 'Parties as Utility Maximizers', *American Political Science Review*, **67** (2), 490–98.

Wittman, D.A. (1977), 'Candidates with Policy Preferences: A Dynamic Model', *Journal of Economic Theory*, **14** (1), 180–89.

Wittman, D.A. (1983), 'Candidate Motivation: A Synthesis of Alternative Theories', *American Political Science Review*, **77** (1), 142–57.

Wittman, D.A. (1990), 'Spatial Strategies when Candidates have Policy Preferences', in J.M. Enelow and M.J. Hinich (eds), *Advances in the Spatial Theory of Voting*, Cambridge: Cambridge University Press, pp. 66–98.

Wolf Jr, Charles (1993), *Markets or Governments: Choosing between Imperfect Alternatives*, Cambridge, MA: MIT Press (2nd edition).

Woodside, K. (1983), 'The Political Economy of Policy Instruments: Tax Expenditures and Subsidies in Canada', in M.M. Atkinson and M.A. Chandler, *The Politics of Canadian Public Policy*, Toronto: University of Toronto Press, pp. 173–97.

Woodside, K. (1986), 'Policy Instruments and the Study of Public Policy', *Canadian Journal of Political Science*, **19** (4), 775–93.

Woodside, K. (1992), 'Trade and Industrial Policy: Hard Choices', in M.M. Atkinson (ed.), *Governing Canada: Institutions and Public Policy*, Toronto: Harcourt Brace Jovanovich, pp. 241–74.

Wright, M. (1988), 'Policy Community, Policy Network and Comparative Industrial Policies', *Political Studies*, **36** (4), 593–612.

Young, R.A. (1991), 'Budget Size and Bureaucratic Carreers', in Blais and Dion (1991), pp. 33–58.

Young, S.D. (1991), 'The Role of Business Valuation in the Privatization of Eastern Europe', *Journal of Multinational Financial Management*, **1** (4), 47–65.

Zeckhauser, R.J. and M. Horn (1989), 'The Control and Performance of State-Owned Enterprises,' in P.W. MacAvoy et al., *Privatization and State-Owned Enterprises*, Boston, MA: Kluwer Academic Publishers, pp. 7–57.

Zijlstra, G.J. (1982), *The Policy Structure of the Dutch Nuclear Energy Sector* (s.n.).

OTHER SOURCES QUOTED

Foreign Broadcast Information Service, 29 December, 1992.

Government of Canada, *The Canada–U.S. Free Trade Agreement*, Department of External Affairs, Ottawa 1987.

Government of Canada, *North American Free Trade Agreement*, Ministry of Supply and Services, Ottawa 1993.

Hospodarske noviny, 29 January 1993, p. 16.

Magyar Hirlap, 14 October, 1992a, p. 11.

Magyar Hirlap, 24 November 1992b, p. 10.

Magyar Hirlap, 29 December 1993c, p. 8.

Magyarorszag, 29 December 1992, p. 7.

PlanEcon Report, April 1993, vol. 9, no. 13–14.

PlanEcon Report, July 1993, vol. 9, no. 26–7.

PlanEcon Report, November 1995a, vol. 11, no. 32–3.

PlanEcon Report, November 1995b, vol. 11, no. 34–5.

Polityka, 2 May 1992, p. 12.

Programma uglubleniya ekonomicheskikh reform (Program for the Deepening of the Economic Reforms), Moscow 1992.

Prseglad Rzadowy, 1992.

Republika, 10 March 1994.

RFE/RL News Briefs, 11–15 January 1993, p. 10.

Rossiiskaya Gazeta, 10 and 15 January 1992.

Index

sociogenesis in Netherlands 195,
198
traditional approach 17, 21, 22, 23,
24, 27
Van Dijk, J.W.A. 23
Van Gunsteren, H.R. 190, 209
Van Nispen, F.K.M. 1–8, 83, 204–17,
218–21
Van Ommeren, F.J. 76
Van Riel, C.B.M. 19, 76
Van Twist, M.J.W. 89
Van Wissen, L.J.G. 214
Van Woerkom, C.J.M. 24
Vermeend, W.A.F.G. 22
Vermeulen, W.J.V. 20, 23, 24, 81
Vernon, R. 125
Vickers, J. 125
Vining, A.R. 120, 124, 125
visibility 6, 162–81

Von Mises, L. 108, 109

Wamsley, G.L. 16
Weber, M. 200
Weimer, D.L. 6, 120–49
Wildavsky, A. 6–7, 35, 38, 55
Winsemius, P. 92, 104
Wintrobe, R. 215
Wittman, D.A. 107
Wolf Jr, C. 209, 221
Woodside, K. 7, 35, 162–81, 220
World Bank 128, 129
Wright, M. 54

Yarrow, G. 125
Yeltsin, B. 146, 147
Young, S.D. 132

Zeckhauser, R.J. 124, 125
Zijlstra, G.J. 86, 87

Printed and bound by CPI Group (UK) Ltd, Croydon, CR0 4YY

23/04/2025

14660986-0002

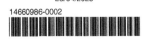